Digital Forensics with Open Source Tools

Digital Forensics with Open Source Tools

Cory Altheide

Harlan Carvey

Technical Editor

Ray Davidson

AMSTERDAM • BOSTON • HEIDELBERG • LONDON
NEW YORK • OXFORD • PARIS • SAN DIEGO
SAN FRANCISCO • SINGAPORE • SYDNEY • TOKYO

SYNGRESS

ELSEVIER

Syngress is an imprint of Elsevier

Acquiring Editor: Angelina Ward
Development Editor: Heather Scherer
Project Manager: Andre Cuello
Designer: Joanne Blank

Syngress is an imprint of Elsevier
225 Wyman Street, Waltham, MA 02451, USA

Library of Congress Cataloging-in-Publication Data
Application submitted

British Library Cataloguing-in-Publication Data
A catalogue record for this book is available from the British Library.

ISBN: 978-1-59749-586-8

Printed in the United States of America

16 17 18 19 20   10 9 8 7 6 5

Typeset by: diacriTech, India

Working together to grow
libraries in developing countries

www.elsevier.com | www.bookaid.org | www.sabre.org

ELSEVIER   BOOK AID
International   Sabre Foundation

For information on all Syngress publications visit our website at *www.syngress.com*

Contents

About the Authors

Cory Altheide is a security engineer at Google, focused on forensics and incident response. Prior to Google, Cory was a principal consultant with MANDIANT, an information security consulting firm that works with the Fortune 500, the defense industrial base, and banks of the world to secure their networks and combat cyber crime. In this role he responded to numerous incidents for a variety of clients in addition to developing and delivering training to corporate and law enforcement customers.

Cory also worked as the senior network forensics specialist in the National Nuclear Security Administration's Information Assurance Response Center (NNSA IARC). In this capacity he analyzed potentially hostile code, performed wireless assessments of Department of Energy facilities, and researched new forensic techniques. He also developed and presented hands-on forensics training for various DoE entities and worked closely with members of the Southern Nevada Cyber Crimes Task Force to develop their skills in examining less common digital media.

Cory has authored several papers for the computer forensics journal *Digital Investigation* and was a contributing author for *UNIX and Linux Forensic Analysis* (2008) and *The Handbook of Digital Forensics and Investigation* (2010). Additionally, Cory is a recurring member of the program committee of the Digital Forensics Research Workshop.

Harlan Carvey (CISSP) is a vice president of Advanced Security Projects with Terremark Worldwide, Inc. Terremark is a leading global provider of IT infrastructure and "cloud computing" services based in Miami, Florida. Harlan is a key contributor to the Engagement Services practice, providing disk forensics analysis, consulting, and training services to both internal and external customers. Harlan has provided forensic analysis services for the hospitality industry and financial institutions, as well as federal government and law enforcement agencies. Harlan's primary areas of interest include research and development of novel analysis solutions, with a focus on Windows platforms. Harlan holds a bachelor's degree in electrical engineering from the Virginia Military Institute and a master's degree in the same discipline from the Naval Postgraduate School. Harlan resides in Northern Virginia with his family.

Acknowledgments

Cory Altheide

First off I want to thank Harlan Carvey. In addition to serving as my coauthor and sounding board, he has been a good friend and colleague for many years. He has proven to be one of the most consistently knowledgeable and helpful individuals I have met in the field. Harlan, thanks again for adding your considerable expertise to the book and for never failing to buy me a beer every time I see you.

I also thank Ray Davidson for his work as technical editor. His early insights and commentary helped focus the book and made me target my subsequent writing on the intended audience.

Tremendous thanks go out to the "usual suspects" that make the open source forensics world the wonderful place it is. First, thank you to Wietse Venema and Dan Farmer for creating open source forensics with "The Coroner's Toolkit." Thanks to Brian Carrier for picking up where they left off and carrying the torch to this day. Simson Garfinkel, you have my gratitude for providing the invaluable resource that is the Digital Forensics Corpora. Special thanks to Eoghan Casey, who first encouraged me to share my knowledge with the community many years ago.

To my parents, Steve and Jeanine Altheide, thank you for buying my first Commodore-64 (and the second… and the third). Thanks to my brother Jeremy Altheide and the Old Heathen Brewing Company for producing some of the finest beers around… someday.

I express infinite gratitude to my incredible wife Jamie Altheide for her never-ending patience, love, and support during the research and writing of this book. Finally, I thank my daughters Winter and Lily for reminding me every day that I will never have all the answers, and that's okay.

Harlan Carvey

I begin by thanking God for the many blessings He's given me in my life, the first of which has been my family. I try to thank Him daily, but I find myself thinking that that's not nearly enough. A man's achievements are often not his alone, and in my heart, being able to write books like this is a gift and a blessing in many ways.

I thank my true love and the light of my life, Terri, and my stepdaughter, Kylie. Both of these wonderful ladies have put up with my antics yet again (intently staring off into space, scribbling in the air, and, of course, my excellent imitations taken from some of the movies we've seen), and I thank you both as much for your patience as for being there for me when I turned away from the keyboard. It can't be easy to have a nerd like me in your life, but I do thank you both for the opportunity to "put pen to paper" and get all of this stuff out of my head. Yes, that was a John Byrne reference.

Finally, whenever you meet Cory, give him a thundering round of applause. This book was his idea, and he graciously asked me to assist. I, of course, jumped at the chance to work with him again. Thanks, Cory.

Introduction

INTENDED AUDIENCE

When writing a technical book, one of the first questions the authors must answer is "Who is your audience?" The authors must then keep this question in mind at all times when writing. While it is hoped that this book is useful to everyone that reads it, the intended audience is primarily two groups.

The first group is new forensic practitioners. This could range from students who are brand new to the world of digital forensics, to active practitioners that are still early in their careers, to seasoned system administrators looking to make a career change. While this book is not a singular, complete compendium of all the forensic knowledge you will need to be successful, it is, hopefully, enough to get you started.

The second audience is experienced digital forensics practitioners new to open source tools. This is a fairly large audience, as commercial, proprietary tools have had a nearly exhaustive hold on working forensic examiners. Many examiners operating today are reliant upon a single commercial vendor to supply the bulk of their examination capabilities. They rely on one vendor for their core forensic platform and may have a handful of other commercial tools used for specific tasks that their main tool does not perform (or does not perform well). These experienced examiners who have little or no experience with open source tools will also hopefully benefit greatly from the content of this book.

LAYOUT OF THE BOOK

Beyond the introductory chapter that follows, the rest of this book is divided up into eight chapters and one Appendix.

Chapter 2 discusses the **Open Source Examination Platform**. We walk through all the prerequisites required to start compiling source code into executable code, install interpreters, and ensure we have a proper environment to build software on Ubuntu and Windows. We also install a Linux emulation environment on Windows along with some additional packages to bring Windows closer to "feature parity" with Linux for our purposes.

Chapter 3 details **Disk and File System Analysis** using the Sleuth Kit. The Sleuth Kit is the premier open source file system forensic analysis framework. We explain use of the Sleuth Kit and the fundamentals of media analysis, disk and partition structures, and file system concepts. We also review additional core digital forensics topics such as hashing and the creation of forensic images.

Chapter 4 begins our operating system-specific examination chapters with **Windows Systems and Artifacts**. We cover analysis of FAT and NTFS file systems, including internal structures of the NTFS Master File Table, extraction and analysis of Registry hives, event logs, and other Windows-specific artifacts. Finally, because malware-related intrusion cases are becoming more and more prevalent, we discuss some of the artifacts that can be retrieved from Windows executable files.

We continue on to **Chapter 5**, **Linux Systems and Artifacts**, where we discuss analysis of the most common Linux file systems (Ext2 and 3) and identification, extraction, and analysis of artifacts found on Linux servers and desktops. System level artifacts include items involved in the Linux boot process, service control scripts, and user account management. User-generated artifacts include Linux graphical user environment traces indicating recently opened files, mounted volumes, and more.

Chapter 6 is the final operating system-specific chapter, in which we examine **Mac OS X Systems and Artifacts**. We examine the HFS+ file system using the Sleuth Kit as well as an HFS-specific tool, HFSXplorer. We also analyze the Property List files that make up the bulk of OS X configuration information and user artifacts.

Chapter 7 reviews **Internet Artifacts**. Internet Explorer, Mozilla Firefox, Apple Safari, and Google Chrome artifacts are processed and analyzed, along with Outlook, Maildir, and mbox formatted local mail.

Chapter 8 is all about **File Analysis**. This chapter covers the analysis of files that aren't necessarily bound to a single system or operating system—documents, graphics files, videos, and more. Analysis of these types of files can be a big part of any investigation, and as these files move frequently between systems, many have the chance to carry traces of their source system with them. In addition, many of these file formats contain embedded information that can persist beyond the destruction of the file system or any other malicious tampering this side of wiping.

Chapter 9 covers a range of topics under the themes of **Automating Analysis and Extending Capabilities**. We discuss the PyFLAG and DFF graphical investigation environments. We also review the *fiwalk* library designed to take the pain out of automated forensic data extraction. Additionally, we discuss the generation and analysis of timelines, along with some alternative ways to think about temporal analysis during an examination.

The **Appendix** discusses some non-open source tools that fill some niches not yet covered by open source tools. These tools are all available free of charge, but are not provided as open source software, and as such did not fit directly into the main content of the book. That said, the authors find these tools incredibly valuable and would be remiss in not including some discussion of them.

WHAT IS NOT COVERED

While it is our goal to provide a book suitable for novice-to-intermediate examiners, if you do not have any experience with Linux at the command line, you may find it difficult to follow along with the tool use examples. While very few of the tools covered are Linux specific, most of the tool installation and subsequent usage examples are performed from a Linux console.

We focus exclusively on dead drive forensic analysis—media and images of systems that are offline. Collection and analysis of volatile data from running systems are not covered. Outside of the Linux platform, current tools for performing these tasks are largely closed source. That said, much of the analysis we go through is equally applicable to artifacts and items recovered from live systems.

Low-level detail of file system internals is intentionally omitted as this material is covered quite well in existing works. Likewise the development of open source tools is not discussed at length here. This is a book that first and foremost is concerned with the operational use of existing tools by forensic practitioners.

Outside of the Appendix, no commercial, proprietary, closed source, or otherwise restricted software is used.

Digital Forensics with Open Source Tools

INFORMATION IN THIS CHAPTER

- Welcome to "Digital Forensics with Open Source Tools"
- What Is "Digital Forensics?"
- What Is "Open Source?"
- Benefits of Open Source Tools

WELCOME TO "DIGITAL FORENSICS WITH OPEN SOURCE TOOLS"

In digital forensics, we rely upon our expertise as examiners to interpret data and information retrieved by our tools. To provide findings, we must be able to trust our tools. When we use closed source tools exclusively, we will always have a veil of abstraction between our minds and the truth that is impossible to eliminate.

We wrote this book to fill several needs. First, we wanted to provide a work that demonstrated the full capabilities of open source forensics tools. Many examiners that are aware of and that use open source tools are not aware that you can actually perform a complete investigation using solely open source tools. Second, we wanted to shine a light on the persistence and availability (and subsequent examination) of a wide variety of digital artifacts. It is our sincere hope that the reader learns to understand the wealth of information that is available for use in a forensic examination.

To continue further, we must define what we mean by "Digital Forensics" and what we mean by "Open Source."

WHAT IS "DIGITAL FORENSICS?"

At the first Digital Forensics Research Workshop (DFRWS) in 2001, digital forensics was defined as:

> *The use of scientifically derived and proven methods toward the preservation, collection, validation, identification, analysis, interpretation, documentation and*

presentation of digital evidence derived from digital sources for the purpose of facilitating or furthering the reconstruction of events found to be criminal, or helping to anticipate unauthorized actions shown to be disruptive to planned operations [1].

While digital forensics techniques are used in more contexts than just criminal investigations, the principles and procedures are more or less the same no matter the investigation. While the investigation type may vary widely, the sources of evidence generally do not. Digital forensic examinations use computer-generated data as their source. Historically this has been limited to magnetic and optical storage media, but increasingly snapshots of memory from running systems are the subjects of examination.

Digital forensics is alternately (and simultaneously!) described as an art and a science. In *Forensic Discovery*, Wietse Venema and Dan Farmer make the argument that at times the examiner acts as a digital archaeologist and, at other times, a digital geologist.

Digital archaeology is about the direct effects from user activity, such as file contents, file access time stamps, information from deleted files, and network flow logs. … Digital geology is about autonomous processes that users have no direct control over, such as the allocation and recycling of disk blocks, file ID numbers, memory pages or process ID numbers [2].

This mental model of digital forensics may be more apropos than the "digital ballistics" metaphor that has been used historically. No one ever faults an archaeologist for working on the original copy of a 4000-year-old pyramid, for example. Like archaeology and anthropology, digital forensics combines elements from "hard" or natural science with elements from "soft" or social science.

Many have made the suggestion that the dichotomy of the art and science of forensic analysis is not a paradox at all, but simply an apparent inconsistency arising from the conflation of the two aspects of the practice: the *science* of forensics combined with the *art* of investigation. Applying scientific method and deductive reasoning to data is the science—interpreting these data to reconstruct an event is the art.

On his Web site, Brian Carrier makes the argument that referring to the practice as "digital forensics" may be partially to blame for some of this. While traditional crime scene forensic analysts are tasked with answering very discrete questions about subsets of evidence posed to them by detectives, digital forensic examiners often wear both hats. Carrier prefers the term "digital forensic investigation" to make this distinction clear [3].

Goals of Forensic Analysis

The goal of any given forensic examination is to find facts, and via these facts to recreate the truth of an event. The examiner reveals the truth of an event by discovering and exposing the remnants of the event that have been left on the system. In keeping with the digital archaeologist metaphor, these remnants are known as *artifacts*. These remnants are sometimes referred to as *evidence*. As the authors deal frequently with lawyers in writing, we prefer to avoid overusing the term *evidence* due to the loaded legal connotations. *Evidence* is something to be used during a legal proceeding, and using this term loosely may get an examiner into trouble. *Artifacts* are traces left behind due to activities and events, which can be innocuous, or not.

As stated by Locard's exchange principle, "with contact between two items, there will be an exchange [4]." This simple statement is the fundamental principle at the core of evidence dynamics and indeed all of digital forensics. Specific to digital forensics, this means that an action taken by an actor on a computer system will leave traces of that activity on the system. Very simple actions may simply cause registers to change in the processor. More complex actions have a greater likelihood of creating longer-lasting impressions to the system, but even simple, discreet tasks can create artifacts. To use a real-world crime scene investigation analogy, kicking open a door and picking a lock will both leave artifacts of their actions (a splintered door frame and microscopic abrasions on the tumblers, respectively). Even the act of cleaning up artifacts can leave additional artifacts—the digital equivalent to the smell of bleach at a physical crime scene that has been "washed."

It is important to reiterate the job of the examiner: to determine truth. Every examination should begin with a hypothesis. Examples include "this computer was hacked into," "my spouse has been having an affair," or "this computer was used to steal the garbage file." The examiner's task is not to prove these assertions. The examiner's task is to uncover artifacts that indicate the hypothesis to be either valid or not valid. In the legal realm, these would be referred to as *inculpatory* and *exculpatory* evidence, respectively.

An additional hitch is introduced due to the ease with which items in the digital realm can be manipulated (or fabricated entirely). In many investigations, the examiner must determine whether or not the digital evidence is consistent with the processes and systems that were purported to have generated it. In some cases, determining the consistency of the digital evidence is the sole purpose of an examination.

The Digital Forensics Process

The process of digital forensics can be broken down into three categories of activity: *acquisition*, *analysis*, and *presentation*.

- *Acquisition* refers to the collection of digital media to be examined. Depending on the type of examination, these can be physical hard drives, optical media, storage cards from digital cameras, mobile phones, chips from embedded devices, or even single document files. In any case, media to be examined should be treated delicately. At a minimum the acquisition process should consist of creating a duplicate of the original media (the *working copy*) as well as maintaining good records of all actions taken with any original media.

- *Analysis* refers to the actual media examination—the "identification, analysis, and interpretation" items from the DFRWS 2001 definition. Identification consists of locating items or items present in the media in question and then further reducing this set to items or artifacts of interest. These items are then subjected

to the appropriate analysis. This can be file system analysis, file content examination, log analysis, statistical analysis, or any number of other types of review.
Finally, the examiner interprets results of this analysis based on the examiner's
training, expertise, experimentation, and experience.

- *Presentation* refers to the process by which the examiner shares results of the
analysis phase with the interested party or parties. This consists of generating a
report of actions taken by the examiner, artifacts uncovered, and the meaning of
those artifacts. The presentation phase can also include the examiner defending
these findings under challenge.

Note that findings from the analysis phase can drive additional acquisitions, each
of which will generate additional analyses, etc. This feedback loop can continue for
numerous cycles given an extensive network compromise or a long-running criminal
investigation.

This book deals almost exclusively with the analysis phase of the process,
although basic acquisition of digital media is discussed.

WHAT IS "OPEN SOURCE?"

Generically, "open source" means just that: the source code is open and available
for review. However, just because you can view the source code doesn't mean you
have license to do anything else with it. The Open Source Initiative has created a
formal definition that lays out the requirements for a software license to be truly open
source. In a nutshell, to be considered open source, a piece of software must be freely
redistributable, must provide access to the source code, must allow the end user to
modify the source code at will, and must not restrict the end use of the software. For
more detail, see the full definition at the Open Source Initiative's site [5].

> **NOTE**
> **Free for Some**
> Note that under the Open Source Initiative's definition, any license that restricts the use of
> software for certain tasks or that restricts distribution among certain groups cannot be an
> open source license. This includes the "Law Enforcement Only" or "Non-Commercial Use"
> restrictions commonly placed on freeware tools in the digital forensics community.

"Free" vs. "Open"

Due to the overloading of the word "free" in the English language, confusion about
what "free" software is can arise. Software available free of charge (*gratis*) is not
necessarily free from restriction (*libre*). In the open source community, "free software" generally means software considered "open source" and without restriction, in
addition to usually being available at no cost. This is in contrast to various "freeware"
applications generally found on Windows system available solely in binary, executable format but at no cost.

This core material of this book is focused on the use of open source software to perform digital forensic examinations. "Freeware" closed source applications that perform a function not met by any available open source tools or that are otherwise highly useful are discussed in the Appendix.

Open Source Licenses

At the time of this writing, there are 58 licenses recognized as "Open Source" by the Open Source Initiative [6]. Since this is a book about the use of open source software and not a book about the intricacies of software licensing, we briefly discuss the most commonly used open source licenses. The two most commonly used licenses are the GNU Public License (GPL) and the Berkeley Software Distribution License (BSD). To grossly simplify, the core difference between these two licenses is that the GPL requires that any modifications made to GPL code that is then incorporated into distributed compiled software be made available in source form as well. The BSD license does not have this requirement, instead only asking for acknowledgment that the distributed software contains code from a BSD-licensed project.

This means that a widget vendor using GPL-licensed code in their widget controller code must provide customers that purchase their widgets the source code upon request. If the widget was driven using BSD license software, this would not be necessary. In other words, the GPL favors the rights of the original producer of the code, while the BSD license favors the rights of the user or consumer of the code. Because of this requirement, the GPL is known as a *copyleft* license (a play on "copyright"). The BSD license is what is known as a *permissive* license. Most permissive licenses are considered GPL compatible because they give the end user authority over what he or she does with the code, including using it in derivative works that are GPL licensed. Additional popular GPL-compatible licenses include the Apache Public License (used by Apache Foundation projects) and the X11/MIT License.

BENEFITS OF OPEN SOURCE TOOLS

There are great many passionate screeds about the benefits of open source software, the ethics of software licensing, and the evils of proprietary software. We will not repeat them here, but we will outline a few of the most compelling reasons to use open source tools that are specific to digital forensics.

Education

When the authors entered the digital forensics field, there were two routes to becoming an examiner. The first was via a law enforcement or military career, and the second was to teach yourself (with the authors representing each of these routes). In either scenario, one of the best ways to learn was by using freely available tools (and in the self-taught scenario, the only way!). Today, there are numerous college programs and training programs available to an aspiring examiner, but there is still something to be said for learning by doing. The authors have been using open source tools throughout their careers in digital forensics, and we both have no doubt that we are far better examiners than we would have been otherwise.

Using open source tools to learn digital forensics has several benefits. First, open source tools innately "show their work." You can execute the tool, examine the options and output, and finally examine the code that produced the output to understand the logic behind the tool's operation. For the purposes of small examination scenarios, you can run the tools on any old hardware you have access to—no multithousand dollar deluxe forensic workstation required. Finally, you also have access to a dedicated community of examiners, developers, and enthusiasts ready to help you—provided you've done a modicum of legwork before firing off questions answered trivially by a Google search.

Portability and Flexibility

Another key benefit to the tools covered in this book by and large is that they are all *portable* and *flexible*. By portable we mean that you can easily take your toolkit with you as you move from one system to another, from one operating system to another, or from one job to another. Unless you personally license an expensive proprietary tool, your toolkit may not come with you if you move from one company to another. Any product-specific expertise you built up could end up worthless. If you are currently employed in law enforcement, any law enforcement–only tools you are currently using won't be available to you should you decide to go into the private sector.

If *portability* means you can choose where you use your tools, *flexibility* means you can choose how you use your tools. You can use open source tools on your local system or you can install them on a remote server and use them over a remote shell. You can install them on a single system or you can install them on thousands of systems. You can do all this without asking the software provider for permissions, without filling out a purchase order, and without plugging a thousand hardware copy protection dongles into a thousand machines.

Price

In addition to being open source, all of the tools covered in this work are free of cost. This is great for individuals looking to learn forensics on their own, students taking formal coursework in digital forensics, or examiners looking to build a digital forensics capability on a budget. This is also a great benefit for anyone already using a full complement of commercial tools. Adding a set of open source tools to your toolkit will usually cost you nothing, save for a bit of time. Even if you continue using proprietary, commercial tools on a daily basis, you can use the tools in this book as an adjunct to cover gaps in your tools coverage or to validate or calibrate your tools' findings and operation.

Ground Truth

Arguably the biggest benefit open source software provides to the examiner is the code itself. As renowned philosopher Alfred Korzybski once said, "the map is not the territory." Being able to review the source code that you then compile into a working program is invaluable. If you have the skill and desire, you can make changes to the function of the code. You can verify fixes and changes between versions directly without having to simply trust what your software provider is telling you.

Using the Sleuth Kit as an example, we have no less than three different ways to review bug fixes in the software. First, we can review the change log files included with each release. Most proprietary software vendors will include something similar when a new version is released. Second, we can review the freely accessible bug trackers maintained at the Sleuth Kit project site [7]. Most proprietary forensic software vendors will *not* provide open access to their full list of bugs and fixes. Finally, we can take the previous version of the source code and compare it with the newer version automatically via the *diff* command, highlighting exactly which changes have occurred. The first option is reading the map. The last option is surveying the territory.

Additionally, with open source software the function of the code can be reviewed directly. The authors have had experiences where proprietary forensic products have produced demonstrably erroneous results, but these tests were performed in a "black box" scenario. Known input files were generated and processed, and precalculated expected results compared to the output from the proprietary tool, and false negatives were discovered. The authors had to bypass the tool's internal logic and implement correct function externally. Had the tool been open source, the error in processing could have been identified directly in the code, fixed, and subsequently fixed in the main code repository, identifying and solving the problem for all users of the code.

In the previous scenario, the lack of access to the source code acted as an additional layer of abstraction between the examiners and the truth. Each layer of abstraction is a possible source for error or distortion. Since the goal of the examiner is to uncover truth, it is in the examiner's interest to ensure that the possible layers of abstraction are minimized. If your findings are ever brought into question, being able to show the actual source code used to generate data you interpreted could be incredibly valuable.

SUMMARY

The world of digital forensics has a long history of relying heavily on closed-source tools.

Armed with an understanding of what we are doing, why we are doing it, and why we choose to use the tools we do, we can move on to the next chapter and begin building an open source examination platform.

References

[1] A Road Map for Digital Forensic Research, Digital Forensics Research Workshop, 2001 (p. 16), (accessed 05.01.11).

[2] Dan Farmer & Wietse Venema, Forensic Discovery—Chapter 1: The spirit of forensic discovery. http://www.porcupine.org/forensics/forensic-discovery/chapter1.html, (accessed 05.01.11).

[3] Digital Investigation and Digital Forensic Basics. http://www.digital-evidence.org/di_basics.html.

[4] W. Jerry Chisum, & Brent E. Turvey, Profiling 1(1) (2000). http://www.profiling.org/journal/vol1_no1/jbp_ed_january2000_1-1.html, (accessed 05.01.11).

[5] The Open Source Definition|Open Source Initiative, http://opensource.org/docs/osd.

[6] Open Source Licenses by Category|Open Source Initiative. http://opensource.org/licenses/category.

[7] Trackers—SleuthKitWiki. http://wiki.sleuthkit.org/index.php?title=Trackers. (accessed 07.01.2011).

Open Source Examination Platform

PREPARING THE EXAMINATION SYSTEM

Before using many of the open source forensics tools explored in the chapters to come, you will need to ensure that your system is prepared to build said tools. As they are "open source," the bulk of these tools are distributed primarily in source form, that is, you'll need to generate the executable code yourself. In other cases, the tools will be scripts that require a specific interpreter to run. This chapter deals with the setup required to perform examinations with open source tools using Linux and Windows hosts.

For each platform we will go through the following steps.

Building Software

Because we are going to be working with open source software, we are going to need to be able to take that source code and convert it into usable form. At a high level this is known as building, and we will need to have one or more working build environments on the systems we are planning to use open source applications on. This chapter sets up a generic development environment that can be used to build open source applications written in the C and C++ languages and to build (or install) any libraries these applications require.

Installing Interpreters

Some of the open source applications we will be using are written in interpreted (or "scripting") languages, such as Perl, Python, or Ruby. To run these programs we will need the appropriate interpreter, and usually we will need some means to install prerequisite modules that the applications rely upon.

Working with Image Files

A key part of forensic examination is working with image files—forensic copies of media. This is easier on some platforms, but is necessary on all—if we can't open the container, we can't get at the contents. An important part of setting up an examination system is ensuring that you can access work with image files directly. While the forensic tools worked with in later chapters can access image files directly, having multiple means to access them is an effective means of verifying the operation of our tools. Having this capability also serves as a hedge in case our forensic tools fail to process a given image file properly.

There are two general classes of image files we will be working with: *raw images* and *forensic containers*. Raw image files are exactly what they sound like—a pure bit-for-bit copy of source media. Forensic containers are special file formats designed with forensic use in mind. Generally these will contain equivalent data found in a raw image and will also contain checksum information or metadata about the container. In addition, forensic container formats may allow for compression and encryption.

Working with File Systems

Finally, there will be times when we as examiners will need to interact with the file systems contained in image files using native system functionality (but still in a forensically sound manner). For example, to examine an Ext4 file system we'll need to use native system capabilities rather than a forensic utility simply because (at the time of writing) there are no open source forensic utilities that can interpret Ext4 file systems.

USING LINUX AS THE HOST

Using Linux as the base is the most common way to set up an open source forensics platform, and throughout the book will be our "supported" use case. In the examples we are using Ubuntu, but if you have a different distribution you prefer using already it's entirely possible to do so. We will use the Ubuntu package manager *apt* to install software throughout the book; however, none of the software we are installing is Ubuntu-specific, and most of the packages we install should be available via the package manger in your distribution of choice.

> **TIP**
>
> **Brief Linux Command Line Refresher**
>
> Ideally you will come into this book with some Linux experience. If it's been a while (or you're brand new), here's a refresher list of the basic terminal commands you'll need to use to navigate and work with files:
>
> - *cd* **c**hanges **d**irectories. "cd .." goes up a directory, "cd /" goes to the top of the directory structure, and "cd ~" goes to your home directory.
> - *ls* **l**ists the contents of a directory (equivalent to "dir" in a Windows command prompt). "ls" will list the current directory, and "ls -l" will provide a verbose listing.
> - *pwd* will print the current directory you are in, in case you get lost.
> - *mkdir* will create a new directory
> - *cp* will **c**o**p**y a file. "cp -r" will copy a directory and all items in the subdirectory.
> - *mv* will rename (or, **m**o**v**e) a file or directory
> - *rm* will delete (or, **rem**ove) a file. "rm -r" is required to delete a directory (and all its subdirectories!)
> - *cat* will dump the contents of a file to the screen. Long files can be viewed a page at a time using *less* or *more*.
> - The pipe character "|" is used to chain the output from one command to the input of the next. The greater than sign ">" is used to send the output to a named file instead of the screen. Double arrows ">>" append the output instead of overwriting.
> - Finally, *man* and *info* can be used to get usage information for any command.

Extracting Software

Linux source code is usually distributed in compressed archives known as *tarballs*. To extract these we will use the tar command along with a handful of flags.

To extract tarballs with *tgz* or *tar.gz* extensions (GZippped tarballs), use the command:

```
tar xzf {filename}
```

To extract tarballs with *tbz*, *tbz2*, *tar.bz2*, or *tar.bz* extensions (BZipped tarballs), use this command:

```
tar xjf {filename}
```

In either case you can add the -v option for verbose mode, which will display the name and path of extracted files to the console as the command progresses.

We'll need to install a few pieces of software before we can begin building programs from source code. On Ubuntu, the "build-essential" meta-package will get us started. Build-essential is basically a grouping of packages *essential* for *building* software. To install this package we'll used the apt-get command. The apt-get command is part of the "Advanced Packaging Tool," the main method for installing precompiled software packages on Debian-derived Linux distributions (including Ubuntu). Because installing packages is a system administration function, on Linux systems we will need to act with *super-user* or *root* privileges in order to do so. We will use the sudo command to run *apt-get* with super-user privileges.

```
user@ubuntu:~$ sudo apt-get install build-essential
[sudo] password for user:
The following extra packages will be installed:
  dpkg-dev fakeroot g++ g++-4.4 libstdc++6-4.4-dev patch
    xz-utils
Suggested packages:
  debian-keyring debian-maintainers g++-multilib g++-4.4-
    multilib gcc-4.4-doc
  libstdc++6-4.4-dbg libstdc++6-4.4-doc diffutils-doc
The following NEW packages will be installed:
  build-essential dpkg-dev fakeroot g++ g++-4.4 libstdc++6-4.4-
    dev patch xz-utils
0 upgraded, 8 newly installed, 0 to remove and 0 not upgraded.
Need to get 7571kB of archives.
After this operation, 24.6MB of additional disk space will be
  used.
Do you want to continue [Y/n]? Y
```

While we now have the basics of our build environment installed, we will come back to the *apt-get* command to install development libraries required by many of the applications we will be installing later. Most open source applications will come with a README or INSTALL document that will contain information regarding what additional libraries. Be sure to reference this prior to attempting to build software.

For more information on installing software on Ubuntu, please see the Ubuntu Help Guide [1].

GNU Build System

The majority of the software we will be building uses the "GNU Autotools" system to prepare and execute a build [2]. Building software that uses this system generally consists of running three commands, in sequence:

1. `./configure`
2. `make`
3. `(sudo) make install`

Configure

If the application being built has any configurable options, the included `configure` script is the method we will use to set them. Generally the configure script will respond to the `--help` flag by displaying all the available configuration options. We can use the configure script from LibEWF library as an example. We will discuss the operation of this library in detail shortly—for now it's enough to know that it is a prerequisite for the operation of our forensic platform. We have truncated the output that follows due to space considerations—most configure scripts will allow you to tune many options related to the building and subsequent installation of the software.

```
user@ubuntu:~/src/libewf-20100226$ ./configure --help
'configure' configures libewf 20100226 to adapt to many kinds of
   systems.
Usage: ./configure [OPTION]... [VAR=VALUE]...
...
Optional Features:
...
  --enable-wide-character-type
              enable wide character type support (default is no)
  --enable-static-executables
              build the ewftools as static executables (default is
              no)
  --enable-low-level-functions
              use libewf's low level read and write functions in
              the ewftools (default is no)
  --enable-low-memory-usage
              enable low memory usage (default is no)
  --enable-verbose-output enable verbose output (default is no)
  --enable-debug-output   enable debug output (default is no)
  --enable-python    build python bindings (pyewf) (default is no)
  --enable-v2-api    enable experimental version 2 API (default is no)
...
```

Here we can see handful of libewf-specific configuration options that may be of interest to us. Referencing the included README file tells us that libewf relies on zlib (the deflate/zip compression library) and libcrypto (the OpenSSL library). Different distributions will have these libraries packaged under different names, but in general these can be located fairly easily by searching for the development name of the libraries at hand using the apt-cache search command or equivalent command for your distribution.

```
user@ubuntu:~$ apt-cache search openssl | grep dev
libssl-ocaml-dev - OCaml bindings for OpenSSL
libcurl4-openssl-dev - Development files and documentation for
   libcurl (OpenSSL)
libssl-dev - SSL development libraries, header files and documentation
user@ubuntu:~$ apt-cache search zlib | grep dev
lib32z1-dev - compression library - 32 bit development
libmng-dev - M-N-G library (Development headers)
libzlcore-dev - zlibrary core - development files
libzltext-dev - zlibrary text model/viewer - development files
zlib1g-dbg - compression library - development
zlib1g-dev - compression library - development
libcryptokit-ocaml-dev - cryptographic algorithm library for
   OCaml - development
libniftiio1-dev - IO libraries for the NIfTI-1 data format
libtrf-tcl-dev - Tcl data transformations - development files
libzzip-dev - library providing read access on ZIP-archives -
   development
```

From the results, we see that we need the "zlib1g-dev" and "libssl-dev" libraries, which can be installed using the following command:

```
user@ubuntu:~$ sudo apt-get install zlib1g-dev libssl-dev
...
Setting up libssl-dev (0.9.8k-7ubuntu8) ...
```

With our libraries installed, we are ready to execute the configure script. Upon execution, the configure script will check the build system to ensure that all the libraries required to build (and subsequently execute) the program are present, functional, and of the correct version.

```
user@ubuntu:~/src/libewf-20100226$ ./configure --enable-wide-
   character-type --enable-low-level-functions
checking for a BSD-compatible install... /usr/bin/install -c
checking whether build environment is sane... yes
...
config.status: executing libtool commands
configure:
Building:
   libuna support:              local
   libbfio support:             local
   libcrypto EVP support:          yes
   libcrypto MD5 support:          evp
   libcrypto SHA1 support:         evp
   guid support:             libuuid
Features:
   Wide character type support:          yes
   ewftools are build as static executables:        no
   ewftools use low level read and write functions: yes
   Python (pyewf) support:          no
   Verbose output:            no
   Debug output:          no
   Experimental version 2 API:          no
```

Note that this particular configuration script provides the name of the library providing the included functionality: "guid support: libuuid." If the README or INSTALL documentation is missing, incomplete, or simply incorrect, simply attempting to run the configure script is a trial-and-error method that may provide more information about what libraries you need to complete the build.

WARNING

"./configure not found"

Very simple programs that don't have any third-party library dependencies may not have a configure script. Some of these may provide a prebuilt makefile, but if this isn't the case you may need to compile the code directly. Check for a README or INSTALL document or, barring that, read the source itself for an indication of how to proceed with building the software.

A successful execution of the configure script will generate a "makefile"—a build script read by the `make` command, which brings us to the next step in the build process.

Make

The `make` command reads through the "makefile" generated by the configure script, and proceeds to compile and link each of the executable files and libraries that make up the program at hand. This can take some time and will generate a lot of output while it is executing. A highly edited sample of what you can expect from a typical *make* execution appears here:

```
user@ubuntu:~/src/libewf-20100226$ make
Making all in include
make[1]: Entering directory '/home/user/src/libewf-20100226/
  include'
...
make[1]: Entering directory '/home/user/src/libewf-20100226/
  liberror'
/bin/bash ../libtool --tag=CC -- mode=compile gcc -DHAVE_CONFIG_H -I.
  -I../common  -I../include -I../common-  g -O2 -Wall -MT
  liberror_error.lo -MD -MP -MF .deps/liberror_error.Tpo -c -o
  liberror_error.lo liberror_error.c
libtool: compile:  gcc -DHAVE_CONFIG_H -I. -I../common -I../
  include -I../common -g -O2 -Wall -MT liberror_error.lo -MD -MP
  -MF .deps/liberror_error.Tpo -c liberror_error.c -fPIC -DPIC
  -o .libs/liberror_error.o
...
make[1]: Leaving directory '/home/user/src/libewf-20100226'
```

Once the "make" completes, the final step is to actually install the application. Executing

```
sudo make install
```

will copy the finished executables, libraries, documentation (if present), and any additional materials to their configured locations—generally under the "/usr/local/" directory.

NOTE

Other Build Systems

GNU Autotools does not stand alone in the pantheon of build systems for open source software. While it is the most venerable and still most common build system in use, there are others in use in various projects. Two of the most common are *cmake* and *scons*. *Scons* is python based and is therefore a popular build system for python-heavy programs. *Cmake* is an intermediary build layer used by cross-platform applications—it generates native build files for each target—Makefiles for Unix-like systems, Visual Studio Solution files for Windows targets, etc.

Version Control Systems

In addition to packaged tarballs of source code, many open source projects are available via *version control systems*. These services enable tracking of code changes among a distributed group of participants. Version control systems offer many capabilities geared toward ensuring clean and easy collaboration on development; however, for our use, we will only be "checking out" code—retrieving a copy of the source code from the repository. The end result will be a directory tree of code similar to what we would have after extracting a tarball.

Sometimes, code that is still under active development may only be available via a source checkout from a version control system; in other cases, the development version of an application may have capabilities required to perform a successful examination. As always, validate that any tools you use perform the functions they are designed for in a verifiable, repeatable manner, but above all work on copies or extracted data rather than original data.

Popular open source version control systems include

- cvs
- subversion
- git
- mercurial

We will discuss the operation of these tools to perform source code checkouts when we build tools that require this.

TIP

CERT Forensic Tools Repository

The examples throughout this book use Ubuntu as our base operating system. If you are a Fedora user, you may want to use the CERT Linux Forensics Tools Repository. This repository provides a prebuilt set of forensic packages for Fedora 10, 11, 12, and 13, including many of the tools discussed throughout this book.

http://www.cert.org/forensics/tools/

Installing Interpreters

In addition to compiling executable code, we will need to be able to execute programs written in interpreted languages. To do so, we will need to install the appropriate interpreters—Perl, Python, and Ruby. On most Linux distributions the Perl and Python interpreters (and a handful of modules) will be already be installed. We'll want to install the Python 3 interpreter in addition to our currently installed version, and we'll need to install the Ruby interpreter. We will also explore how to install various modules in each of the interpreters.

Perl

Perl is one of the older nonshell scripting languages still in common use. Its longevity is one of its core strengths—over many years of use Perl has built up an impressive number of open source libraries and modules available for reuse.

To check our installed version of perl we can issue the following command:

```
user@ubuntu:~$ perl -v
This is perl, v5.10.1 built for x86_64-linux-gnu-thread-multi
```

The core repository for Perl modules is known as CPAN (the Comprehensive Perl Archive Network). Packages in CPAN can be installed from the terminal using the -MCPAN option to perl. Upon executing this command for the first time your CPAN preferences will be set up—defaults are fine for our usage so hit enter when prompted to accept them.

```
user@ubuntu:~$ perl -MCPAN -e shell
...
cpan[1]> help
Display Information                        (ver 1.9402)
   command  argument       description
cpan [n] quit
...
```

Python

Like Perl, Python will be present on most Linux distributions by default. We can check the python version we have installed with the -V flag:

```
user@ubuntu:~$ python -V
Python 2.6.5
```

In addition to the Python 2.6 interpreter we want a parallel installation of the Python 3 interpreter. Python 3 represents a major change from the 2.x series and as such is not directly backward compatible with existing programs written for Python 2.x. Because we will be using a few programs targeted for the newer Python, we will need both. We can install Python 3 directly using the following command:

```
user@ubuntu:~$ sudo apt-get install python3-minimal
[sudo] password for user:
Reading package lists... Done
Building dependency tree
Reading state information... Done
The following extra packages will be installed:
  python3.1 python3.1-minimal
Suggested packages:
  python3.1-doc python3.1-profiler
The following NEW packages will be installed:
  python3-minimal python3.1 python3.1-minimal
0 upgraded, 3 newly installed, 0 to remove and 0 not
  upgraded.
Need to get 4,995kB of archives.
After this operation, 17.7MB of additional disk space will
  be used.
Do you want to continue [Y/n]?
```

Unlike Perl and Ruby, Python doesn't have a "standard" package management system. Python modules are instead expected to be handled by the operating system's package manager or installed by the user manually. As we use programs that need specific packages we will install using both methods. That said, Python **does** have a centralized packaged repository, and there are several unofficial package managers available that leverage this repository. The most widely used is easy_install, provided by the "python-setuptools" package. We can install this for Python 2.x and 3.x using the following command:

```
user@ubuntu:~$ sudo apt-get install python-setuptools python
  3-setuptools
```

Ruby

Ruby is the third scripting language we will need to ensure is installed. As a younger language, it is not present by default on our Ubuntu installation:

```
user@ubuntu:~$ ruby -v
The program 'ruby' is currently not installed. You can install
  it by typing:
sudo apt-get install ruby
```

As just shown, we can install via apt-get. Once this is completed, we can verify the install and check the version with the -v option.

```
user@ubuntu:~$ ruby -v
ruby 1.8.7 (2010-01-10 patchlevel 249) [i486-linux]
```

Ruby packages are managed via RubyGems. This needs to be installed separately:

```
user@ubuntu:~$ sudo apt-get install rubygems
```

The package manager is invoked via the gem command:

```
user@ubuntu:~$ gem
RubyGems is a sophisticated package manager for Ruby. This is a
basic help message containing pointers to more information.
  Usage:
    gem -h/--help
    gem -v/--version
    gem command [arguments...] [options...]
  Examples:
    gem install rake
    gem list --local
    gem build package.gemspec
    gem help install ...
```

We will use tools that require each of these interpreters more throughout the book. For now, ensuring that we have them installed, operational, and can install packages is sufficient.

Working with Images

Although we will be using forensic utilities that can interpret the file system on a raw image, it is in our interest to ensure that we can work with image files using native system functionality as well. This enables us to test our forensic tools for accuracy, provides us a much needed "safety net" in the event our tools don't function properly, and, in some cases, may be the most useful way to access data of interest.

WARNING

Automounting of Volumes on Ubuntu

One of the major benefits of using Linux as a forensic platform is the tremendous power the system provides to an educated examiner. However, as Linux distributions become more and more "user-friendly," the operation of system becomes more and more abstracted away and difficult to access. One example is preventing the automatic mounting of external media. Historically, most Linux distributions did *not* automatically mount file systems— all mounts had to explicitly requested. For forensic examiners, this is terrific; end users, though, were obviously less than enthusiastic about this "feature." Current Ubuntu systems will detect and automatically mount external storage in much the same manner as Windows systems. Given this, examiners should **always** use hardware write blocker devices whenever working with original media.

Any given Linux distribution should have the capability to work with raw image files natively. We will use the `losetup` command to create a "loop device" associated with our disk image. A loop device is a virtual device that allows a disk image to be treated as if it were an actual disk.

```
user@ubuntu:~$ losetup
Usage:
losetup loop_device                 # give info
losetup -a | --all                  # list all used
losetup -d | --detach loop_device   # delete
losetup -f | --find                 # find unused
losetup [ options ] {-f|--find|loop_device} file  # setup
Options:
-e | --encryption <type> enable data encryption with specified
   <name/num>
-h | --help              this help
-o | --offset <num>      start at offset <num> into file
-p | --pass-fd <num>     read passphrase from file descriptor
   <num>
-r | --read-only         setup read-only loop device
-s | --show              print device name (with -f <file>)
-N | --nohashpass        Do not hash the given password (Debian
   hashes)
-k | --keybits <num>     specify number of bits in the hashed
   key given
```

```
                 to the cipher. Some ciphers support several key
                 sizes and might be more efficient with a smaller
                 key size. Key sizes < 128 are generally not
                 recommended
    -v | --verbose      verbose mode
```

To determine the appropriate offset we will use the `mmls` command from the Sleuth Kit to read the partition table from a sample image. We will examine this command and the rest of the Sleuth Kit at length in Chapter 3.

```
user@ubuntu:~$ mmls /mnt/forensic/testimg/testimg.img
DOS Partition Table
Offset Sector: 0
Units are in 512-byte sectors
  Slot  Start      End        Length      Description
00:  Meta  0000000000 0000000000 0000000001 Primary Table (#0)
01:  ----- 0000000000 0000016064 0000016065 Unallocated
02:  00:00 0000016065 0312496379 0312480315 NTFS (0x07)
03:  ----- 0312496380 0312499999 0000003620 Unallocated
```

We want to associate the loop device with the *partition*, not the disk, as this will allow us to mount the file system. To do this we provide losetup with an offset into the image file where we would like the loop device to begin. The output of `mmls` is measured in sectors, and *losetup* expects an offset in bytes, so multiplying 16065 by the default sector size of 512 gives us an offset of 8225280. We also want the device to be read-only (-r).

```
user@ubuntu:~$ sudo losetup -r -o 8225280 /dev/loop0 /mnt/
    forensic/testimg/testimg.img
```

We can test our math by checking for a valid file system at the beginning of the loop device. Using `dd` and the `file` command is one way to do this:

```
user@ubuntu:~$ sudo dd if=/dev/loop0 bs=512 count=1 | file -
1+0 records in
1+0 records out
512 bytes (512 B) copied, 0.0778169 s, 6.6 kB/s
/dev/stdin: x86 boot sector, code offset 0x52, OEM-ID "NTFS   ",
    sectors/cluster 8, reserved sectors 0, Media descriptor 0xf8,
    heads 255, hidden sectors 16065, dos < 4.0 BootSector (0x80)
```

The `file` command confirms that we have a valid file system at the beginning of our loop device. Now we can create a directory to serve as a mount point and mount the loop device.

```
user@ubuntu:~$ sudo mkdir /mnt/testimg
user@ubuntu:~$ sudo mount -o ro /dev/loop0 /mnt/testimg/
user@ubuntu:~$ ls /mnt/testimg/
CONFIG.SYS       IO.SYS    MSOCache    Program Files System
    Volume Information Windows ntldr     python
AUTOEXEC.BAT     Documents and Settings  I386     MSDOS.SYS
    NTDETECT.COM RECYCLER    boot.ini pagefile.sys
```

TIP

Mounting Split Raw Images

If you have ever dealt with sharing of forensic images across different groups you will have likely come across "split raw" images. Due to file size limitations and differing examination preferences and capabilities, raw image files split into 2-Gigabyte chunks are the lowest common denominator when sharing forensic data. Unfortunately, split raw image files aren't directly accessible as a "virtual disk" using the loop device method just described. Historically, this meant the examiner would need to map devices to each segment and then combine them using the Linux *md* functionality. Luckily, Richard Harman has written a perl script called `poorcase` (http://code.google.com/p/poorcase/) that handles this tedium.

Unfortunately, this only lets us access volumes contained in raw disk images. To access volumes inside forensic containers we will need to use software that understands these containers. The two forensic container formats we will need to be able to work with are EWF and AFF. EWF (Expert Witness Format) is the native format generated by Guidance Software's EnCase software. AFF is the Advanced Forensics Format and is an open source forensic container format that provides many benefits over traditional "raw" images. These containers are discussed in more detail in Chapter 3— for now, being able to mount volumes inside the containers is all we're after.

FUSE

FUSE is a Linux kernel module that allows for "File Systems In User Space." In addition to interpreting file systems, various FUSE modules will also interpret volumes or containers and allow for access to their contents. There are many FUSE modules implementing everything from cloud-based file systems to encrypted local file systems to Wikipedia as a file system. We can install a few FUSE modules (and prerequisites for additional FUSE modules) using the following command:

```
user@ubuntu:~$ sudo apt-get install zfs-fuse python-fuse fuse-
   zip sshfs
The following extra packages will be installed:
   libaio1 libewf1 libzip1
The following NEW packages will be installed:
   fuse-zip ifuse libaio1 libzip1 python-fuse sshfs zfs-fuse
0 upgraded, 7 newly installed, 0 to remove and 0 not upgraded.
Need to get 1,917kB of archives.
After this operation, 5,759kB of additional disk space will be
   used.
Do you want to continue [Y/n]?
```

This will install:

- ZFS-Fuse—a driver for Sun's ZFS file system
- Python-Fuse—a python API for implementing FUSE file systems
- Fuse-Zip—a FUSE module that presents ZIP archives as file systems
- SSHFS—a FUSE module that transparently presents remote file systems as local over SSH (SFTP/SCP)

MountEWF

MountEWF is a program that presents an Expert Witness Format forensic image as a raw image. It does this by leveraging the FUSE system via Python. It is not included with libewf directly but can be retrieved from the LibEWF project site [3]. Like a disk, the forensic container can hold multiple mountable file systems, so simply "mounting" the container is not desirable or even feasible. Instead, MountEWF provides a view of raw streams contained in the EWF container at the provided mount point. The raw streams can then be accessed directly using the *losetup* technique discussed previously.

MountEWF is a python script so it does not need to be compiled before running. We can copy it into our path to allow for easier execution:

```
user@ubuntu:~/src/afflib-3.5.12$ sudo cp /home/user/src/mount_
  ewf-20090113.py /usr/local/bin/mount_ewf.py
```

Executing the command with no arguments will provide usage instructions:

```
user@ubuntu:~/src/afflib-3.5.12$ mount_ewf.py
Using libewf-20100226. Tested with libewf-20080501.
Usage:
  mount_ewf.py [options] <filename(s)> <mountpoint>
Note: This utility allows EWF files to be mounted as a filesystem
  containing a flat disk image. <filename> can be any segment of
  the EWF file. To be identified, all files need to be in the same
  directory, have the same root file name, and have the same first
  character of file extension. Alternatively, multiple filenames
  can be specified in different locations in the order to be
  reassembled.
ewf segment filename(s) required.
```

To test mount_ewf without creating an Expert Witness formatted image, we can use the image provided by Lance Mueller for his first forensic practical [4].

```
user@ubuntu:~/images$ mount_ewf.py WinXP2.E01 ~/mount_points/
  ewf/
Using libewf-20100226. Tested with libewf-20080501.
user@ubuntu:~/images$ ls -lath /home/user/mount_points/ewf/
total 2.0G
drwxr-xr-x 5 user user 4.0K 2010-08-20 23:52 ..
dr-xr-xr-x 2 root root 0 1969-12-31 16:00 .
-r--r--r-- 1 root root 2.0G 1969-12-31 16:00 WinXP2
-r--r--r-- 1 root root 293 1969-12-31 16:00 WinXP2.txt
```

The text file listed is the case metadata. The other file is the raw image.

```
user@ubuntu:~/images$ cat /home/user/mount_points/ewf/WinXP2.txt
# Description: WinXP
# Case number: Case 1
# Examiner name: Mueller
# Evidence number: WinXP
# Acquiry date: 2008-01-17T17:05:46
# System date: 2008-01-17T17:05:46
```

```
# Operating system used: Vista
# Software version used: 6.8
ce2211114a461a96bb2c4409b272dbee */home/user/mount_points/ewf/
    WinXP2
```

The last line of the text file is the MD5 hash of the content. We can verify this using the md5sum command.

```
user@ubuntu:~/images$ md5sum /home/user/mount_points/ewf/WinXP2
ce2211114a461a96bb2c4409b272dbee /home/user/mount_points/ewf/
    WinXP2
```

We can verify access to the raw content using the file command:

```
user@ubuntu:~/images$ file /home/user/mount_points/ewf/WinXP2
/home/user/mount_points/ewf/WinXP2: x86 boot sector, code offset
    0x52, OEM-ID "NTFS", sectors/cluster 4, reserved sectors 0,
    Media descriptor 0xf8, heads 128, hidden sectors 63, dos <
    4.0 BootSector (0x80)
```

AFFuse

AFFuse is a FUSE-based program that gives the examiner access to Advanced Forensic Format containers. From an examiner's perspective, AFFuse operates in much the same manner as MountEWF—the forensic container is "mounted" to a directory provided by the examiner. This directory will have a file for each stream inside the AFF container, which can then be accessed as "raw" images via losetup.

AFFuse is part of the AFF library, available at www.afflib.org.

AFFuse requires the FUSE development library, and AFF itself requires the expat library for signature verification. On Ubuntu we can install these with the following command:

```
sudo apt-get install libfuse-dev libexpat1-dev
```

A simple "./configure" should eventually yield the following result:

```
configure: ****************************************
configure: AFFLIB 3.5.12 configuration
configure: Amazon S3 Support:  no
configure: LZMA Compression:   yes
configure: LIBEWF:             yes (requires uuid-dev on Linux)
configure: PYTHON Bindings:    no
configure: QEMU Image Drivers: yes
configure: FUSE:               yes
configure: LIBEXPAT:           yes (needed for AFF signatures)
configure:
configure: CFLAGS:     -g -O2 -D_FORTIFY_SOURCE=2 -Wall
configure: CPPFLAGS:   -D_FILE_OFFSET_BITS=64 -DFUSE_USE_
    VERSION=26 -I/usr/local/include
configure: CXXFLAGS:   -g -O2 -D_FORTIFY_SOURCE=2 -Wall
configure: LIBS:       -lssl -lcrypto -lexpat -lrt -lz -lewf
configure: LDFLAGS: -L/usr/local/lib
```

We can complete the install with `make` and finally `sudo make install`.

Once again, executing the command with no options gives us usage instructions. In this case, the usage instructions are quite verbose as AFFuse is also displaying options that can be passed to the FUSE library and are not AFF specific. We won't be using any of these at the moment so trimming them gives us the following usage:

```
user@ubuntu:~/src/afflib-3.5.12$ affuse
affuse version 3.5.12
Usage: affuse [<FUSE library options>] af_image mount_point
...
Use fusermount -u mount_point, to unmount
```

We can test out AFFuse using an image from Digital Corpora (http://www
.digitalcorpora.com). *Ubnist1.casper-rw.gen3.aff* is an AFF image taken from
a Ubuntu 8.10 thumbdrive. We can mount the AFF container with the following
`affuse` command:

```
user@ubuntu:~/images$ mkdir ~/mount_points/
user@ubuntu:~/images$ mkdir ~/mount_points/aff/
user@ubuntu:~/images$ affuse ubnist1.casper-rw.gen3.aff ~/mount_
  points/aff/
user@ubuntu:~/images$ ls -lath /home/user/mount_points/aff/
total 4.0K
drwxr-xr-x 4 user user 4.0K 2010-08-20 23:47 ..
drwxr-xr-x 2 root root 0 1969-12-31 16:00 .
-r--r--r-- 1 root root 600M 1969-12-31 16:00 ubnist1.casper-rw.
  gen3.aff.raw
```

Listing the contents of the mount point displays a single raw image inside. We
can use the file command to confirm that we have access to the raw content.

```
user@ubuntu:~/images$ file ~/mount_points/aff/ubnist1.casper-rw.
  gen3.aff.raw
/home/user/mount_points/aff/ubnist1.casper-rw.gen3.aff.raw:
  Linux rev 1.0 ext3 filesystem data, UUID=8717883b-0b7b-4149-
  8b76-d97117813599 (needs journal recovery) (large files)
```

XMount

XMount is similar to both MountEWF and AFFuse in that it provides the examiner "raw" access to container files. Where it differs is that rather than simply presenting a raw "dd" style image, XMount can also present the contents of the container as a VirtualBox or VMWare format disk image. It converts on the fly via FUSE and is tremendously useful for a Linux-based examiner who wishes to boot a virtual instance of an imaged system. XMount will redirect any writes to a cache file in a directory specified by the examiner. XMount is available from https://www.pinguin.lu/index
.php. To install XMount, execute the basic "`./configure; make; sudo make install`" sequence described previously.

```
user@ubuntu:~$ uname -a
Linux ubuntu 2.6.32-21-generic #32-Ubuntu SMP Fri Apr 16
   08:10:02 UTC 2010 i686 GNU/Linux
```

Next, we can change directories to "/lib/modules/2.6.32-21-generic/kernel/fs"—this is the subdirectory where file system kernel modules for our running kernel are located.

```
user@ubuntu:/lib/modules/2.6.32-21-generic/kernel/fs$ ls
9p   affs autofs befs binfmt_aout.ko btrfs   cifs configfs dlm
  exofs   fat   fscache gfs2 hfsplus isofs jfs    minix nfs
  nfsd   nls ocfs2 qnx4 reiserfs smbfs   sysv udf xfs
adfs afs autofs4 bfs binfmt_misc.ko cachefiles coda cramfs   efs
  exportfs freevxfs fuse   hfs hpfs   jffs2 lockd ncpfs nfs_
  common nilfs2 ntfs omfs quota romfs   squashfs ubifs ufs
```

Another way to check file system support in our current kernel is to browse through the kernel's configuration ("/boot/config-2.6.32-21-generic", for example) until we see the section entitled "File systems."

```
#
# File systems
#
CONFIG_EXT2_FS=y
CONFIG_EXT2_FS_XATTR=y
CONFIG_EXT2_FS_POSIX_ACL=y
CONFIG_EXT2_FS_SECURITY=y
# CONFIG_EXT2_FS_XIP is not set
CONFIG_EXT3_FS=y
CONFIG_EXT3_DEFAULTS_TO_ORDERED=y
CONFIG_EXT3_FS_XATTR=y
CONFIG_EXT3_FS_POSIX_ACL=y
CONFIG_EXT3_FS_SECURITY=y
CONFIG_EXT4_FS=y
CONFIG_EXT4_FS_XATTR=y
CONFIG_EXT4_FS_POSIX_ACL=y
CONFIG_EXT4_FS_SECURITY=y
# CONFIG_EXT4_DEBUG is not set
CONFIG_JBD=y
# CONFIG_JBD_DEBUG is not set
CONFIG_JBD2=y
# CONFIG_JBD2_DEBUG is not set
CONFIG_FS_MBCACHE=y
CONFIG_REISERFS_FS=m
 . . .
```

USING WINDOWS AS THE HOST

Setting up a working build environment on a Windows system is a bit more complex than on Linux or OS X. Many of the items we take for granted on a Linux system aren't present on a default Windows system. An out-of-the-box Windows system doesn't have a compiler or any of the interpreters we will need. It doesn't have native capability to mount or examine image files and only supports a handful of file systems. Luckily, we can set up a reasonable development environment suitable for building open source forensics tools without too much trouble. That said, we can turn a Windows host into a capable open source forensics platform; better, stronger, faster. We have the technology.

Building Software

There are a couple different methods for building software on Windows, and they each have advantages and disadvantages regarding different use cases. For our purposes the best approach is going to be implementation of a Unix-like environment on our Windows system via *Cygwin*. Per www.cygwin.com, "Cygwin is a Linux-like environment for Windows." Cygwin provides this environment through *cygwin1.dll*, a Linux-emulation layer between Linux tools and the Windows operating system. Through Cygwin we can compile and use Linux-targeted source code on our Windows examination workstation. Using a Cygwin environment ensures that we have the highest available compatibility with the bulk of open source forensics utilities, as these are usually written and tested on Unix-like systems.

To install Cygwin, download and execute the installer (setup.exe).

Using the Cygwin installer, we will install the following packages, which can be located using the search box at the top of the package installer window, seen in Figure 2.1.

- automake
- make
- cmake
- cvs
- subversion
- mercurial
- gcc
- gcc-g++
- git
- python
- perl
- ruby
- mintty

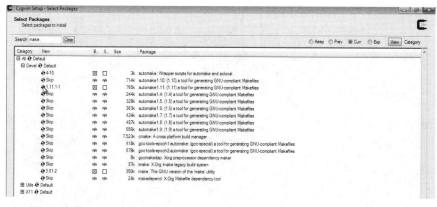

FIGURE 2.1

Cygwin setup.

This will give us a working Unix-like development environment. We should be able to use the majority of the utilities discussed in later chapters, barring any utilities that require native Linux functionality to work—for example, any FUSE-based utilities will not function under Cygwin.

> **TIP**
>
> **Visual Studio and MinGW**
> Compiling "native" Windows code will usually require the use of Microsoft's Visual Studio. While the full version of Visual Studio is commercial software, Microsoft releases "Express" versions of Visual Studio targeted toward specific languages at no cost. We won't cover the installation or operation of Visual Studio in this book, but be aware that this may be an option worth exploring.
>
> MinGW (Minimal Gnu for Windows) is another option for producing "native" Windows binaries from open source software. MinGW is a port of the GNU C-Compiler and GNU Binutils to Windows, which allows developers to produce truly native Windows binaries that don't rely on external DLLs to function. This differs from the Cygwin approach, which produces binaries dependent on the functionality exposed by the cygwin1.dll file to operate. Additionally, developers can *cross-compile* native Windows code from non-Windows development systems. If you are interested in learning more about MinGW, please refer to http://www.mingw.org/.

Installing Interpreters

We already installed the perl, python, and ruby interpreters via the Cygwin installer. We can verify the versions of each of the interpreters installed by opening up the *mintty* terminal emulator from the Start Menu and passing the appropriate "version" flag to each interpreter (see Figure 2.2). These installations will serve us well when

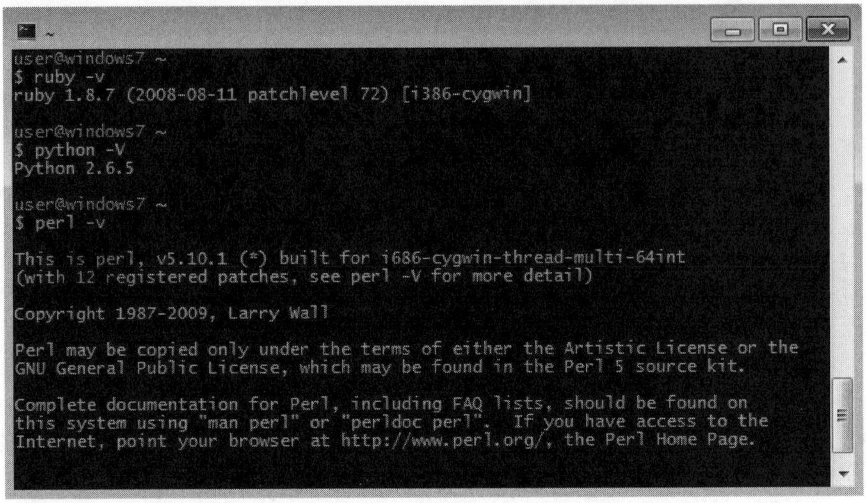

FIGURE 2.2

Verifying the Cygwin installs of Perl, Python, and Ruby.

working in Cygwin environment but we will need "native" interpreters for some of the code we will be running later.

Perl—ActiveState

ActiveState's Perl distribution [5] is the de facto Windows Perl in use today. It provides the Perl interpreter in an easy-to-use and easy-to-manage installer and includes a graphical package manger (shown in Figure 2.3) to handle modules. Installation is the straightforward "Click next/Accept defaults" until the installer exits.

Python

Installing Python on Windows isn't quite as obvious of a proposition as installing Perl. While ActiveState provides its own Windows Python distribution, there are also "native" Windows installers that provide functional basic Python installations. At the time of this writing the consensus seems to be that if you are going to be doing Windows-specific python development, the ActiveState installer provides some nice benefits. That said, the official Windows installer (shown in Figure 2.4) will be sufficient to run any of the python scripts covered in this book. You can choose to install either or both, as you can have multiple installations in different directories.

At the time of this writing, Python 2.x and Python 3.x are both in active parallel development and use. Python 3 is *not* directly backward compatible with Python 2—Python 2 scripts need to be rewritten for 3. Given this, there is a lot of existing Python 2 code, so we will definitely need at least a Python 2 installation. There is also

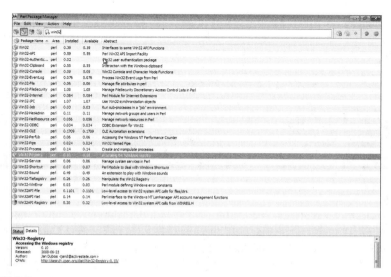

FIGURE 2.3

The Perl Package Manager installed with ActiveState Perl.

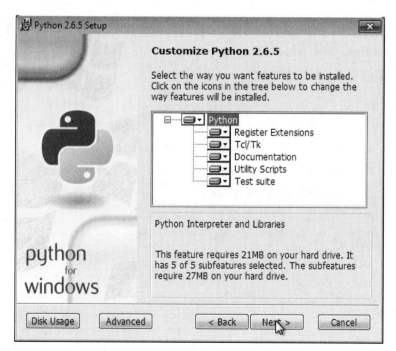

FIGURE 2.4

The Windows native installer for Python 2.6.5.

a growing set of Python 3 code, so it is in our best interest to have a parallel Python 3 environment installed as well. Given this, the current newest versions at the time of writing of Python are 2.6.5 and 3.1.2.

> **TIP**
>
> **Too Many Pythons...**
> Keeping track of the latest Python installer can be a chore, especially given the current 2.x/3.x split. Wesley Chun, author of *Core Python Programming*, provides a constantly updated matrix of Python versions for Linux, Mac, and Windows at www.corepython.com.

Ruby

Getting Ruby on Windows is trivial using the installer from www.rubyinstaller.org. During installation, ensure that both checkboxes shown in Figure 2.5 are checked— this will let you run command-line ruby scripts without specifying the path of the interpreter and will ensure that ruby programs launched from Explorer are associated with this ruby installation.

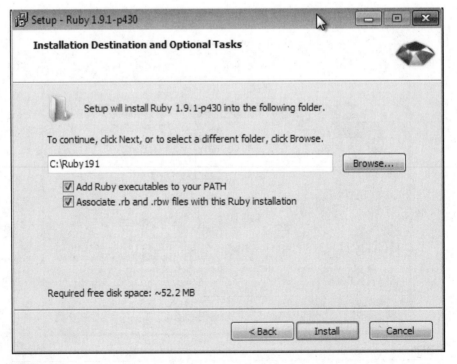

FIGURE 2.5

Ruby installer configuration options.

Working with Images

Windows doesn't have any native equivalent to the `losetup` command we used to access image files as disks. Fortunately, Olof Lagerkvist has written the open source *ImDisk*, which brings much of the same functionality to the Windows world. After downloading and running the ImDisk installer (http://www.ltr-data.se/opencode.html/#ImDisk), we need to manually start the ImDisk service the first time and configure it to automatically start in the future. To do so, we'll need to start a command prompt with *administrator access* (see Figure 2.6).

Entering these lines shown in Figure 2.7 in the administrator shell will set the ImDisk service to start automatically in the future and will start it now manually.

FIGURE 2.6

Starting an administrator shell—Windows 7.

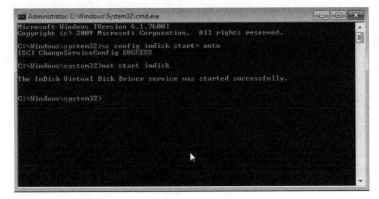

FIGURE 2.7

Starting ImDisk service manually.

The ImDisk service is located in the Control Panel, as shown in Figure 2.8. Upon launching the application and selecting "Mount New," you should be greeted with a screen similar to Figure 2.9.

There are many options to experiment with here, but for our purposes the most important are the path to the image file and the "Read-only media" checkbox.

FIGURE 2.8

Locating the IMDisk entry in the Control Panel.

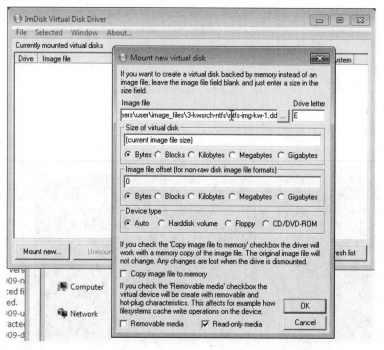

FIGURE 2.9

Mounting an NTFS volume image.

Checking this will ensure that we don't make any inadvertent writes to our image file. Figure 2.10 shows the ImDisk service after successfully mounting a test NTFS image from the Digital Forensic Tool Testing collection. http://dftt.sourceforge.net/.

Figures 2.11 and 2.12 show that the image file now appears exactly like a normal volume.

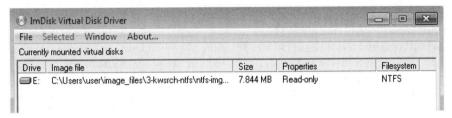

FIGURE 2.10

ImDisk displaying the mounted image.

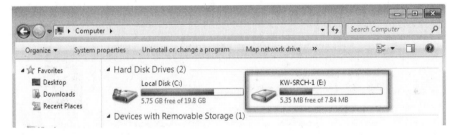

FIGURE 2.11

ImDisk mounted volume as shown in Explorer.

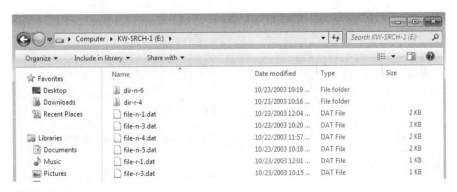

FIGURE 2.12

Browsing the contents of an ImDisk mounted volume.

> **WARNING**
> **Potential ImDisk Pitfall**
> Remember that when you access a file system from a Windows machine using your Windows examination machine, you are doing so using standard Windows functionality. If you attempt to access files on the mounted file system that your current user doesn't have permission to access, you will not be able to access them!

Working with File Systems

While Windows doesn't have the breadth of file system support our Ubuntu examination system has by default, there are some open source programs that allow Windows to access some commonly encountered non-Windows file systems. It's important to note that in both cases, the forensic software we will be using is capable of interpreting both of these file systems directly.

Ext2Fsd is an open source Ext2 file system driver for Windows systems available from http://www.ext2fsd.com/. Using this we can examine Ext 2 (and Extended 3, minus the journal) file systems directly. Note that during installation we have the option to enable write support on Ext2/3 volumes as well—this is not recommended but depending on your use case this may be necessary (see Figure 2.13). When

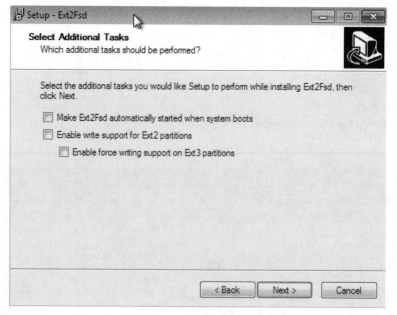

FIGURE 2.13

Deselecting all options during Ext2Fsd configuration.

FIGURE 2.14

Finishing Ext2Fsd installation.

completing the installation, you will have the option to assign drive letters to any connected Ext2 and 3 volumes—deselect this (Figure 2.14).

HFS Explorer (available from http://www.catacombae.org/hfsx.html) is an application that can read the HFS and HFS+ file systems used on Mac OS X disks (including some CDs/DVDs and the DMG container files used frequently on Macs). On installation, it will associate itself with DMG containers by default (Figure 2.15). This is generally a safe option, as we have no other means of accessing these files.

Figure 2.16 shows HFS Explorer being used to examine a DMG container. Individual files can be extracted out for examination using the "Extract" button. The "Info" button will display detailed information about the currently highlighted file or directory, including time stamps and ownership information. Under the "Tools" menu, the "File System Info" option provides a plethora of detailed information about the file system.

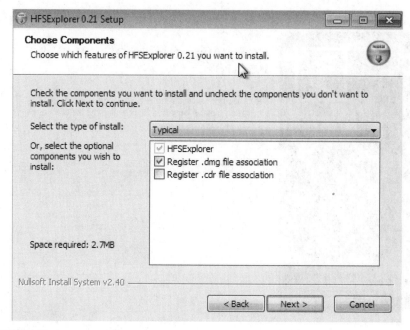

FIGURE 2.15

HFS Explorer installation.

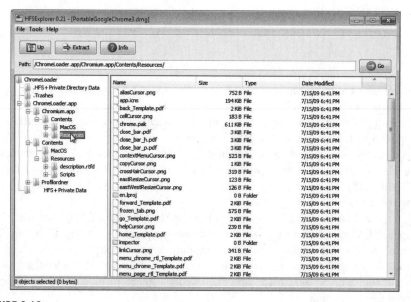

FIGURE 2.16

Navigating a DMG file with HFSExplorer.

SUMMARY

While using open source forensic tools has certain advantages, preparing the platform to build and execute these tools can be daunting to a newcomer. In this chapter we have gone through the process of building a development workstation that we will use to compile and run tools going forward. Additionally, we discussed the installation of various utilities that allow examiners utilizing Windows systems to use many of the tools and scripts we will be working with throughout the book.

References

[1] InstallingSoftware—Community Ubuntu Documentation. https://help.ubuntu.com/community/InstallingSoftware, (accessed 24.08.10).

[2] GNU Build System—automake. http://www.gnu.org/software/hello/manual/automake/GNU-Build-System.html, (accessed 24.08.10).

[3] libewf—Browse /mount_ewf at SourceForge.net. http://sourceforge.net/projects/libewf/files/mount_ewf/, (accessed 24.08.10).

[4] Computer Forensics, Malware Analysis & Digital Investigations: Forensic Practical. http://www.forensickb.com/2008/01/forensic-practical.html, (accessed 24.08.10).

[5] ActivePerl Downloads—Perl Binaries for Windows, Linux and Mac|ActiveState. http://www.activestate.com/activeperl/downloads, (accessed 24.08.10).

Disk and File System Analysis

MEDIA ANALYSIS CONCEPTS

At its most basic, forensic analysis deals with *files* on *media*—deleted files, files in folders, files in other files, all stored on or in some container. The goal of media analysis is to identify, extract, and analyze these files and the file systems they lie upon. *Identification* includes determining which active and deleted files are available in a volume. *Extraction* is the retrieval of relevant file data and metadata. *Analysis* is the process in which we apply our intelligence to the data set and ideally come up with meaningful results.

Note that these are not necessarily discrete procedural steps. In fact, some examination processes will seem to straddle two or more of these—carving, for example, can easily be described as both identification and extraction. Nonetheless, we feel that this is a suitable model for describing *why* we as examiners are taking a particular action.

This chapter focuses primarily on the concepts behind identifying and extracting file system artifacts, and information *about* files. Deep analysis of the artifacts found in content of the files and the artifacts of interest found in specific file systems will not be covered here as this analysis makes up the bulk of Chapters 4 through 8.

While we discuss the file system analysis concepts that will be of the most use to an examiner, a full analysis of every conceivable artifact and nuance of each file system is outside the scope of this book. For greater detail on this topic, the authors highly recommend *File System Forensic Analysis* by Brian Carrier [1], the authoritative work on the subject.

File System Abstraction Model

In the aforementioned *File System Forensic Analysis*, the author puts forth a file system abstraction model to be used when describing the functions of file systems and the artifacts generated by these functions. For readers with networking backgrounds, this model is not unlike the OSI model used to describe communications systems.

As described by Carrier, the logical progression of any file system, from low level to high level, is:

- Disk

  A *disk* refers to a physical storage device—a SCSI or SATA hard drive, or a Secure Digital Card from a digital camera, for example. Analysis of items at this level is usually beyond the capabilities of most examiners—physical media analysis of conventional hard drives requires extensive specialized training and knowledge, access to a clean room, and expensive electron microscopy equipment. With the rise of flash media and Solid State Disks, however, analysis of media at this level may be in the realm of possibility for a larger pool of examiners.

- Volume

  A *volume* is created using all or part of one or more disks. A single disk may contain several volumes, or a volume may span several disks, depending on configuration. The term "partition" is often used interchangeably for a volume; Carrier makes a distinction wherein a "partition" is limited to a single physical disk, and a volume is a collection of one or more partitions. Put simply, a volume describes a number of sectors on a disk(s) in a given system. Please see Figure 3.1 for a simplified display of the delineation between a disk and volumes present on the disk.

- File System

  A *file system* is laid down on a volume and describes the layout of files and their associated metadata. Items in the file system layer include metadata specific to and solely used for the file system's operation—the Ext2 superblock is a good example.

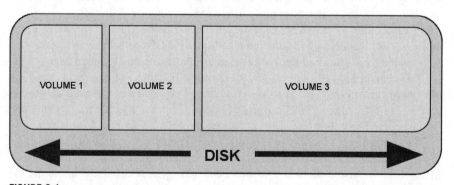

FIGURE 3.1

Disk and volumes.

- Data Unit

  A *data unit* is the smallest available freestanding unit of data storage available in a given file system. On Unix-derived file systems these are known as *blocks*. These are generally some power of 2 multiple of the physical sector size of the disk. Historically the sector size of every disk was 512 bytes—most modern file systems will use 4096 bytes (4K) or larger as the smallest addressable *data unit*. The information available at the data unit layer is simple: the content of that data unit. If that data unit is allocated to a JPEG image, the data unit will contain a portion of JPEG data. If the data unit was allocated to a text file, the data unit will contain text.

- Metadata

  Metadata refers to *data about data*. Given that the *data unit layer* holds data in a file system, the *metadata layer* then contains data about the data units. On Unix-derived file systems these metadata units are called *inodes*. The exact content of metadata units depends on the actual file system being discussed, but generally this layer will at least consist of file time stamps, file ownership information, and data units allocated to this metadata unit. We'll discuss the specific artifacts for each file system in the relevant sections later.

- File Name

  The *file name* layer is where humans operate. Unsurprisingly, this layer consists of file and folder/directory names. Once again, artifacts available in this layer vary depending on the file system. At the very least, file names have a pointer to their corresponding metadata structure.

Because this abstraction model is built with the design of Unix-derived file systems in mind, some of the separations do not map directly to the designs of file systems for other platforms. However, a good understanding of this model is imperative to truly understanding the significance of file system artifacts on *any* file system.

THE SLEUTH KIT

To process file system artifacts, we will use *The Sleuth Kit* (www.sleuthkit.org). The Sleuth Kit (TSK) is the suite of file system forensic tools originally created by Brian Carrier as an updated version of the older *Coroner's Toolkit*. The Coroner's Toolkit (TCT) was designed specifically to perform forensic analysis of compromised Unix-like systems. While being a very powerful set of early forensic tools, TCT had major shortcomings, including a lack of portability between systems and a lack of support for non Unix-like file systems. Carrier developed the Sleuth Kit to provide a highly portable, extensible, and useful open source forensics toolkit.

Installing the Sleuth Kit

The Sleuth Kit natively supports processing raw disk images (split or not), but it can also import the ability to process additional image formats from the LibEWF and

AFFLib packages installed in Chapter 2. Note that we could install precompiled Sleuth Kit packages using the Ubuntu package manager. Retrieving the source code directly and compiling ourselves minimizes the number of intermediaries involved in producing executable code. It also ensures that we have the latest version of our core tools and libraries, as package repositories may take some time to update.

Note that when executing the Sleuth Kit's configure script (./configure), you should see the following lines toward the end of the script's output:

```
checking afflib/afflib.h usability... yes
checking afflib/afflib.h presence... yes
checking for afflib/afflib.h... yes
checking for af_open in -lafflib... yes
checking libewf.h usability... yes
checking libewf.h presence... yes
checking for libewf.h... yes
checking for libewf_open in -lewf... yes
configure: creating ./config.status
```

This confirms that LibEWF and AFFLib are installed properly and will be used by the Sleuth Kit.

With these development libraries installed, and the Sleuth Kit configured, finishing the build and install is a simple matter executing make followed by sudo make install. This will install the suite of command-line tools that make up the Sleuth Kit.

WARNING

Got Root?

If you plan to use Sleuth Kit tools with an attached disk as the target (as opposed to an image file) remember that you will need *root* privileges. This can be accomplished either by becoming root via the "su-" command or by executing the command with root privileges using the "sudo" command, as shown in Chapter 2.

Sleuth Kit Tools

Mastering 21 separate command line utilities may seem daunting if you are not used to operating via command prompt frequently. That said, the bulk of Sleuth Kit tools are named in a logical manner, which indicates the file system layer they operate upon and the type of output you should expect from them. Since the Sleuth Kit comes from a Unix-derived pedigree, this naming is quite clear if you are familiar with the Linux command line.

The common prefixes found in the Sleuth Kit tools that indicate the file system layer of the tool are:

- "mm-": tools that operate on volumes (aka "media management")
- "fs-": tools that operate on file system structures
- "blk-": tools that operate at the data unit (or "block") layer
- "i-": tools that operate at the metadata (or "inode") layer
- "f-": tools that operate at the file name layer

There are two additional layers that don't map directly into the file system model as described:

- "j-": tools that operate against *file system journals*
- "img-": tools that operate against *image files*

Common suffixes found in Sleuth Kit tools that indicate the expected function of the tool are:

- "-stat": displays general information about the queried item—similar to the "stat" command on Unix-like systems
- "-ls": lists the contents of the queried layer, such as the "ls" command on Unix-like systems
- "-cat": dumps/extracts the content of the queried layer, such as the "cat" command on Unix-like systems

Additionally, a handful of tools provided by the Sleuth Kit don't follow this naming scheme. These are described under the "Miscellaneous Tools" section.

To demonstrate use of the Sleuth Kit, we will proceed through each layer, describing each tool present in that layer. Additionally, we will examine the use and output of the most important tools using a Linux Ext3 file system as our demonstration target.

NOTE

Sleuth Kit Disk Layer Tools

Current versions of the Sleuth Kit do not provide any tools for operating at the disk layer. Because the Sleuth Kit is a file system forensic analysis framework, this should not be surprising. That said, versions of the Sleuth Kit prior to 3.1.0 did include two tools at this layer that you may encounter in older forensic live CD distributions.

The `disk_stat` tool will show if the disk has a *Host Protected Area* (HPA) present. A HPA is one method that can be used to artificially restrict the number of sectors addressable by the operating system accessing a hard drive.

The `disk_sreset` will allow you to temporarily remove an HPA from a disk. This is a nonpermanent change—the HPA will return the next time the disk is powered on. Temporarily removing the HPA using `disk_sreset` enables a subsequent image capture operation to grab the entire disk, including the protected area.

Another method for restricting the displayed number of sectors is via *Device Configuration Overlay*. Both this and HPA can be detected and removed using the `hdparm` utility, which is included by default on most Linux distributions.

Other non-Sleuth Kit tools that operate at the disk layer include all of the imaging tools discussed in the *Forensic Imaging* section later in the chapter.

Volume Layer Tools

The `mmstat` command will display the type of volume system in use on the target image file or disk.

The `mmls` command parses and displays the media management structures on the image file or disk (i.e., the partition table). Note that unlike the `fdisk` command, `mmls` will clearly show nonallocated spaces before, after, or between volumes.

Here we have an example image from Digital Forensics Tool Testing archive.

```
user@forensics:~$ mmls 10-ntfs-disk.dd
DOS Partition Table
Offset Sector: 0
Units are in 512-byte sectors
  Slot Start End Length Description
00: Meta 0000000000 0000000000 0000000001 Primary Table (#0)
01: ----- 0000000000 0000000062 0000000063 Unallocated
02: 00:00 0000000063 0000096389 0000096327 NTFS (0x07)
03: 00:01 0000096390 0000192779 0000096390 NTFS (0x07)
04: ----- 0000192780 0000192783 0000000004 Unallocated
```

We can see here that the primary partition table was found in the first sector of the disk and that there are two volumes present—the first from sector 63 through sector 96389 and the second from sector 96390 through sector 192779. The `mmls` output also makes it clear that there are four "extra" sectors after the end of the last volume in addition to the standard 63 sector gap before the first volume.

Another important benefit of using mmls instead of a tool such as `fdisk` is that the offsets to individual volumes are presented as counts of 512-byte sectors. These offsets can be passed directly to higher level Sleuth Kit tools to specify a volume to analyze.

The `mmcat` streams the content of the specified volume to STDOUT (usually the console). This can be used to extract a specific volume of interest for analysis using tools that may not be able to operate on the container format or disk directly.

File System Layer Tools

The `fsstat` command displays file system information. Data of particular interest in the output of this command vary depending on the file system being examined but may include volume names, data unit sizes, and statistical information about the state of the file system. We will use output from an Ext3 file system to present the tool. Analysis of Ext3-specific information is covered in detail in Chapter 5.

```
user@forensics:~$ fsstat ubnist1.casper-rw.gen3.aff
FILE SYSTEM INFORMATION
--------------------------------------------
File System Type: Ext3
Volume Name:
Volume ID: 9935811771d9768b49417b0b3b881787
Last Written at: Tue Jan 6 10:59:33 2009
Last Checked at: Sun Dec 28 12:37:56 2008
Last Mounted at: Tue Jan 6 10:59:33 2009
Unmounted properly
Last mounted on:
Source OS: Linux
Dynamic Structure
Compat Features: Journal, Ext Attributes, Resize Inode, Dir Index
InCompat Features: Filetype, Needs Recovery,
Read Only Compat Features: Sparse Super, Has Large Files,
Journal ID: 00
Journal Inode: 8
```

As you can see from the partial tool output just given, the fsstat tool provides some basic file system information, including some information that may be of key investigative value, such as the last written and last mounted information. After this general information, the output of fsstat will be highly file system dependent. In the case of Ext3, statistical and layout information is provided about metadata and content structures present on the disk:

```
METADATA INFORMATION
------------------------------------
Inode Range: 1 - 38401
Root Directory: 2
Free Inodes: 36976
Orphan Inodes: 35, 20, 17, 16,
CONTENT INFORMATION
------------------------------------
Block Range: 0 - 153599
Block Size: 4096
Free Blocks: 85287
...
```

Note that this tool provides the block size used on the file system. This is important information when carving data from unallocated space.

Data Unit Layer Tools

The blkstat command displays information about a specific data unit. Generally, this will simply be allocation status; however, on Ext file systems, the block group to which the block is allocated is also displayed.

```
user@forensics:~$ blkstat ubnist1.casper-rw.gen3.aff 521
Fragment: 521
Allocated
Group: 0
```

The blkls command lists details about data units. Blkls can also be used to extract all unallocated space of the file system. This is useful to do prior to attempting to carve data from a file system. The following example extracts all of the unallocated space from our sample image file into a single, flat file.

```
user@forensics:~$ blkls ubnist1.casper-rw.gen3.aff > ubnist1.
  casper-rw.gen3.unalloc
user@forensics:~$ ls -lath ubnist1.casper-rw.gen3.unalloc
-rw-r----- 1 cory eng 331M Sep 2 20:36 ubnist1.casper-rw.gen3.
  unalloc
```

The blkcat command will stream the content of a given data unit to STD-OUT. This is similar in effect to using dd to read and write a specific block. The next example uses blkcat to extract block 521, which we view courtesy of the xxd binary data viewer, which is included with the vim editor package on most distributions.

```
user@forensics:~$ blkcat ubnist1.casper-rw.gen3.aff 521 | xxd |
  head
0000000: 0200 0000 0c00 0102 2e00 0000 0200 0000 ........
0000010: 0c00 0202 2e2e 0000 0b00 0000 1400 0a02 ........
0000020: 6c6f 7374 2b66 6f75 6e64 0000 0c00 0000 lost+found.....
0000030: 1400 0c01 2e77 682e 2e77 682e 6175 6673 ......wh..wh.aufs
0000040: 011e 0000 1400 0c02 2e77 682e 2e77 682e .........wh..wh.
0000050: 706c 6e6b 015a 0000 1400 0c02 2e77 682e plnk.Z......wh.
0000060: 2e77 682e 2e74 6d70 021e 0000 0c00 0402 .wh..tmp.......
0000070: 726f 6673 025a 0000 0c00 0302 6574 6300 rofs.Z.....etc.
0000080: 045a 0000 1000 0502 6364 726f 6d00 0000 .Z...cdrom......
0000090: 031e 0000 0c00 0302 7661 7200 013c 0000 ......var..<..
```

The `blkcalc` command is used in conjunction with the unallocated space extracted using `blkls`. With *blkcalc*, we can map a block from `blkls` output back into the original image. This is useful when we locate a string or other item of interest in the `blkls` extract and want to locate the location of the item in our forensic image.

Metadata Layer Tools

The `istat` command displays information about a specific metadata structure. In general, any of the information listed as being contained in a metadata structure (ownership, time information, block allocations, etc.) will be displayed. As always, the exact information displayed is file system dependent. We will explore file system-specific information in subsequent chapters.

What follows is the `istat` output for inode 20 on our test Ext3 file system. Output common to other file systems includes allocation status, ownership information, size, and time stamp data. Addresses of the inode's data units will also be present but are handled in different manners by different file systems, as shown later.

```
user@forensics:~$ istat ubnist1.casper-rw.gen3.aff 20
inode: 20
Allocated
Group: 0
Generation Id: 96054594
uid / gid: 0 / 0
mode: rrw-r--r--
size: 123600
num of links: 0
Inode Times:
Accessed:        Tue Jan 6 10:59:33 2009
File Modified:   Wed Jan 7 07:59:47 2009
Inode Modified:  Wed Jan 7 07:59:47 2009
Deleted:         Wed Dec 31 16:00:17 1969
Direct Blocks:
28680 0 0 0 0 0 28681
0 0 0 0 0 0 28683
0 0 0 0 0 28684 0
0 0 0 0 0 28685
Indirect Blocks:
28682
```

The `ils` command lists the metadata structures, parsing and displaying the embedded dates, ownership information, and other relevant information. This is one of the commands that can be used to generate a *bodyfile* for timeline generation using the *mactime* command (see "Miscellaneous Tools"). Timelines are key to the investigations presented in Chapter 9.

As you can see from the argument list, the examiner can tune the `ils` output to view as much (or as little) data as necessary.

```
user@forensics:~$ ils
Missing image name
usage: ils [-emOpvV] [-aAlLzZ] [-f fstype] [-i imgtype] [-b
  dev_sector_size] [-o imgoffset] [-s seconds] image [images]
  [inum[-end]]
    -e: Display all inodes
    -m: Display output in the mactime format
    -O: Display inodes that are unallocated, but were sill open
        (UFS/ExtX only)
    -p: Display orphan inodes (unallocated with no file name)
    -s seconds: Time skew of original machine (in seconds)
    -a: Allocated inodes
    -A: Unallocated inodes
    -l: Linked inodes
    -L: Unlinked inodes
    -z: Unused inodes (ctime is 0)
    -Z: Used inodes (ctime is not 0)
    -i imgtype: The format of the image file (use '-i list' for
        supported types)
    -b dev_sector_size: The size (in bytes) of the device
        sectors
    -f fstype: File system type (use '-f list' for supported
        types)
    -o imgoffset: The offset of the file system in the image
        (in sectors)
    -v: verbose output to stderr
    -V: Display version number
```

For example, if we wanted to list all inodes that are allocated or that have been used at some point, we can do so with the `-a` and `-Z` flags:

```
user@forensics:~$ ils -aZ ubnist1.casper-rw.gen3.aff
...
st_ino|st_alloc|st_uid|st_gid|st_mtime|st_atime|st_ctime|st_
  crtime|st_mode|st_nlink|st_size
1|a|0|0|1230496676|1230496676|1230496676|0|0|0|0
2|a|0|0|1231268373|1230496676|1231268373|0|755|15|4096
7|a|0|0|1230496676|1230496676|1230496676|0|600|1|4299210752
8|a|0|0|1230496679|0|1230496679|0|600|1|16777216
11|a|0|0|1230496676|1230496676|1230496676|0|700|2|16384
12|a|0|0|1230469846|1230469846|1231311252|0|444|19|0
13|a|0|0|1230615881|1225321841|1230615881|0|755|9|4096
...
```

The `icat` command streams the data unit referenced by the specified meta data address. For example, if "file1.txt" points to inode 20, which then points to blocks 30, 31, and 32, the command "`icat` *{image_file}* 20" would produce the same output that "`cat` file1.txt" would from the mounted file system.

The `ifind` command finds the metadata structure referenced by the provided file name *or* the metadata structure that references the provided data unit address. For example, to find the inode that owns block 28680, we can do the following:

```
user@forensics:~$ ifind -d 28680 ubnist1.casper-rw.gen3.aff
20
```

File Name Layer Tools

The `fls` command lists file names (deleted and allocated). By default it does not traverse the entire file system so you will only see the root directory of the volume being examined. This is one of the commands we can use to generate a *bodyfile* for timeline generation using the `mactime` command (see "Miscellaneous Tools"). A simple "`fls` *image*" will produce a terse directory listing of the root directory of the file system.

```
user@forensics:~$ fls ubnist1.casper-rw.gen3.aff
d/d 11:       lost+found
r/r 12:       .wh..wh.aufs
d/d 7681:     .wh..wh.plnk
d/d 23041:    .wh..wh..tmp
d/d 7682:     rofs
d/d 23042:    etc
d/d 23044:    cdrom
d/d 7683:     var
d/d 15361:    home
d/d 30721:    tmp
d/d 30722:    lib
d/d 15377:    usr
d/d 7712:     sbin
d/d 13:       root
r/r * 35(realloc):    .aufs.xino
d/d 38401:    $OrphanFiles
```

Note that the ".aufs.xino" file is listed with an asterisk—this indicates that it is deleted. The (realloc) indicates that the inode the name references has been real-located to another file.

The `fls` man page provides more background into the various options that can be passed to the command. For interactive use, particularly important `fls` arguments include:

```
-d: Display deleted entries only
-l: Display long version (like ls -l)
-m: Display output in mactime input format with
dir/ as the actual mount point of the image
```

```
-p: Display full path for each file
-r: Recurse on directory entries
-u: Display undeleted entries only
-z: Time zone of original machine (i.e. EST5EDT or GMT)
    (only useful with -l)
-s  seconds: Time skew of original machine (in seconds)
    (only useful with -l & -m)
```

Note that the time zone argument does not apply if you are using -m to create a mactime input file. This is only used when displaying time information to the console.

The ffind command finds file names that reference the provided metadata number. Using inode 20, which we located via the ifind command, we can discover the name associated with this inode.

```
user@forensics:~$ ffind ubnist1.casper-rw.gen3.aff 20
File name not found for inode
```

Unfortunately, no name currently points to this inode—it is *orphaned*. Just to sate our curiosity, we can check the adjacent inodes.

```
user@forensics:~$ ffind ubnist1.casper-rw.gen3.aff 19
/root/.pulse-cookie
user@forensics:~$ ffind ubnist1.casper-rw.gen3.aff 21
/root/.synaptic/lock
```

Miscellaneous Tools
The mactime command generates a timeline based on processing the *bodyfile* produced by ils and/or fls. To generate a timeline using the Sleuth Kit, first we need to generate the *bodyfile*. This is simply a specifically ordered pipe-delimited text file used as the input file for the mactime command.

```
user@forensics:~$ ils -em ubnist1.casper-rw.gen3.aff > ubnist1.
  bodyfile
user@forensics:~$ fls -r -m "/" ubnist1.casper-rw.gen3.aff >>
  ubnist1.bodyfile
```

This produces a text file with the metadata information of each file or inode on a single line.

```
md5|file|st_ino|st_ls|st_uid|st_gid|st_size|st_atime|st_mtime|st_
  ctime|st_crtime
0|<ubnist1.casper-rw.gen3.aff-alive-1>|1|-/----------
  |0|0|0|1230496676|1230496676|1230496676|0
0|<ubnist1.casper-rw.gen3.aff-alive-2>|2|-/drwxr-
  xr-x|0|0|4096|1230496676|1231268373|1231268373|0
0|<ubnist1.casper-rw.gen3.aff-alive-3>
  |3|-/----------|0|0|0|0|0|0|0
0|<ubnist1.casper-rw.gen3.aff-alive-4>
  |4|-/----------|0|0|0|0|0|0|0
```

```
0|<ubnist1.casper-rw.gen3.aff-alive-5>
 |5|-/----------|0|0|0|0|0|0|0
0|<ubnist1.casper-rw.gen3.aff-alive-6>
 |6|-/----------|0|0|0|0|0|0|0
0|<ubnist1.casper-rw.gen3.aff-alive-7>|7|-/rrw-------
 |0|0|4299210752|1230496676|1230496676|1230496676|0
...
0|/lost+found|11|d/drwx------
 |0|0|16384|1230496676|1230496676|1230496676|0
0|/.wh..wh.aufs|12|r/rr--r-
 -r--|0|0|0|1230469846|1230469846|1231311252|0
0|/.wh..wh.plnk|7681|d/drwx------
 |0|0|4096|1230469846|1230469897|1230469897|0
0|/.wh..wh.plnk/1162.7709|7709|r/rrw-r-
 -r--|0|0|186|1225322232|1225322232|1230469866|0
```

When generating a timeline for an actual investigation we will want to set the time zone that data originated in and possibly some additional file system-specific information. However, to generate a simple comma-separated timeline, we can issue the following command:

```
user@forensics:~$ mactime -b ubnist1.bodyfile -d > ubnist1.timeline.csv
```

Timeline analysis is quite useful when performed properly. We will discuss timeline analysis in Chapter 9.

The sigfind command is used to search a source file for a binary value at given offsets. Given a sequence of hexadecimal bytes, sigfind will search through a stream and output the offsets where matching sequences are found. Sigfind can be sector or block aligned, which can be of value when searching through semistructured data such as memory dumps or extracted unallocated space. This is useful for locating files based on header information while minimizing noisy false positives that may occur when simply searching through a data stream using something like the grep command.

Using the sigfind tool is quite simple.

```
-sigfind [-b bsize] [-o offset] [-t template] [-lV] [hex_
   signature] file
        -b bsize: Give block size (default 512)
        -o offset: Give offset into block where signature
           should exist (default 0)
        -l: Signature will be little endian in image
        -V: Version
        -t template: The name of a data structure template:
           dospart, ext2, ext3, fat, hfs, hfs+, ntfs, ufs1, ufs2
```

As an example, we can use sigfind to locate (at least portions of) PDF files on our test Ext3 image. PDF documents begin with the characters "%PDF." Converting these ASCII characters to their hex equivalent gives us "25 50 44 46." Using sigfind, we look for this at the start of every cluster boundary (which was discovered earlier using the fsstat tool).

```
user@forensics:~$ sigfind -b 4096 25504446 ubnist1.casper-rw.gen3.aff
Block size: 4096 Offset: 0 Signature: 25504446
Block: 722 (-)
Block: 1488 (+766)
Block: 1541 (+53)
Block: 1870 (+329)
Block: 82913 (+81043)
...
```

The output of the tool provides the offset in blocks into the image where the hit signature matched and in parentheses provides the offset from the previous match. Sigfind also has a number of data structure templates included, which makes identifying lost partitions or file system structures simple.

The hfind command is used to query hash databases in a much faster manner than grepping through flat text files.

The sorter command extracts and sorts files based on their file type as determined by analysis of the file's content. It can also look up hashes of extracted files and perform file extension verification.

Finally, the srch_strings command is simply a standalone version of the *strings* command found in the GNU *binutils* package. This tool is included to ensure that the Sleuth Kit has string extraction capability without requiring that the full *binutils* package be installed on systems where it is not normally present.

Image File Tools

We can think of the image file as a new intermediary layer that replaces the disk layer in our file system stack. Because this layer is created by an examiner, we generally don't expect to find any forensically interesting items here. However, depending on the forensic format, relevant information may be available.

The img_stat command will display information about the image format, including any hash information and other case-relevant metadata contained in the image. This tool is generally only useful when executed against forensic image container types. Here is the img_stat information from our Ext3 test image:

```
user@forensics:~$ img_stat ubnist1.casper-rw.gen3.aff
IMAGE FILE INFORMATION
--------------------------------------------
Image Type: AFF
Size in bytes: 629145600
MD5: 717f6be298748ee7d6ce3e4b9ed63459
SHA1: 61bcd153fc91e680791aa39455688eab946c4b7
Creator: afconvert
Image GID: 25817565F05DFD8CAEC5CFC6B1FAB45
Acquisition Date: 2009-01-28 20:39:30
AFFLib Version: "3.3.5"
```

The img_cat command will stream the content of an image file to STDOUT. This is a convenient way to convert a forensic container into a "raw" image.

Journal Tools

Many modern file systems support *journaling*. To grossly simplify, journaling file systems keep a journal of changes they are preparing to make and then they make the changes. Should the system lose power in the middle of a change, the journal is used to replay those changes to ensure file system consistency. Given this, it is possible that the journal may contain data not found anywhere else in the active file system.

The jls command lists items in the file system journal, and the jcat command streams the content of the requested journal block to STDOUT. As the information provided by these tools is highly file system specific, we will discuss the use of both of them in the relevant file system sections in the following chapters.

PARTITIONING AND DISK LAYOUTS

The two primary partitioning schemes in use today are the "Master Boot Record (MBR)" and the "GUID Partition Table (GPT)." The GPT scheme was developed as a replacement for the aging MBR scheme. The MBR partitioning method originally only allowed for four primary partitions and disks of up to 2 Terabytes, a size that is quite possible to exceed nowadays. The GPT format supports disks up to 8 Zettabytes in size and 128 primary partitions, along with many more improvements. The partition table is not likely to contain any information of relevance to most investigations. Forensic analysis of the partition table is usually limited to recovery of volumes when the partitioning structures are missing or corrupted.

Partition Identification and Recovery

Identification of deleted or otherwise missing partitions can be performed using the sigfind tool mentioned earlier. The tool includes a number of predefined data structure templates that will locate the tell-tale marks of a partition table or file system header. We can test this using the 10th test image from the Digital Forensic Tool Testing project (http://dftt.sourceforge.net/test10/index.html). The "dospart" template looks for the hex value "55AA" in the last two bytes of each sector, a structure common to MBR partitions.

```
user@ubuntu:~/10-ntfs-autodetect$ sigfind -t dospart 10-ntfs-
  autodetect/10-ntfs-disk.dd
Block size: 512 Offset: 510 Signature: 55AA
Block: 0 (-)
Block: 63 (+63)
Block: 96389 (+96326)
Block: 96390 (+1)
```

We can compare this with mmls output for the same image:

```
DOS Partition Table
Offset Sector: 0
Units are in 512-byte sectors
  Slot Start End Length Description
00: Meta 0000000000 0000000000 0000000001 Primary Table (#0)
01: ----- 0000000000 0000000062 0000000063 Unallocated
02: 00:00 0000000063 0000096389 0000096327 NTFS (0x07)
03: 00:01 0000096390 0000192779 0000096390 NTFS (0x07)
04: ----- 0000192780 0000192783 0000000004 Unallocated
```

We can see that sigfind located the 0x55AA signature in the boot sector (0), the beginning and end of the first volume (63 and 96389), and the beginning of the next volume (96390).

NOTE

Other Media Management Schemes

The Sleuth Kit is able to recognize two other volume layer layouts: Sun *slices* (used by Solaris) and BSD *disklabels* (used by BSD-based operating systems). We don't cover analysis of either platform in this book, but should you need to, you can use the Sleuth Kit on these volumes as well.

Additionally, the TestDisk tool from CGSecurity can be used to recover partitions in the case of disk corruption or intentional spoiling. TestDisk can operate on both raw and Expert Witness/E01 format files used by EnCase. An excellent tutorial on the use of TestDisk is provided at the CGSecurity site [2]. Testdisk can be installed on Ubuntu via *apt-get*. The source code and precompiled binaries for DOS, Windows, OS X, and Linux are also available from the CGSecurity site (www.cgsecurity.org).

Redundant Array of Inexpensive Disks

Redundant Array of Inexpensive Disks (RAID) is designed as a means to take multiple physical disks and address them as a single logical unit.

The most commonly used basic RAID levels are:

- **RAID 0** refers to a setup of at least two disks that are "striped" at a block level. Given two disks (0 and 1), block A will be written to disk 0, block B will be written to disk 1, and so on. This increases write speeds and does not sacrifice any storage space, but increases the fragility of data, as losing a single drive means losing half of your blocks.
- **RAID 1** is the opposite of RAID 0—blocks are mirrored across pairs of drives. This increases read speeds and reliability, but reduces the amount of available storage to half of the physical disk space.

- **RAID 5** requires at least three disks and performs striping across multiple disks in addition to creating *parity blocks*. These blocks are also striped across disks and are used to recreate data in the event a drive is lost.

Additionally, there are "nested" or "hybrid" RAID setups that combine two of these RAID levels in sequence. For example, a RAID 50 or 5+0 set would be a pair of RAID5 sets that are subsequently striped.

The Sleuth Kit has no built-in capability for dealing with RAID. The *PyFLAG* suite discussed in Chapter 9 includes a command line python utility called *raid_guess.py* that can be used to reconstruct a RAID map when given a set of disk images [3]. That said, the authors recommend using the original hardware the RAID is housed in to perform imaging whenever possible. There are many different RAID implementations in use, and recreating the logical structure after the fact can be perilous.

SPECIAL CONTAINERS

In addition to file systems in volumes on physical media, you may have to deal with file systems in other containers. One example is the Macintosh-specific DMG container discussed in the previous section. The other two major containers you are likely to encounter are *Virtual Machine Disk Images* and *Forensic Containers*.

Virtual Machine Disk Images

Virtualization applications such as VMWare, VirtualBox, Virtual PC, and QEMU allow users to run a full "virtual machine" within the host operating system. Generally, they store the file systems used by these virtual machines as virtual disk images— container files that act as a "disk" for purposes of virtualization software. If it acts like a disk for virtualization software, we should be able to get it to act as a disk for purposes of extracting artifacts. The most common virtual disk format today is *VMDK*, used by VMWare's virtualization products.

A VMWare virtual disk is defined using a *descriptor file* that defines the file(s) that makes up that particular virtual disk, as well as specifications of the "disk" being presented to the virtual machine. A disk is originally formed from the base file (or files in the case where the disk is created as a series of 2-GB split chunks). As users create snapshots of a virtual machine, files containing changes from the base image called *delta links* are created, and a new descriptor file containing information about the base and delta files is created.

The full VMDK specification is available from VMWare at http://www.vmware.com/app/vmdk/?src=vmdk.

AFFLib supports VMDK containers natively, and Sleuth Kit will import this functionality if built with AFF support. We can use any of the sleuth kit tools directly against a VMDK by specifying the "afflib" parameter to the image type argument (- i).

> **TIP**
>
> **Creating VMDKs from Raw Images**
> In some circumstances it is useful to be able to access a raw image in a virtual machine. Two projects are available that provide just this functionality. LiveView (http://liveview .sourceforge.net/) is a graphical application targeted for use on Windows with limited Linux support that will create all the files needed to generate a VMWare-bootable virtual machine. Raw2VMDK (http://segfault.gr/projects/lang/en/projects_id/16/secid/28/) is a command line utility that simply generates a valid VMDK file that points to your existing raw image. You can then use this VMDK in any number of ways. For example, the VMDK can be added as a secondary (read-only) disk attached to a forensics-oriented virtual machine.

> **NOTE**
>
> **Other Virtual Disk Formats**
> While the most common, VMWare's VMDK is by no means the only virtual disk format in use.
>
> **VDI** is the virtual disk format used by Sun's open source virtualization platform VirtualBox.
> **VHD** is the format used by Microsoft's Virtual PC product, as well as the "built-in" virtualization capability found in Windows 7 and Server 2008.
> **QCOW2** is the format used currently by the open source QEMU project.
>
> Should you need to do so, these disk formats can be converted into either VMDKs or raw images suitable for forensic processing using either the *qemu-img* utility (part of the QEMU package) or the *vboxmanage* utility from VirtualBox.

Forensic Containers

We have already spent a little time working with forensic containers, but we have not gone into detail about what exactly they are. In general, container formats geared toward forensic imaging have some functionality above and beyond what we get with a raw disk image. This can include things such as internal consistency checking, case information management, compression, and encryption. We can, of course, perform any of these tasks with a raw image as well. The difference is for a forensic container format, these functions are built into the format, reducing the administrative overhead involved with things such as ensuring that the hash and case notes for a given image are kept with that image at all times.

EWF/E01

The most commonly used forensic container format is the *Expert Witness Format* (EWF), sometimes referred to as the "E01" format after its default extension. This native format is used by Guidance Software's *EnCase* forensic suite. This "format" has changed somewhat from one release of EnCase to the next and is not an open standard. That said, the LibEWF library supports all modern variants of image files generated by EnCase in this format.

The structure of this format has been documented by its original author, Andy Rosen of ASRData, with further documentation performed by Joachim Metz during his work on the LibEWF project [4]. The EWF format supports compression, split files, and stores case metadata (including an MD5 or SHA1 hash of the acquired image) in a header data structure found in the first segment of the image file. Examiners interested in the inner workings of the EWF format should reference these documents.

AFF

The Advanced Forensics Format (AFF) is an open source format for storing disk images for forensics, as well as any relevant metadata. AFF is implemented in the LibAFF package we installed previously. The Sleuth Kit supports AFF image files through this library. AFF images can be compressed, encrypted, and digitally signed. An interesting feature of the AFF format is that metadata stored in the image file are extensible—arbitrary information relevant to the case can be stored directly in the image file in question.

AFF images can be stored in one of three methods:

- AFF—This is the default format of an AFF container; this is a single image file containing forensic data as well as case metadata.
- AFD—This format contains metadata in the image, but splits the image file into fixed-size volumes. This can be useful when transporting or archiving images via size-limited file systems or media.
- AFM—This format stores the image file as a single, solid container but stores metadata in an external file.

HASHING

One of the key activities performed at many different points throughout an examination is generation of a cryptographic hash, or *hashing*. A cryptographic hash function takes an arbitrary amount of data as input and returns a fixed-size string as output. The resulting value is a *hash* of data. Common hashing algorithms used during a forensic examination include MD5 and SHA1. MD5 produces a 128-bit hash value, while SHA1 produces a 160-bit hash value. Longer versions of SHA can be used as well; these will be referred to by the bit length of the hash value they produce (e.g., SHA256 and SHA512).

For hash functions used in forensic functions, modification of a single bit of input data will produce a radically different hash value. Given this property, it is easy to determine one of the core uses for hashing in forensic analysis: verification of the integrity of digital evidence. A hash generated from the original evidence can be compared with a hash of the bit-stream image created from this evidence— matching hashes show that these two items are the same thing. Additionally, taking an additional hash after completing examination of a forensic copy can show that the examiner did not alter source data at any time.

Other characteristics of hash functions make them valuable for additional forensic uses. Because a hash is calculated by processing the content of a file, matching hashes across various files can be used to find renamed files, or to remove "known good" files from the set of data to be examined. Alternately, the hashes of files of interest can be used to locate them irrespective of name changes or other metadata manipulations.

Many programs that implement the MD5 and SHA* algorithms are available for a variety of platforms. For simply generating a hash of a single file, the md5sum or sha1sum programs present on nearly on Linux systems are sufficient. Using these programs to generate hash lists of multiple files or multiple nested directories of files can be quite tedious. To solve this problem, Jesse Kornblum has produced the md5deep and hashdeep utilities.

Md5deep is a suite of hashing utilities designed to recurse through a set of input files or directories and produce hash lists for these. The output is configurable based on the examiners requirements and, despite the name, the suite includes similar tools implementing SHA* and other hashing algorithms. Hashdeep is a newer utility developed as a more robust hash auditing application. It can be used to generate multiple hashes (e.g., MD5 and SHA1 hashes) for files and can be used to subsequently audit the set of hashed data. After generating a base state, hashdeep can report on matching files, missing files, files that have been moved from one location to another, and files that did not appear in the original set. Full usage information and tutorials, source code, and binaries for Windows are available at the md5deep site [5].

As stated earlier, the fact that a change in a single input bit will change many bits in the final hash value is one of the valuable characteristics of hash functions for purposes of proving a file's content or integrity. If you instead want to prove that two files are *similar* but not identical, a standard hashing approach will not help—you will only be able to tell that two files are different, not *how* different. Jesse Kornblum's ssdeep was developed to provide this capability, which Jesse calls "context triggered piecewise hashes" "fuzzy hashing [6]." To simplify, fuzzy hashing breaks the input file into chunks, hashes those, and then uses this list to compare the similarity of two files. The hashing window can be tuned by the end user.

We can see the basic operation of ssdeep in the console output that follows. The author generated a paragraph of random text and then modified capitalization of the first word. The MD5 hashes are wildly different:

```
MD5 (lorem1.txt) = ea4884844ddb6cdc55aa7a95d19815a2
MD5 (lorem2.txt) = 9909552a79ed968a336ca3b9e96aca66
```

We can generate fuzzy hashes for both files by running ssdeep with no flags:

```
ssdeep,1.1--blocksize:hash:hash,filename
24:FPYOEMR7S1PYzvH6juMtTtqULiveqrTFIoCPddBjMxiAyejao:
   9YfQ7qYza6MdtiHrTKoCddBQxiwd,"/home/cory/ssdeep-test/lorem1.txt"
24:1PYOEMR7S1PYzvH6juMtTtqULiveqrTFIoCPddBjMxiAyejao:dYfQ
   7qYza6MdtiHrTKoCddBQxiwd,"/home/cory/ssdeep-test/lorem2.txt"
```

By inspecting both sets of fuzzy hashes visually, we can identify that they match, except for the first byte, which is where our modification occurred. Alternately, we can run ssdeep in directory mode by passing the -d flag, which will compare all files in a directory:

```
user@ubuntu:~/ssdeep-test$ ssdeep -d *
/home/user/ssdeep-test/lorem2.txt matches /home/user/ssdeep-
   test/lorem1.txt (99)
```

Full usage information and tutorials, source code, and binaries for Windows are available at the ssdeep site [7].

NOTE

Hash Collisions

Over the past few years there have been some publicized attacks against the MD5 algorithm in which researchers were able to generate two different files that generated the same MD5 hash value. All of the attacks made public thus far have been in the category of *collision attacks*. In a collision attack, a third party controls both files. This scenario is not applicable for most of the tasks we use hashing for in forensic analysis, such as verifying an image file has not been altered or verifying a file against a set of known good or bad hashes. That said, tools such as hashdeep can use multiple hash algorithms (in addition to nonhash data like file size) to strengthen the confidence of a hashset.

CARVING

A wise forensic examiner once said "when all else fails, we carve." Extraction of meaningful file content from otherwise unstructured streams of data is a science and an art unto itself. This discipline has been the focus of numerous presentations at the Digital Forensics Research Workshop over the years, and advancements continue to be made to this day. At its most basic, however, the process of carving involves searching a data stream for file headers and magic values, determining (or guessing) the file end point, and saving this substream out into a carved file. Carving is still an open problem and is an area of ongoing, active experimentation. Numerous experimental programs are designed to implement specific new ideas in carving, as well as more utilitarian programs geared toward operational use.

TIP

hachoir-subfile

The hachoir-subfile program can be used to intelligently identify files within binary streams, including unallocated space from disk images. It operates in a manner similar to the sigfind, but uses intelligence about file formats to provide a much stronger signal that an actual file has been located, minimizing false positives. While not a carving tool in and of itself, it can be used to positively identify files inside of a stream for subsequent manual extraction. The *hachoir* suite of programs is discussed in detail in Chapter 8.

Foremost

Foremost is a file carving program originally written by Jesse Kornblum and Kris Kendall at the Air Force Office of Special Investigations and later updated by Nick Mikus of the Naval Postgraduate School. It uses defined headers, footers, and knowledge of the internal structures for supported file types to aid in carving. A complete list of the file types supported natively by foremost can be found in the program's man page, but suffice it to say it includes the usual suspects: JPEG images, office documents, archive files, and more. If necessary, additional file types can be defined in a custom *foremost.conf* file. We will discuss the analysis of files and their content in Chapter 8.

Foremost can be installed easily using apt-get on Ubuntu or by retrieving and compiling the source (or supplied binaries) from the foremost project page at Source-Forge: http://foremost.sourceforge.net/. Options that may be particularly important include:

```
-d - turn on indirect block detection (for UNIX file-systems)
-i - specify input file (default is stdin)
-a - Write all headers, perform no error detection (corrupted
     files)
-w - Only write the audit file, do not write any detected files
     to the disk
-o - set output directory (defaults to output)
-c - set configuration file to use (defaults to foremost.conf)
-q - enables quick mode. Search are performed on 512 byte
     boundaries.
```

We can perform a basic run of foremost using the Digital Forensics Research Work-stop 2006 carving challenge file as input [8]. We will use the -v flag to increase the verbosity of the output.

```
user@ubuntu:~/dfrws $ foremost -v -i dfrws-2006-challenge.raw
Foremost version 1.5.4 by Jesse Kornblum, Kris Kendall, and Nick Mikus
Audit File
Foremost started at Sat Dec 10 21:51:55 2010
Invocation: foremost -v -i dfrws-2006-challenge.raw
Output directory: /home/user/dfrws/output
Configuration file: /usr/local/etc
Processing: dfrws-2006-challenge.raw
|------------------------------------------------------------
File: dfrws-2006-challenge.raw
Start: Sat Jan 1 21:51:55 2011
Length: Unknown

Num     Name (bs=512)    Size      File Offset     Comment
0:      00003868.jpg     280 KB    1980416
1:      00008285.jpg     594 KB    4241920
2:      00011619.jpg     199 KB    5948928
3:      00012222.jpg       6 MB    6257664
```

```
4:      00027607.jpg      185 KB      14134784
5:      00031475.jpg      206 KB      16115200
6:      00036292.jpg      174 KB      18581504
7:      00040638.jpg      292 KB      20806656
8:      00041611.jpg        1 MB      21304832
9:      00045566.jpg      630 KB      23329792
10:     00094846.jpg      391 KB      48561152
11:     00000009.htm       17 KB      4691
12:     00004456.htm       22 KB      2281535
13:     00027496.htm      349 KB      14078061
14:     00028244.htm       50 KB      14460928
15:     00029529.htm      183 KB      15118957
16:     00032837.doc      282 KB      16812544
17:     00045964.doc       71 KB      23533568
18:     00028439.zip      157 KB      14560768
19:     00030050.zip      697 KB      15385752
20:     00045015.zip      274 KB      23047680
21:     00007982.png        6 KB      4086865     (1408 x 1800)
22:     00033012.png       69 KB      16902215    (1052 x 360)
23:     00035391.png       19 KB      18120696    (879 x 499)
24:     00035431.png       72 KB      18140936    (1140 x 540)
*|
Finish: Sat Jan 1 21:51:57 2011
25 FILES EXTRACTED

jpg:= 11
htm:= 5
ole:= 2
zip:= 3
png:= 4
```

Note that due to the intentional fragmentation of this test image, the bulk of these extracted files will not be identical to the original items. Simson Garfinkel presented research at the Digital Forensics Research workshop in 2007 that indicated that the majority of files on any give volume will be contiguous and that most fragmented files are simply split into two fragments, with a single block splitting the halves [9].

TIP

Additional Carving Utilities

Scalpel is a file carver forked from Foremost version 0.69 and completely rewritten with an eye toward increasing performance. The latest public release of scalpel is version 1.60, released in December 2006. The authors have presented papers referencing advanced versions of scalpel with parallelized carving support and GPU acceleration, but at the time of this publication these have not been released publicly [10].

PhotoRec is an advanced, cross-platform carving program distributed as part of the TestDisk program mentioned in the *Partition Identification and Recovery* section. Like TestDisk, CGSecurity provides an extensive guide that details use of the tool on their Web site [11].

The most common scenario for carving in an actual investigation is the attempted retrieval of deleted data for which metadata are no longer present or no longer linked. In these cases, extracting the unallocated space of the volume into a contiguous block using `blkls` has the potential to eliminate fragmentation caused by currently allocated blocks.

FORENSIC IMAGING

In creation of a forensic image, we are trying to capture an accurate as possible representation of source media. This is not unlike the police lines set up at a physical crime scene. These lines are put in place to minimize the amount of change that occurs in a crime scene, which in turn gives the crime scene investigators the most accurate data possible.

Imagine, then, if the crime scene investigators could create a *copy* of the actual crime scene. In the real world this is madness, but this is what we aim to do with creation of a forensic image.

A good forensic imaging process generates an exact duplicate (or a container that holds an exact duplicate) of the source media under investigation. By *exact duplicate* we mean exactly that—we aim to acquire a complete sector-for-sector, byte-for-byte copy of original media. There should be no on-disk information present on source media that do not appear in our forensic image. An ideal imaging process should not alter original media, fail to acquire any portion of original media, nor introduce any data not present on source media into the image file.

A traditional forensic analyst examining a gun used in a homicide works on the original. Why doesn't the computer forensic examiner do the same? Examiners generate forensic images for several reasons. The primary reason is to provide an *exact copy* of original media to examine. For the traditional analyst, the actual weapon is the *best evidence*. In the case of digital evidence, we can make a duplicate of source media that matches the original in every way. Working with original digital evidence can be very dangerous because the original can be altered or destroyed with relative ease. By only accessing the original media once, to generate our forensic image, we minimize our opportunities to alter the original accidentally. Another benefit of working on an image is if we make a mistake and somehow end up altering the image file in some way, we can generate a new exact duplicate from the intact original media.

Deleted Data

Another reason examiners use forensic imaging is for *completeness*. Simply examining an active file system as presented by the operating system is not sufficiently thorough for a forensic examination. Most volumes contain reams of potentially interesting data outside of the viewable, allocated files on a mounted file system. This includes several categories of "deleted data."

- *Deleted* files are the "most recoverable." Generally this refers to files that have been "unlinked"—the file name entry is no longer presented when a user views a directory, and the file name, metadata structure, and data units are marked as "free." However, the connections between these layers are still intact when forensic techniques are applied to the file system. Recovery consists of recording the relevant file name and metadata structures and then extracting the data units.
- *Orphaned* files are similar to *deleted* files except the link between the file name and metadata structure is no longer accurate. In this case, recovery of data (and metadata structure) is still possible but there is no direct correlation from the file name to recovered data.
- *Unallocated* files have had their once-allocated file name entry and associated metadata structure have become unlinked and/or reused. In this case, the only means for recovery is carving the not-yet-reused data units from the unallocated space of the volume.
- *Overwritten* files have had one or more of their data units reallocated to another file. Full recovery is no longer possible, but partial recovery may depend on the extent of overwriting. Files with file names and/or metadata structures intact that have had some or all data units overwritten are sometimes referred to as *Deleted/ Overwritten* or *Deleted/Reallocated*.

File Slack

As mentioned previously, the minimum space that can be allocated on a volume is a single block. Assuming a 4K block size, on a standard drive with 512-byte sectors, this means the ASCII text file containing a single byte—the letter 'a'—will consume eight sectors on the disk. We provided the 'a'—where did the other 4095 bytes written to the disk come from?

The answer is, as always, it depends. Different file systems and operating systems handle this differently, but generally the process goes:

- The cluster to be used is marked as "allocated" and assigned to the file's metadata structure.
- The 'a' followed by 511 null bytes (hex 00) are placed in the first sector.

Astute readers will note that we didn't state how the next seven sectors are written to the disk. That's not an oversight—they aren't written to the disk. They retain whatever data were last stored in them during their *previous* allocation. This is what is known as *file slack* or *slack space*.

Figure 3.2 demonstrates the generation of file slack using three successive views of the same eight blocks on a disk. At first the row consists of new, empty, unallocated blocks. Then, file A is created, has eight blocks allocated to it, and those eight blocks are filled with data. File A is then "deleted" and sometime later the first five blocks are reallocated and overwritten with the content from File B. This leaves three of the blocks containing data from File A unallocated but recoverable.

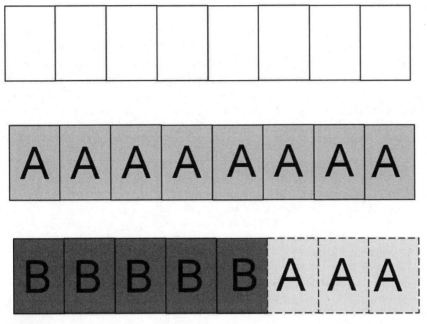

FIGURE 3.2

File slack.

NOTE

RAM Slack

While all modern operating systems pad the written sector with null bytes, this was not always the case. MS-DOS and older DOS-based versions of Microsoft Windows would pad the rest of the sector out with whatever contents of memory happened to be next to data being written. These data, between the end of allocated data and the beginning of previously allocated data, became known as *RAM slack*. Given this, RAM slack could potentially contain data that were never written to the disk, such as cryptographic keys or passphrases.

TIP

Volume or Disk?

When creating a forensic image, most of the time an examiner will use the physical disk (e.g., */dev/sda*) as input. However, in some circumstances you may be better off imaging the volume or volumes of interest (e.g., */dev/sda1*). One example is when dealing with a RAID array. Imaging physical disks requires the capability to rebuild the RAID from these disk images at a later date, which (as mentioned previously) can be difficult. Depending on the type of RAID and the utilities available to you as an examiner, this may prove to be difficult or impossible. Another example is in the case of Storage Area Network volume—with many of these systems, removing and imaging the physical drives are simply not options.

dd

The dd command is the most basic open source tool available to create a forensic image. Because it is nearly universally present on any Unix-like operating system and is the basis for several other forensic imaging utilities, learning its operation is valuable to any examiner. Put simply, dd copies data from one place to another. The user can provide various arguments and flags to modify this simple behavior, but the basic syntax of the tool is fairly clear. The excerpt from the tool help given here has the basic options you need to understand in bold.

```
user@forensics:~$ dd --help
Usage: dd [OPERAND]…
  or: dd OPTION
Copy a file, converting and formatting according to the operands.
  bs=BYTES force ibs=BYTES and obs=BYTES
  cbs=BYTES convert BYTES bytes at a time
  conv=CONVS convert the file as per the comma separated symbol list
  count=BLOCKS copy only BLOCKS input blocks
  ibs=BYTES read BYTES bytes at a time
  if=FILE read from FILE instead of stdin
  iflag=FLAGS read as per the comma separated symbol list
  obs=BYTES write BYTES bytes at a time
  of=FILE write to FILE instead of stdout
  oflag=FLAGS write as per the comma separated symbol list
  seek=BLOCKS skip BLOCKS obs-sized blocks at start of output
  skip=BLOCKS skip BLOCKS ibs-sized blocks at start of input
  status=noxfer suppress transfer statistics
```

So, to make a simple clone from one drive to another, we would invoke the tools like so:

```
dd if=/dev/sda of=/dev/sdb bs=4096
```

This takes reads from the first disk, 4096 bytes at a time, and writes the content out to the second disk, 4096 bytes at a time. If we did not provide the *block size* (bs=) argument, dd would default to reading and writing a single 512-byte sector at a time, which is quite slow.

Cloning a disk is interesting but of limited use for an examiner. For the most part, we are interested in creating a *forensic image file*—a file that contains all of the content present on the source disk. This, also, is simple to do using the same syntax.

```
user@forensics:~$ sudo dd if=/dev/sdg of=dd.img bs=32K

[sudo] password for user:
60832+0 records in
60832+0 records out
1993342976 bytes (2.0 GB) copied, 873.939 s, 2.3 MB/s
```

The key items of interest in the console output for the dd command are "records in" and "records out" lines. First, they match, which is good—this indicates that we did not lose any data due to drive failures, failure to write the output file fully, or any other reason. Second, the "60832+0" records indicate that exactly this many 32K blocks were both read and written. If we had imaged a drive that was not an exact multiple of 32K in size, the "+0" would instead show "+1," indicating that a partial record was read (and written).

Some of the other options of forensic interest present in the base dd command are the conv (convert) option. If imaging a failing or damaged hard drive, the conv=noerror,sync option can be used to ignore read errors, writing blocks of NULL characters in the output file for every block that was unable to be read. Additionally, in the case of a dying drive, supplying the iflag=direct option (use direct I/O, bypassing the kernel drive cache) and reducing the block size to 512 bytes will ensure that the amount of unrecoverable data is kept to a minimum.

> **WARNING**
> **Bad Sectors**
> Note that using dd with the conv=noerror argument is **not** the recommended course of action when attempting to image a damaged hard drive. Given the option, we recommend using GNU ddrescue, a specialized version of dd designed to deal with retrieving data from uncooperative drives. However, in some cases your only option may be to either retrieve a partial image using dd or retrieve nothing at all.

dcfldd

While dd can and has been used to acquire forensically sound images, versions of dd are available that are specifically designed for forensic use. The first of these to be examined is dcfldd, created for the Defense Computer Forensics Laboratory by Nick Harbour. The dcfldd project forked from GNU dd, so its basic operation is quite similar. However, dcfldd has some interesting capabilities that aren't found in vanilla dd. Most of the capabilities revolve around hash creation and validation, logging of activity, and splitting the output file into fixed-size chunks. The extended dcfldd functions, as well as base dd functions, can be reviewed by passing the --help flag to the dcfldd command.

Unsurprisingly, performing the same image acquisition that was done with dd using dcfldd is quite similar. In fact, if we did not want to take advantage of the additional features of dcfldd, we could use the exact same arguments as before and would get the same results. In the code section following, we reimage the same device as previously, but at the same time generate a log of the md5 and sha1 hashes generated of each 512 megabyte chunk of the disk.

```
user@forensics:~$ sudo dcfldd bs=32k if=/dev/sdg of=dcfldd.img
  hashwindow=512M hash=md5,sha1 hashlog=dcfldd.hashlog
60672 blocks (1896Mb) written.
60832+0 records in
60832+0 records out
```

dc3dd

The last dd variant we will examine is dc3dd, a forensically oriented version created by Jesse Kornblum for the Department of Defense Cyber Crime Center. dc3dd is developed as a patch applied to GNU dd, rather than a fork, so dc3dd is able to incorporate changes made in the mainline dd more rapidly than dcfldd. dc3dd has all of the same extended features found in dcfldd and has core dd features currently absent in the latest dcfldd release.

We can provide the same arguments to dc3dd that were used previously with dcfldd.

```
user@forensics:~$ sudo dc3dd bs=32k if=/dev/sdg of=dc3dd.img
  hashwindow=512M hash=md5,sha1 hashlog=dc3dd.hashlog
[sudo] password for user:
warning: sector size not probed, assuming 512
dc3dd 6.12.3 started at 2010-09-03 17:34:57 -0700
command line: dc3dd bs=32k if=/dev/sdg of=dc3dd.img
  hashwindow=512M hash=md5,sha1 hashlog=dc3dd.hashlog
compiled options: DEFAULT_BLOCKSIZE=32768
sector size: 512 (assumed)
md5  0- 536870912: 07c416f8453933c80319c2d89e5533ad
sha1 0- 536870912: a222f5835ed7b7a51baaa57c5f4d4495b1ca1e79
md5 536870912- 1073741824: acac88a20c6d6b364714e6174874e4da
sha1 536870912- 1073741824:
  5b69440a15795592e9e158146e4e458ec8c5b319
md5 1073741824- 1610612736: ed9b57705e7ae681181e0f86366b85e6
sha1 1073741824- 1610612736:
  bc5369977d9a2f788d910b5b01a9a1e97432f928
md5 1610612736- 1993342976: 812c94592ec5628f749b59a1e56cd9ab
sha1 1610612736- 1993342976:
  bb789315a814159cdf2d2803a73149588b5290ee
md5 TOTAL: 58e362af9868562864461385ecf58156
sha1 TOTAL: 8eaba11cb49435df271d8bc020eb2b46d11902fe
3893248+0 sectors in
3893248+0 sectors out
1993342976 bytes (1.9 G) copied (??%), 908.424 s, 2.1 M/s
dc3dd completed at 2010-09-03 17:50:06 -0700
```

Note that dc3dd produces a hash log to the console as well as writing it out to the file passed in the hashlog= argument. Additionally, it presents the sector count rather than the block count as a summary upon completion.

> **TIP**
>
> **Creating "Expert Witness Format" Images**
>
> It is likely that you will have to provide forensic images for use by a third party at some point in your career. Depending on the capabilities and experience of the other party, you may wish to provide them with images in the "Expert Witness Format" discussed in the *Forensic Containers* section. Note that EnCase is entirely capable of reading from "raw" images, but should you receive a specific request to provide images in this format, you can comply using open source tools.
>
> The `ewfacquire` utility is a part of the LibEWF package and provides a robust console interface for generating EWF image files. It is invoked simply by providing the `ewfacquire` command with an input source. The program will prompt the user for information required to generate the image file.
>
> The **guymager** application is a graphical forensic imaging utility that can be used to generate raw, AFF, and EWF image files. Note that guymager uses LibEWF for its EWF support, so functionally these two tools should be the same when generating EWF containers.

SUMMARY

This chapter discussed the core concepts of disk and file system analysis. In addition, it explored many of the fundamental concepts of forensic analysis, such as forensic imaging, dealing with forensic containers, and hashing. Through use of the Sleuth Kit, we have shown how to exploit a file system for artifacts of forensic interest. Subsequent chapters will build upon this foundation to examine and analyze higher level artifacts.

References

[1] B. Carrier, 2005. File System Forensic Analysis. Addison-Wesley, Boston, MA.
[2] TestDisk Step By Step—CGSecurity. http://www.cgsecurity.org/wiki/TestDisk_Step_By_Step.
[3] RAID Recovery—PyFLAG. http://pyflag.sourceforge.net/Documentation/articles/raid/reconstruction.html.
[4] libewf—Browse /documentation/EWF file format at SourceForge.net. http://sourceforge.net/projects/libewf/files/documentation/EWF%20file%20format/.
[5] Getting Started with Hashdeep. http://md5deep.sourceforge.net/start-hashdeep.html.
[6] J. Kornblum, Identifying almost identical files using context triggered *piecewise hashing*. Paper presented at Digital Forensics Research Workshop, 2006. Elsevier, (accessed 13.09.10).
[7] Getting Started with ssdeep. http://ssdeep.sourceforge.net/usage.html.
[8] Digital Forensics Research Workshop 2006 File Carving Challenge. http://www.dfrws.org/2006/challenge/dfrws-2006-challenge.zip.
[9] S.L. Garfinkel, Carving contiguous and fragmented files with *fast object validation*. Paper presented at Digital Forensics Research Workshop, 2007.
[10] Scalpel: A Frugal, High Performance File Carver. http://www.digitalforensicssolutions.com/Scalpel/.
[11] PhotoRec Step By Step – CGSecurity, http://www.cgsecurity.org/wiki/PhotoRec_Step_By_Step (retrieived Jan 9, 2011).

Windows Systems and Artifacts

INTRODUCTION

Like any operating system, Windows systems offer a wealth of artifacts. In the case of the Windows operating system, there may be a greater wealth of artifacts than on some other operating systems. As such, those artifacts are unique to the operating system. This chapter addresses and discusses a number of artifacts unique and specific to Windows systems.

WINDOWS FILE SYSTEMS

Windows systems support two primary file systems: FAT and NTFS. "FAT" stands for "file allocation table," and "NTFS" stands for "New Technology File System." FAT file systems come in several different flavors and are supported by a number of operating systems, (although drivers are available that allow other operating systems to access NTFS-formatted volumes) including Linux and MacOSX. In contrast, the NTFS file system is not as widely supported, but does provide administrators with the ability to set access control lists (ACLs) on file objects within the file system.

File Allocation Table

The FAT file system is perhaps one of the simplest file systems available and has been widely available on Microsoft operating systems, starting with MS-DOS.

FAT was the primary file system on MS-DOS systems and floppy diskettes and was also used extensively on Windows 3.x and Window 95 and 98. This file system is still used on removable storage devices such as thumb drives, as well as compact flash cards used in digital cameras. The FAT file system is supported by other operating systems, so it makes a good medium for moving from one system (Linux, MacOSX) to another (Windows); if you're conducting analysis via a Linux system, you can save extracted files and data and easily access it later from a Windows system. However, keep in mind that the FAT file system doesn't possess the same security mechanisms as other file systems, including NTFS (discussed later in this chapter).

The FAT file system comes in a number of different flavors; FAT12, FAT16, FAT32, and exFAT. FAT is also considered to be a rather simple file system in that it possesses relatively few data structures. With the FAT file system, the disk or volume is broken up in to clusters of a specific size, based on the version of FAT used. For example, for FAT12, the cluster size ranged from 512 bytes to 8 kilobytes (KB). For FAT16 [1], the cluster size ranges from 512 bytes to 64 KB.

NOTE

Cluster Sizes

Using larger cluster sizes to support larger disks makes the FAT file system inefficient, as small files, smaller than the cluster size, are written to a cluster. As such, the remaining space in the cluster is wasted.

Microsoft provides a Knowledge Base article that describes the FAT32 file system [2] from a high level. As part of this description, Microsoft states that the FAT32 file system can support disks up to 2 terabytes (TB), but that Windows 2000 only supports partitions up to 32 gigabytes (GB) in size. Using 4-KB clusters, FAT32 uses space more efficiently; cluster sizes can range from 512 bytes to 32 KB. The primary difference between FAT16 and FAT32 is the logical partition size.

On disk, the FAT file system begins with the boot sector (Microsoft Knowledge Base article 140418 [3] provides a detailed description of the FAT boot sector) and is followed by FAT areas 1 and 2 (the second FAT area is a copy of the first), the root folder, files, and other folders. The FAT maps to each cluster within the volume and tells the operating system how each cluster is used; whether it's used, in use as part of a file, or the end of the file.

Files are laid out within the FAT volume in clusters and are referenced by 32-byte entries that contain the address of the starting cluster number for the file. If a file consumes more than one cluster, then the starting cluster ends with the number of the next cluster and so on until the last cluster is reached. This final cluster is marked with an end-of-file indicator (0xffff).

> **NOTE**
>
> **Recovering Deleted Files**
>
> Nick Harbour, a malware reverse engineer with consulting firm Mandiant, wrote an open source Unix command line tool for recovering deleted files from FAT file systems called "fatback." The tool is referenced from Nick's Web site, rnicrosoft.net, and is available for download from SourceForge.net (the project can be found on the Web at http://sourceforge .net/projects/fatback/).

According to the "File Times" article [4] on the Microsoft Developer Network (MSDN) site, FAT file times maintain a resolution of 10 milliseconds for creation times, a resolution of 2 seconds for the last modification or write time, and a resolution of a day for last accessed times. Also, the FAT file system stores its MAC times in the local system time format.

New Technology File System

The NTFS is perhaps the most widely used file system on Windows systems, as it offers a number of advantages over the FAT file system, including the ability to set access control lists (ACLs, or permissions) on file objects, journaling, compression, and a host of other capabilities not offered on the FAT file system.

MFT

The most notable source of valuable information for an analyst from the NTFS file system is the Master File Table (MFT). The location of the starting sector of the MFT can be found in the boot sector of the disk, and every file and directory in the volume has an entry in the MFT. Each MFT entry is 1024 bytes in size, making the MFT very simple to parse. Each MFT record, or entry, begins with ASCII string "FILE" (if there is an error in the entry, it will begin with "BAAD") and consists of one or more (most often, more) attributes, each with their own identifier and structure. Figure 4.1 illustrates a portion of an MFT entry.

The first 42 bytes of each MFT entry comprise a header structure with 12 elements, and the remaining 982 bytes depend largely on the values within the header and the

```
00000000h: 46 49 4C 45 30 00 03 00 64 6F 11 01 00 00 00 00 ; FILE0...do......
00000010h: 01 00 01 00 38 00 01 00 A0 01 00 00 00 04 00 00 ; ....8... .......
00000020h: 00 00 00 00 00 00 00 00 06 00 00 00 00 00 00 00 ; ................
00000030h: 50 00 00 00 00 00 00 00 10 00 00 00 60 00 00 00 ; P...........`...
00000040h: 00 00 18 00 00 00 00 00 48 00 00 00 18 00 00 00 ; ........H.......
00000050h: 26 B8 8D B1 12 55 C4 01 26 B8 8D B1 12 55 C4 01 ; &.□±.UÄ.&.□±.UÄ.
00000060h: 26 B8 8D B1 12 55 C4 01 26 B8 8D B1 12 55 C4 01 ; &.□±.UÄ.&.□±.UÄ.
00000070h: 06 00 00 00 00 00 00 00 00 00 00 00 00 00 00 00 ; ................
00000080h: 00 00 00 00 00 01 00 00 00 00 00 00 00 00 00 00 ; ................
00000090h: 00 00 00 00 00 00 00 00 30 00 00 00 68 00 00 00 ; ........0...h...
```

FIGURE 4.1

Excerpt of an MFT record, or entry.

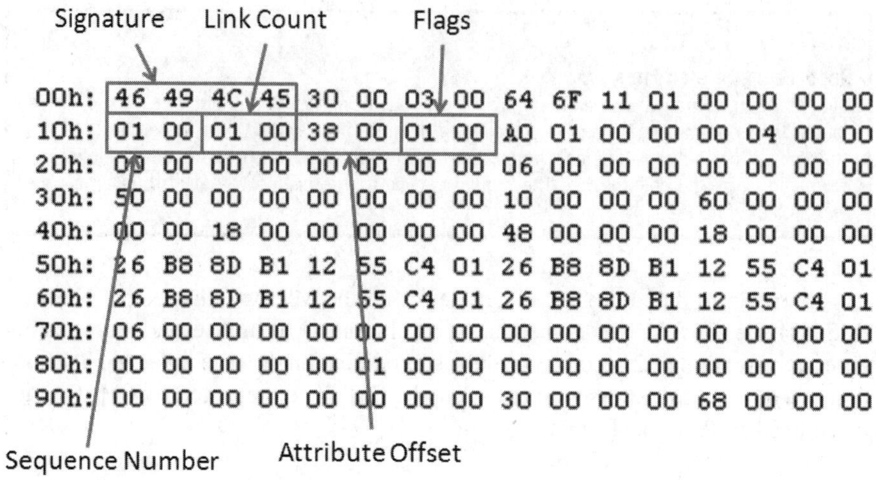

FIGURE 4.2

MFT record header items (in little Endian order).

various attributes contained within the entry. Not all of the elements within the header of the MFT entry are immediately useful to a forensic analyst; however, Figure 4.2 illustrates five of the elements that are immediately useful.

As illustrated in Figure 4.2 (which is a portion extracted from Figure 4.1), we see the "FILE" signature visible at the beginning of the record. Then we see the sequence number or value, which is incremented when the entry is allocated or unallocated. Because this particular MFT entry is actually the first record within the MFT and refers to the file "$MFT," it stands to reason that the sequence number is 1. Next is the link count, which refers to the number of directories that have entries for this record (hard links cause this value to incremented). Next is the offset with the record to the first attribute; if you look at offset 0x38 within the record, you'll see that the first attribute has an identifier of 0x10, or 16. Finally, we see the flags value, which tells us if the entry is allocated (if the 0x01 bit is set) and if the entry is a directory (if the 0x02 bit is set). In short, from these two values, we can determine if the entry is allocated or deleted, and if it is for a file or directory. When the header is parsed, pseudocode for this may be represented as follows:

```
if ($mft{flags} & 0x0001) - allocated; else unallocated/deleted
if ($mft{flags} & 0x0002) - folder/directory; else file
```

The flags value visible in Figure 4.2 is "0x01," which indicates an allocated file. A value of 0x00 would indicate a deleted file, and a value of 0x03 would indicate an allocated directory.

> **TIP**
> **MFT Records**
> MFT records are not deleted once they have been created; new records are added to the MFT as needed, and records for deleted files are reused.

As mentioned previously, only the first 42 bytes are structured; after that, the rest of the MFT entry consists of one or more attribute fields. There is no formal specification or statement that says there needs to be specific attributes within an MFT entry, but for the most part, you can expect to find a $STANDARD_INFORMATION and a $FILE_NAME attribute in most MFT entries. This section looks at these two attributes, as they provide time stamp information, which is valuable to forensic analysts. We will also take a brief look at the $DATA attribute and leave the remaining attributes as an exercise for the interested and curious reader.

The header of each attribute contains a 16-byte header, which identifies the type of attribute, the overall length of the attribute, and whether the attribute is resident to the MFT entry or not, among other elements.

NOTE

MFT Metadata Files

The first 16 entries of the MFT contain information about metadata files; however, they may not all be used. Those that are not used are left in an allocated state and only contain basic information.

Using this header information, we can parse through the MFT entry and extract valuable information from each attribute. For example, the $STANDARD_INFORMATION attribute (which is always resident) exists for every file and directory entry and has an identifier of 0x10 (i.e., 16). This attribute contains the file times for the MFT entry (well, three of them, anyway) that we see when we type "dir" at the command prompt; the modified time, last accessed time, and the creation (born) date of the file or directory, also referred to as "MAC" times. The attribute contains a fourth time value that specifies the last time that the MFT entry was altered. All together, these times are referred to as "MACE" (with the "E" referring to the MFT entry modification time) or "MACB" (with the "C" referring to the MFT entry modification time) times.

WARNING

File Times

NTFS file times are recorded in Universal Coordinated Time (UTC) format, which is analogous to Greenwich Mean Time. This is true for all of the times; in each MFT entry, a file record will likely have at least 8 times associated with it; many times, 12 or more. On the FAT file system, file times are maintained in local system time format.

The $FILE_NAME attribute (identifier 0x30, or 48) is also found with most file and directory MFT entries; in fact, many MFT entries will have more than one $FILE_NAME attribute. Like the $STANDARD_INFORMATION attribute, this attribute is always resident and also contains four time values; however, these time values are usually set when the file is created on the system. Unlike file times in the $STANDARD_INFORMATION attribute, these file times are not affected by normal system activity or malicious tampering and can therefore be used to determine indicators of nefarious activity, and steps can be taken to obfuscate the time when a system was infected. The following code sample (*parseSIAttr()* function) provides an example of how the $STANDARD_INFORMATION attribute can be parsed:

```
sub parseSIAttr {
        my $si = shift;
        my %si;
        my ($type,$len,$res,$name_len,$name_ofs,$flags,$id,
            $sz_content,$ofs_content)
                = unpack("VVCCvvvVv",substr($si,0,22));
        my $content = substr($si,$ofs_content,$sz_content);
        my ($t0,$t1) = unpack("VV",substr($content,0,8));
        $si{c_time} = getTime($t0,$t1);
        my ($t0,$t1) = unpack("VV",substr($content,8,8));
        $si{m_time} = getTime($t0,$t1);
        my ($t0,$t1) = unpack("VV",substr($content,16,8));
        $si{mft_m_time} = getTime($t0,$t1);
        my ($t0,$t1) = unpack("VV",substr($content,24,8));
        $si{a_time} = getTime($t0,$t1);
        $si{flags} = unpack("V",substr($content,32,4));
        return %si;
}
```

TIP

GetTime

The *getTime()* function seen within the code listing for the *parseSIAttr()* attribute just given consists of code borrowed from Andreas Schuster that translates the 64-bit FILETIME object time stamps into a 32-bit Unix time that can be further translated to a human readable time via the Perl built-in *gmtime()* function. That code appears as follows:

```
sub getTime($$) {
        my $lo = shift;
        my $hi = shift;
        my $t;
        if ($lo == 0 && $hi == 0) {
                $t = 0;
        } else {
                $lo -= 0xd53e8000;
                $hi -= 0x019db1de;
                $t = int($hi*429.4967296 + $lo/1e7);
        };
        $t = 0 if ($t < 0);
        return $t;
}
```

This code is very useful for parsing and translating any FILETIME object, regardless of from where it is extracted.

On a normal system, many MFT entries may have two $FILE_NAME attributes: one to hold the full name of the file (or directory) and one to hold the DOS, 8.3 filename. For example, if a file is named "myreallylongfile.txt," the 8.3 file name will appear as "myreal~1.txt." This is kept for compatibility with older file systems and those that do not support long file names. So it is not unusual on a normal Windows system to have a number of MFT entries with two $FILE_NAME attributes with nearly identical contents. The following code sample (*parseFNAttr()* function) provides an example of how a $FILE_NAME attribute from an MFT entry can be parsed and available data extracted:

```
sub parseFNAttr {
        my $fn = shift;
        my %fn;
        my ($type,$len,$res,$name_len,$name_ofs,$flags,$id,
            $sz_content,$ofs_content)
                = unpack("VVCCvvvVv",substr($fn,0,22));
        my $content = substr($fn,$ofs_content,$sz_content);
        $fn{parent_ref} = unpack("V",substr($content,0,4));
        $fn{parent_seq} = unpack("v",substr($content,6,2));
        my ($t0,$t1) = unpack("VV",substr($content,8,8));
        $fn{c_time} = getTime($t0,$t1);
        my ($t0,$t1) = unpack("VV",substr($content,16,8));
        $fn{m_time} = getTime($t0,$t1);
        my ($t0,$t1) = unpack("VV",substr($content,24,8));
        $fn{mft_m_time} = getTime($t0,$t1);
        my ($t0,$t1) = unpack("VV",substr($content,32,8));
        $fn{a_time} = getTime($t0,$t1);
        $fn{flags} = unpack("V",substr($content,56,4));
        $fn{len_name} = unpack("C",substr($content,64,1));
        $fn{namespace} = unpack("C",substr($content,65,1));
        $fn{len_name} = $fn{len_name} * 2 if ($fn{namespace} > 0);
        $fn{name} = substr($content,66,$fn{len_name});
        $fn{name} = cleanStr($fn{name}) if ($fn{namespace} > 0);
        $fn{name} =~ s/\x0c/\x2e/g;
        $fn{name} =~ s/[\x01-\x0f]//g;
        return %fn;
}
```

The final attribute we discuss is the $DATA attribute (identifier 0x80, or 128). This attribute contains or refers to the actual content of the file. If the nonresident flag in the attribute header is not set, then the content of the file is resident within the $DATA attribute of the MFT entry, following the header and two additional structures. This is generally true for short text files, for example, or other files less than 700 bytes. If data are nonresident, then "data runs," or where data are located on the disk, need to be translated.

Example code for parsing $DATA attribute data runs is very involved and is not presented here. Similarly, code for extracting information from resident $DATA attributes is trivial and consists of parsing some additional information (size of content and offset to content) after the attribute header.

Some open source tools are available for parsing the MFT (specifically, $STANDARD_INFORMATION and $FILE_NAME attributes) and making time-stamped data available to the analyst. One is David Kovar's analyzemft.py Python script, found on the Web at http://www.integriography.com/projects/analyzeMFT. Another is the mft.pl Perl script, from which the *parseSIAttr()* and *parseFNAttr()* functions were extracted, which is available in the WinForensicAnalysis Google Code projected, located on the Web at http://code.google.com/p/winforensicaanalysis.

Brian Carrier's "The SleuthKit" (TSK) tools are probably the best known tools for collecting a wide range of file system and file system metadata information from acquired images and even live systems. For example, in order to collect a listing of file system $STANDARD_INFORMATION attribute file times from an acquired image, an analyst may use a command similar to the following:

```
C:\tsk>fls -f ntfs -m C:/ -p -r G:\case\xp.img > G:\case\files\
  bodyfile.txt
```

This command produces what is known as a "bodyfile," which is an intermediate file format used to store this information before converting it to a timeline of file system activity. In some instances, the analyst may need to add the "-o" switch in order to identify the offset to the partition that appeared on the live system as the "C:\" drive; this offset information can be determined manually via a hex editor or by using mmls.exe.

An analyst can also collect this very same information from a live, remote system using F-Response. If the analyst has connected to the remote system properly and has mounted the system's C:\ drive as F:\ on their own system, they may then use a command similar to the following in order to collect $STANDARD_INFORMATION attribute file times for the files in the C:\ partition:

```
C:\tsk>fls -f ntfs -m C:/ -p -r \\.\F: > g:\case\files\bodyfile.txt
```

The complete set of TSK tools, along with documentation and usage information, can be found on the Web at the SleuthKit Web site, http://www.sleuthkit.org.

NTFS Alternate Data Streams
Another interesting feature of the NTFS file system is alternate data streams (ADS), or "ADSs." ADSs have been part of the NTFS file system since the first version of Windows NT 3.1 and were included for compatibility with the Macintosh Hierarchal File System (HFS). HFS utilized resource forks for maintaining file metadata, and ADSs provided interoperability when moving files from one file system (HFS) to another (NTFS). ADSs are actually an additional stream associated with a file, and while all versions of Windows include a means for creating arbitrary ADSs (some versions of Windows actually create and use specific ADSs), it wasn't until Windows Vista that native functionality became available for viewing arbitrary ADSs. As of Windows Vista, the 'dir /r' command would

allow an analyst to search for arbitrary ADSs on a live system. However, Windows systems running the NTFS file system have long had the native ability to create and use arbitrary ADSs.

In order to demonstrate how to create an arbitrary ADS, create a new directory called "ads" (via the DOS *md* or *mkdir* command, if you like), open a command prompt to or *cd* to that directory, and type the following command:

```
C:\ads>echo "this is an ADS" > myfile.txt:ads.txt
```

If you type the *dir* command, you'll see that the file "myfile.txt" exists and is zero bytes in size. We just echo'd a string that is 14 bytes in length into a file (apparently), so where did it go? If we use the 'type' command to attempt to view the string we just entered into the ADS, on Windows XP we'll get an error message about the syntax of the command. Type the following command:

```
C:\ads>notepad .\myfile.txt:ads.txt
```

When the Notepad window opens, we can see the string we typed in . . . where did it come from? The string was stored in the alternate data stream, which is a file but is denoted by the colon in the name. ADSs can be added or attached to files or to directory listings (using a command such as "C:\ads>:ads.txt").

Some Windows applications will actually employ specific ADSs. With Windows XP Service Pack 2, the Attachment Manager would add an ADS called "Zone.Identifier" to files downloaded via Internet Explorer or as OutLook attachments. These ADSs were usually no more than 26 or 28 bytes in length and simply identified the files as having been downloaded via zone 3. Whenever a user would attempt to open or execute a downloaded file, they would be presented with a warning, asking if they were sure that they wanted to launch the file in question.

ADSs can also be used to "hide" executable content. On many versions of Windows, executable image files (.exe files) can be hidden in and run from ADSs. Not only will Perl run scripts that are "hidden" in ADSs, but Windows Scripting Host files can also be "hidden" in and run from ADSs.

Again, ADSs are artifacts specific to the NTFS file system. Many commercial forensic applications will display ADSs in red within the graphical user interface (GUI) of the application. Dave Roth [6] has published a Perl script named "list-datastreams.pl" that can be used on a live system to locate ADSs. This script uses Dave's Win32::API::Prototype module and relies on native Windows application programming interface (API) functions.

File System Summary

NTFS.com has a comparison of file systems [7] that provides an excellent overview of the differences between versions of the FAT file system and NTFS. Perhaps the best, most authoritative source of information available on file systems in general (including but not limited to FAT and NTFS) is Brian Carrier's *File System Forensic Analysis* [8].

REGISTRY

The Windows Registry is an extremely valuable source of forensics artifacts to any analyst. The Registry is a binary, hierarchal database [9] that contains configuration for the Windows system, replacing the INI files of Windows 3.1. The Windows Registry contains operating system and application configuration settings and information. In addition, the Registry records information specific to users, essentially tracking a user's activity in order to organize and optimize the user's experience while interacting with the system.

For the most part, users don't interact directly with the Registry. Any interaction is usually through an installation routine or program, such as a Microsoft Installer file. System administrators may interact more directly with the Registry, through the Registry Editor (regedit.exe), which is a native utility that ships with all versions of the Windows operating system. A view of the Registry via the Registry Editor is illustrated in Figure 4.3.

As seen in Figure 4.3, the Registry appears to have a familiar folder-based structure. This isn't actually the case, but is instead an abstraction provided by the Registry Editor. To really understand what the Registry "looks like," we first have to understand that it's not really a bunch of folders or directories. To begin with, the Registry itself exists as a bunch of files on the hard drive, as illustrated in Figure 4.4.

As illustrated in Figure 4.4, files that comprise the Registry and contain information about the system and applications are located in the Windows\system32\config directory. Additional files that contain user-specific information and application settings are found in the user profile directories (i.e., NTUSER.DAT and USRCLASS.DAT).

The Registry's binary structure consists of "cells," the two most important of which are keys and values. There are several other cell types, but these additional

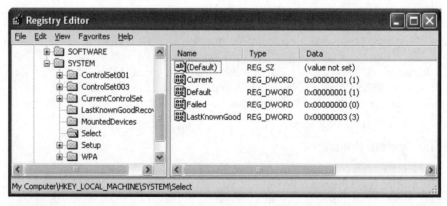

FIGURE 4.3

View of the Windows Registry via the Registry Editor.

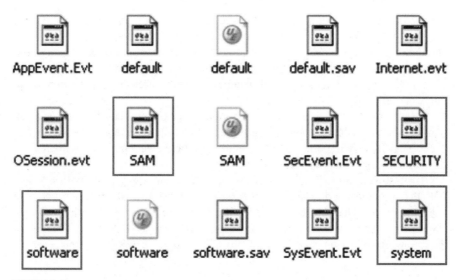

FIGURE 4.4

Registry files on disk.

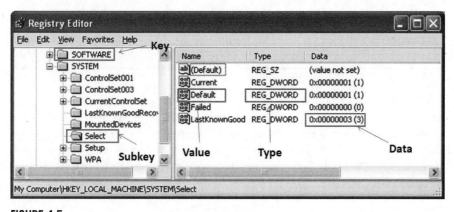

FIGURE 4.5

Registry nomenclature.

cell types serve as pointers to additional keys (also known as "subkeys") and values. Registry keys (the folders in Figure 4.3) can point to or "contain" additional keys (subkeys), as well as values. Values are simply that—values that contain data. Values do not point to keys. Figure 4.5 illustrates this nomenclature.

Figure 4.5 provides an excellent illustration of the various visual elements of the Registry, in particular the cells that we'll be discussing. In the left-hand pane of the Registry Editor, we see the keys and subkeys displayed as folders. When we click on one of the keys, we will likely see (depending on the key) something similar to what appears in the right-hand pane, which illustrates the Registry values and data they can contain. As mentioned earlier, this information is actually contained in files within the file system; if the files are accessed on a binary basis, we can access the various key and value cells and extract the information we're interested in.

In order to really understand how important the Registry can be to an analyst, we need to start by looking at the Registry on a binary basis. Registry key cells (i.e., "keys") can be very important due to the information they contain within their structure, which is illustrated in Figure 4.6.

As illustrated in Figure 4.6, the structure of a Registry key starts with a 4-byte DWORD (double word) that comprises the size of the key, which when read as a signed integer produces a negative value (in Figure 4.6, the size is -96 bytes; as we can see from the hexadecimal view, the key structure is indeed 96 bytes). Using Perl, the following code can be used to parse the DWORD value as a signed integer:

```
Unpack("l",$dword)
```

> **NOTE**
>
> When a Registry key is deleted, much like a file, it really doesn't "go" anywhere. In fact, when a key is deleted, the size value is changed to a positive value. In the fall of 2008, Jolanta Thomassen released a Perl script that became known as "regslack," which uses this property to parse through a hive file and retrieve deleted keys. Regslack is available in the Downloads section of the RegRipper.net Web site.

This is followed by the key node identifier "nk," which tells us that this is a key (as opposed to a value) node, or cell. Immediately after the node identifier is a 2-byte value that describes the node type; in Figure 4.6, that value is 0x2C, which identifies a root key cell. The other value you would expect to find is 0x20, which identifies a regular key cell. The key structure also contains a LastWrite time, a 64-bit

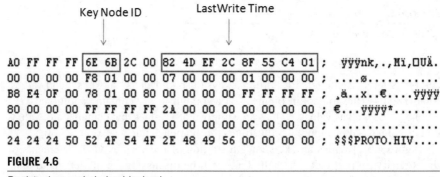

FIGURE 4.6

Registry key node in hexidecimal.

FILETIME object that marks the number of 100-nanosecond epochs since midnight of 1 January 1601. This value is analogous to a file's last modification time and can be very valuable to an analyst, as it indicates when a change occurred to the key. These changes can include values or subkeys being added or removed, or a value being modified. Table 4.1 provides a list of the elements within the key cell structure that are most important to forensic analysts, along with their position within the structure and their size.

The other type of cell within the Registry that we're interested in is the value cell. Figure 4.7 illustrates a hexadecimal view of a value cell.

Value cells do not contain nearly as much information as a key cell. Perhaps most importantly, they do not contain any time-stamped information, such as a key cell's LastWrite time. Value cells do, however, contain important information in that information contained in their data is what constitutes the operating system and application configuration settings within the Registry.

Table 4.2 provides a list of relevant value cell structure details. As with the key cell, the first 4 bytes of a value cell (as illustrated in Figure 4.7) contain the size of the cell.

Table 4.1 Registry Key Cell Structure Details

Offset (bytes)	Size (bytes)	Description
0	4	Size
4	2	Node ID ("nk," or 0x6B6E)
6	2	Node Type (0x2C or 0x20)
8	8	LastWrite time
20	4	Offset to this key's parent key
24	4	Number of subkeys
32	4	Offset to the list of subkey records
36	4	Number of values
44	4	Offset to the value list
48	4	Offset to security identifier record
76	2	Length of the key name

```
                Value Node ID        Value Type

D8 FF FF FF 76 6B 0B 00 12 00 00 00 68 03 00 00 ; Øÿÿÿvk......h...
01 00 00 00 01 00 3D E1 43 75 72 72 65 6E 74 55 ; ......=áCurrentU
73 65 72 00 00 00 00 00 E8 FF FF FF 55 00 53 00 ; ser.....èÿÿÿU.S.
45 00 52 00 4E 00 41 00 4D 00 45 00 00 00 3D E1 ; E.R.N.A.M.E...=á
```

FIGURE 4.7

Registry value node in hexidecimal.

Table 4.2 Registry Value Cell Structure Details

Offset (bytes)	Size (bytes)	Description
0	4	Size (as a negative number)
4	2	Node ID ("vk," or 0x6B76)
6	2	Value name length
8	4	Data length
12	4	Offset to data
16	4	Value type

Reading key and value information from the Registry is relatively straightforward using a variety of open source tools. On live Windows systems, the Win32::TieRegistry Perl module (Python has the winreg module available for the same purpose) would be one way to extract information from both local and remote systems.

WARNING

Win32::TieRegistry Module

Tools such as the Win32::TieRegistry Perl module rely on the underlying native Windows API and, as such, are not cross-platform; that is, they will not run on default MacOSX or Linux installations.

Unlike native tools such as the Registry Editor (regedit.exe) or reg.exe, you can write Perl scripts that allow you to extract the LastWrite time from Registry keys in a programmatic fashion, allowing you to parse or sort the information as necessary. The Win32::TieRegistry module is part of the standard distribution of Perl available from the ActiveState Web site.

TIP

RegScan

A number of Perl scripts available use the Win32::TieRegistry Perl module. One is regscan.pl, available in a zipped archive in the Downloads section of the RegRipper.net Web site. This Perl script allows you to extract information about Windows services found in the Registry on a live, running system.

When working with images acquired from systems (either the entire image or just Registry hives extracted from these systems), we would opt for the Parse::Win32Registry Perl module, in part because it provides us with a cross-platform means for extracting necessary information. The Win32::TieRegistry module utilizes the API available on Windows systems, and therefore provides access to Registry data on the live systems. The Parse::Win32Registry module accesses hive files on a binary level, providing a layer of abstraction so that we can access a Registry value simply by providing a key path (such as "Software/Microsoft/Windows/CurrentVersion").

> **WARNING**
> **F-Response**
> If you're using F-Response as a means for extending your incident response reach and/or capability, you would think that you're interacting with a live system, so Perl scripts written using the Win32::TieRegistry module would be your "tool of choice." Well, you're not using the API to extract data from the hive files; instead, when using F-Response, you'll be interacting with hive files (and other files, as well) on a binary level, so tools using the Parse::Win32Registry module will be most useful to you.

RegRipper is an open source Perl application available for parsing Registry hives extracted from an image, from within a mounted image, or from a system accessed via F-Response. RegRipper is available in the Downloads section of the RegRipper .net Web site.

RegRipper uses the Parse::Win32Registry module in order to interact with Registry hive files. Because this application uses "plugins," or small files containing Perl code, to extract specific information, the main script, rr.pl, is really a GUI interface to an "engine" that runs these plugins. Figure 4.8 illustrates the RegRipper GUI.

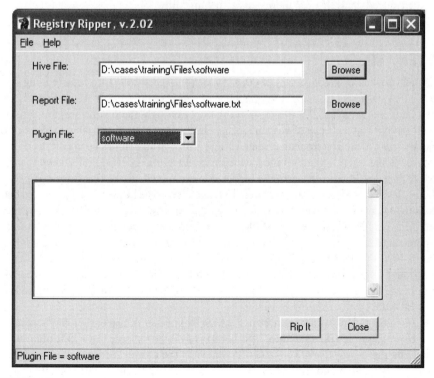

FIGURE 4.8

RegRipper GUI, ready to rip a Software hive.

The RegRipper package also includes a command line interface tool called rip.pl, which allows you to run specific plugins against a hive or (like rr.pl) run lists of plugins (contained in a text file called a "plugins file") against the hive. Rip.pl is extremely useful for getting targeted information from a hive, as well as testing newly created plugins. After all, RegRipper is open source, and the author invites and strongly encourages others to write their own plugins for their own needs.

NOTE

RegRipper in Linux Distributions

RegRipper is included on a number of forensic-oriented, Linux-based toolkit distributions, including PlainSight and the SANS Investigative Forensic Toolkit. The rip.pl script can be run in an environment in which the Parse::Win32Registry can be installed; the RegRipper GUI can be installed and run from a Linux environment in which WINE (found on the Web at http://www.winehq.org/) has been installed.

A number of Registry keys and values may be of interest to an analyst during an examination. *Windows Registry Forensics* [10] from Syngress Publishing, Inc was published in January 2011 and goes into a great deal of detail regarding additional and advanced analysis of Windows Registry hive files.

EVENT LOGS

Earlier versions of Windows (NT, 2000, XP, and 2003, specifically) utilized a logging system known as Event Logging. Information about the structures that make up Event Logs can be found at the MSDN site [11]. Interestingly enough, these structures are defined well enough that tools can be written to parse the event records from within the logs on a binary level, as well as from unallocated space. This can sometimes be important, as the header of the Event Log (.evt) file (see the ELF_LOGFILE_HEADER structure at the MSDN site) will indicate a certain number of event records in the file, but parsing on a binary level may reveal several additional event records. The header contains a value that tells the Microsoft API where the oldest event record is located (StartOffset) and another that tells the API where the "end of file" record is located (EndOffset). Based on normal operation of the Event Logging system, there may be times when valid event records can be found within the "hidden" space within the Event Log file.

Event Log records all contain a "magic number" or unique identifier (Microsoft refers to it as a signature), which is "LfLe" (0x654c664c in hex), as illustrated in Figure 4.9.

As indicated by information from the MSDN site mentioned earlier, the header of the Event Log file (illustrated in Figure 4.9) is 48 bytes in size. This is further indicated by the 4-byte DWORD value that brackets the header record (i.e., is found at both the beginning and the end of the record); in this case, that value is 0x30, or 48. This is important to remember, as the header of an event record (not the header of the Event Log file, as illustrated in Figure 4.9) is 56 bytes in size, which does not

> **NOTE**
>
> **Hidden Event Records**
> There have been a number of instances in which "hidden" event records have been found in an Event Log file. In one instance, the analyst extracted a copy of an .evt file from an acquired image and was able to open it in the Event Viewer on her analysis system. A review of the event records, as well as parsing the header information, indicated that there were a specific number of event records in the Event Log file. However, parsing the Event Log file on a binary basis revealed two additional records.
>
> In another instance, an analyst extracted copies of several Event Log files from an acquired image and parsed them on a binary basis. She suspected that a user had cleared the Event Logs and, when opening copies of the Event Log files in Event Viewer, found that one was reportedly empty. However, parsing the "empty" Event Log revealed five "hidden" event records.

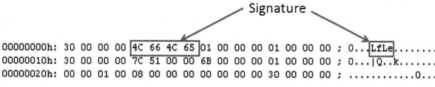

FIGURE 4.9

Event Log header illustrating the signature.

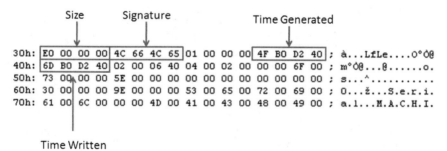

FIGURE 4.10

EVENTLOGRECORD structure elements.

include the actual content of the file. Complete details of the Event Log record (i.e., EVENTLOGRECORD) structure are also available at the MSDN site; several key elements of the structure are illustrated in Figure 4.10.

As with the header structure of the Event Log file, event records are also bracketed by size values. In Figure 4.10, the event record is 224 (0xE0) bytes in size. The event record structure contains information about the record itself, including offsets to and lengths of strings, the user security identifier (SID), if applicable, and data held within the event record. As illustrated in Figure 4.10, two time stamps are embedded within the event record structure as well: when the event in question was generated and when it was actually written to the Event Log. These time stamps are written as 32-bit Unix times and are translated easily into more easily readable dates using, for example, the Perl *gmtime( )* function.

Given the information within the structure, open source tools, such as evtparse.pl (available from the Google Code *winforensicanalysis* project), can be written and used to parse the information from Event Log files. Other tools, such as evtrtp.pl (also available from the Google Code *winforensicanalysis* project), can be used to approach parsing and analysis of the contents of Event Log files in a different manner. Instead of simply extracting and displaying the event record information, evtrpt.pl keeps track of that information and displays statistics about the frequency of various event identifiers (IDs) and sources for the event records. Sample output from a System Event Log (sysevent.evt) from a Windows XP system is shown here:

```
Event Source/ID Frequency

Source                    Event ID    Count
----------                --------    -----
DCOM                      10005       4
Dhcp                      1005        1
EventLog                  6005        7
EventLog                  6006        6
EventLog                  6009        7
EventLog                  6011        1
NetBT                     4311        3
PlugPlayManager           256         3
Print                     20          1
SRService                 115         1
Serial                    2           2
Server                    2504        1
Service Control Manager   7011        1
Service Control Manager   7035        27
Service Control Manager   7036        36
Setup                     60054       1
Setup                     60055       1
W32Time                   35          3

Total: 106
-------------------------------
Event Type Frequency

Type                               Count
-------                            -----
Error                              9
Info                               91
Warn                               6

Total: 106
-----------------------------
Date Range (UTC)
Fri Jun 18 09:05:19 2004 to Fri Jan 18 00:53:41 2008
```

As you can see, evtrpt.pl provides something of an "at-a-glance" of what information would be available from the Event Log file being parsed, including not only the various event sources and IDs, but also the date range of all records found in the file. This information can be useful to an analyst looking for activity that occurred on the system at a specific time. For example, an analyst may be parsing the Application Event Log looking for specific event IDs associated with antivirus scanning applications (as the event source), looking for logins via the Security Event Log, or looking for specific events in the System Event Log. If none of these events exists within the Event Log or the date range of the available event records does not cover the window of compromise or the specific time frame of the incident, the analyst can save herself considerable time by moving on to other sources of data.

Grokevt (found on the Web at http://projects.sentinelchicken.org/grokevt/) is another open source tool for parsing Event Log files.

Later versions of Windows (i.e., Vista and beyond) use the Windows Event Log mechanism, which supersedes the Event Logging mechanism of earlier versions of Windows. Part of this change included a change in the structure of events recorded and how those events are recorded. This new Windows Event Log format is much more complex, and details about the schema used can be found at the MSDN Windows Event Log Reference site [12].

Andreas Schuster has written and maintains a Perl-based tool for parsing Windows Event Logs from Vista and above systems, called evtxparse.pl. You can download a copy of evtxparse.pl via Andreas' blog, which can be found on the Web at http://computer.forensikblog.de.

PREFETCH FILES

Beginning with Windows XP, the operating system was capable of performing "prefetching." The actual mechanics of how prefetching is performed aren't significant; suffice to say that the purpose of prefetching is to allow regularly used applications to load faster by prestaging segments of loaded code in a specific location so that instead of searching for it (resulting in page faults), the operating system would know exactly where to find that code. This is a simple explanation, to be sure, but again, the specifics of how prefetching is performed aren't what we're interested in; instead, we're interested in prefetch file metadata.

Windows XP, Vista, and Windows 7 conduct application prefetching by default; Windows 2003 and 2008 have the ability to do so, but that functionality is disabled by default (all versions of Windows after Windows XP perform boot prefetching). What this means is that when an application is launched, a prefetch file for that application is created. This file is located in the C:\Windows\Prefetch directory and ends with the extension ".pf." That way, the next time that application is launched, the prefetch directory is checked for a prefetch file and, if one exists, the code within the file is used to launch the application.

These prefetch files appear in the C:\Windows\Prefetch directory, and their names start with the name of the executable image file for the application. For example, if a user runs Notepad, an application prefetch file that starts with "notepad.exe" will appear in the Prefetch directory. Following the name, there is a dash and several hexadecimal characters that make up the hash of the path to the file. The file name ends with ".pf." Looking back to our Notepad example, a prefetch file for the application could look like "NOTEPAD.EXE-336351A9.pf."

What this means to an analyst is that when a prefetch file is found, it's an indication that an application was run on that system. These prefetch files also contain metadata that can be very useful to an analyst. For example, the creation date of the file will tell the analyst when the application was first run, assuming that a previous prefetch file wasn't deleted and a new one created in its place. The prefetch file itself contains a 64-bit time stamp indicating when it was last run, as well as a count of how many times the application has been run. On Windows XP, the 64-bit "last run" time stamp is at offset 0x78 (120 bytes) within the file, and the run count is a 4-byte (DWORD value) located at offset 0x90 (144 bytes). Metadata at these offsets are illustrated in Figure 4.11.

On Vista and Windows 7 systems, the 64-bit "last run" time stamp can be found at offset 0x80 (128 bytes) within the binary contents of the prefetch file, and the run count is (again, 4 bytes) located at offset 0x98 (152 bytes).

Additional information can also be extracted from metadata within a prefetch file. For example, embedded within the prefetch file is information about the volume from which the executable image file was run, as well as strings indicating the paths to modules loaded by the executable image when it was run. The Perl script pref.pl (available at the *winforensicanalysis* Google Code project) can retrieve these metadata from prefetch files from Windows XP, as well as from Vista and Windows 7 systems. An example of the volume information available in the Notepad prefetch file appears as follows:

```
Volume Path        : \DEVICE\HARDDISKVOLUME1
Volume Creation Date: Fri Jan 1 22:24:09 2010 Z
Volume Serial Number: A424-CE42
```

One of the interesting file paths in the available strings embedded within this particular prefetch file is "\DEVICE\HARDDISKVOLUME1\ADS\MYFILE.TXT:ADS.TXT"; you will probably recognize this file path from the discussion of ADSs in the NTFS section earlier in this chapter.

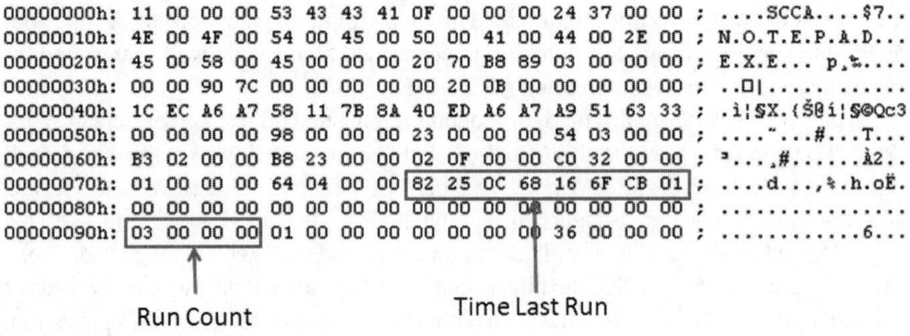

```
00000000h: 11 00 00 00 53 43 43 41 0F 00 00 00 24 37 00 00 ; ....SCCA....$7..
00000010h: 4E 00 4F 00 54 00 45 00 50 00 41 00 44 00 2E 00 ; N.O.T.E.P.A.D...
00000020h: 45 00 58 00 45 00 00 00 20 70 B8 89 03 00 00 00 ; E.X.E... p.¸....
00000030h: 00 00 90 7C 00 00 00 00 00 20 0B 00 00 00 00 00 ; ..□|..... ......
00000040h: 1C EC A6 A7 58 11 7B 8A 40 ED A6 A7 A9 51 63 33 ; .ì¦§X.{Š@í¦§©Qc3
00000050h: 00 00 00 00 98 00 00 00 23 00 00 00 54 03 00 00 ; ....˜...#...T...
00000060h: B3 02 00 00 B8 23 00 00 02 0F 00 00 C0 32 00 00 ; ³...¸#......À2..
00000070h: 01 00 00 00 64 04 00 00 82 25 0C 68 16 6F CB 01 ; ....d...‚%.h.oË.
00000080h: 00 00 00 00 00 00 00 00 00 00 00 00 00 00 00 00 ; ................
00000090h: 03 00 00 00 01 00 00 00 00 00 00 00 36 00 00 00 ; ............6...
```

Run Count   Time Last Run

FIGURE 4.11

Metadata found in a Prefetch file (Windows XP).

SHORTCUT FILES

Windows shortcut files are shell artifacts created under a number of circumstances, such as when a user double-clicks a file or when an application is installed (i.e., a shortcut file may be created on the desktop). Most shortcut files appear in the Windows Explorer shell with an associated icon that may represent the type of file that is referring to, and when a user double-clicks the shortcut, the appropriate application is launched to load or run the target file.

Due to their file extension (.lnk), Windows shortcut files are often referred to as LNK files. Jesse Hager has done some considerable work to parse the structure of LNK files, and a copy of his paper can be found in the Downloads section of the *8bits* project on Google Code. The various structure elements and sizes, with a few corrections, can also be found on the Web at http://www.stdlib.com/art6-Shortcut-File-Format-lnk.html. While Windows shortcuts are files within the file system, and as such have their own MACB times, the embedded elements within the structure of LNK files contain the MACB times of the target file that the shortcut points to, as well as the path (among other data). This information can be used to demonstrate access to files, particularly those that may be on network shares or removable storage locations.

A number of open source resources are available for parsing LNK files. A Perl script for parsing LNK files can be found linked at the "JAFAT: Archive of Forensics Tools" site at http://jafat.sourceforge.net/files.html. There is an example of JAVA code that will reportedly parse information from LNK files that can be found on the Web at http://www.javafaq.nu/java-example-code-468.html.

TIP

A Bit of History

While working on this book, I found a Lisp script for NTEmacs that could reportedly be used to parse and display information from Windows shortcut files. While there probably aren't many forensic analysts using NTEmacs or Lisp tools for analysis, the script was technically open source!

WINDOWS EXECUTABLES

Executable files on Windows systems follow the portable executable (PE), common object file format (COFF) specification [13]. What this means is that under normal circumstances, files with specific extensions (i.e., .exe, .dll, .sys, .ocx) will follow a particular binary structure format. This section discusses the format of PE files; however, it will not discuss any of the various tricks that malware authors will use to obscure and obfuscate the malicious programs that they attempt to place on systems. This is more a subject for a larger text on malware reverse engineering, and there are several books available that cover this subject nicely, the best of which will be mentioned later in this section.

A detailed breakdown of the various structures (including the structure element names, sizes, and meanings) within a PE file is available via the ImageHlp Structures site [14].

These details can assist (and have assisted) analysts with writing their own tools and utilities, as well as modifying others, for use in "normal" PE file analysis, as well as in static malware analysis.

PE files start with the letters "MZ" as the first two characters in the binary contents of the file, as illustrated in Figure 4.12.

> **TIP**
>
> **Where Does "MZ" Come From?**
> The "MZ" at the beginning of a PE file are the initials of Mark Zbikowski, one of the original architects of MS-DOS, OS/2, and Windows NT.

The "MZ" at the beginning of the PE file marks the beginning of what is referred to as the PE file's "DOS header" or the IMAGE_DOS_HEADER structure and is sometimes referred to as a "magic number." The DOS header is 64 bytes long, and in addition to the "magic number," the only other important element is the 4-byte DWORD at the end of the structure, which points us to the beginning of the IMAGE_NT_HEADER structure, as illustrated in Figure 4.13.

Details of parsing of the remaining structures of PE files are left as an exercise to the reader.

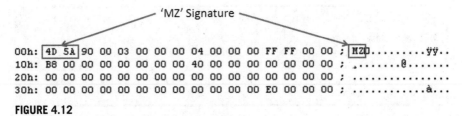

FIGURE 4.12

Binary contents at the beginning of a PE file.

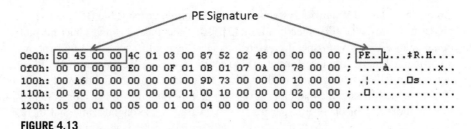

FIGURE 4.13

PE Signature of the IMAGE_NT_HEADER structure.

Many "normal" PE files have additional information embedded within their structure, in particular file version information. This is usually strings maintained in the "resource section" of the file, as the section can contain other "resources," such as icons and bitmaps. Most applications developed by reputable software development companies will include file version information within the resource section of the executable files (EXE as well as DLL files) that ship with the application. Also, "bad guys" have been known to simply rename files loaded on to compromised systems, leaving the resource information in place.

WARNING

Extracting file version information from a PE file is simply one technique of many that an analyst has at her disposal. While some attackers may make use of existing tools and change the names of the files, leaving the file version information in place, others have removed the file version information, or faked it. File version information should never be considered the sole source of information about a PE file during an investigation.

Extracting file version information from a PE file is relatively trivial using tools such as the Perl Win32::FileVersionInfo module. Scripts using this module can be written to display the file version information from files, as follows:

```
C:\Perl>ver.pl  c:\windows\notepad.exe
Filename         : c:\windows\notepad.exe
Type             : Application
OS               : NT/Win32
Orig Filename    : NOTEPAD.EXE
File Description : Notepad
File Version     : 5.1.2600.5512 (xpsp.080413-2105)
Internal Name    : Notepad
Company Name     : Microsoft Corporation
Copyright        : Microsoft Corporation. All rights reserved.
Product Name     : Microsoft« Windows« Operating System
Product Version  : 5.1.2600.5512
Trademarks       :
```

TIP

Installing Perl Modules

If you're using ActiveState Perl distribution, you can search for and install a number of modules that don't ship with the default installation using the Perl Package Manager, or ppm.

Searching for modules that include "win32" in their name is as simple as typing "ppm search win32." Once you find a module, you can install it using "ppm install <module name>"; all dependencies will also be installed.

The *pefile* project [15] on Google Code provides an open source Python module, written by Ero Carrera, for interacting with and extracting information from PE files. The module includes some fairly extensive capabilities beyond just retrieving various elements of the PE structure, including modifying values, and detecting compression utilities that may have been used to obfuscate the file. The project wiki includes usage examples as well. Example Python code for extracting the import table from a PE file using the *pefile* module appears as follows:

```
import pefile
pe = pefile.PE("C:/Windows/notepad.exe")
for entry in pe.DIRECTORY_ENTRY_IMPORT:
  print entry.dll
  for imp in entry.imports:
    print '\t', hex(imp.address), imp.name
```

This simple bit of open source code makes it relatively simple to query the import table of a PE file and determine which dynamic link library (DLL) functions the executable image file accesses when run, giving the analyst a clue as to some potential functions of the file or if the file has been modified.

TIP

Parsing PE Headers

During an examination, I'd run across a DLL that I later determined was loaded by a number of processes on Windows systems. Examining a timeline constructed from file system metadata, I noticed that during the window of initial infection, immediately after several files where created on the system, that the DLL in question had been modified. I looked closer and noticed that during the installation process for a malicious DLL, which had been detected via antivirus application scans, that the DLL had been modified to not only include an additional section to the PE header, but also that the malicious DLL (and its exported function) was referenced by the modified DLL. Being able to examine the import table of a PE file allows an examiner to not only see what the executable file is capable of (based on the imported DLLs and functions) but also what may have been added to the executable file.

In the fall of 2010, the *Malware Analyst's Cookbook* [16] was published by Wiley Publishing, Inc. In this book, the authors provide a "recipe" demonstrating use of the *pescanner.py* Python script for parsing and performing a modicum on analysis on PE files. The script can be installed and run on Linux, MacOSX, and (with some work) Windows systems. The script uses a number of techniques to scan for indications of suspicious elements (i.e., unusual section names, unusual entry points, to name a few) within a particular executable image file (EXE, DLL, etc.). Clam antivirus and Yara (the Yara project can be found on the Web at http://code.google.com/p/yara-project/) signatures can be incorporated into pescanner.py in order to add the ability to not just detect suspicious elements of the PE file, but also perform a modicum of malware detection.

The Win32::Exe Perl module provides a level of modicum of access to the structure of PE files, albeit not to the level of the Python *pefile* module; while being able to read the section information, there's no apparent access (with the current version) to the import or export tables within the PE file.

SUMMARY

There are a number of open source tools and utilities that an analyst can use to explore and retrieve information from the various artifacts produced by and found on Windows systems. Many of these tools and utilities are cross-platform in that they can be run on MacOSX, Linux, or Windows platforms, with the proper configuration (as discussed in Chapter 2). Many of these tools and utilities are actually scripts of some kind (Perl, Python, Ruby, etc.) that an analyst can use or modify to meet their needs (be sure to read the license, if there is one, for the tool first!). Analysts with some programming skill, or access to someone like this, can modify the open source tools to provide whatever necessary information would be most valuable and useful.

The needs of forensic analysis are outstripping the functionality available in commercial forensic analysis applications. As such, analysts need the ability to quickly access or develop the necessary tools and utilities to allow them to be better able to complete the tasks at hand. While there are a number of files on Windows systems that are text based and easily examined or parsed, a number of other files (and file formats) may play a critical role during an examination. Analysts need to be able to access the necessary information quickly and decisively, and open source utilities provide this capability, while providing for documentation and reproducibility.

References

[1] FAT File System, Microsoft TechNet. http://technet.microsoft.com/en-us/library/cc938438.aspx, (accessed 20.12.10).
[2] Description of the FAT32 File System, Microsoft Support. http://support.microsoft.com/kb/154997/, (accessed 20.12.10).
[3] Detailed Explanation of FAT Boot Sector, Microsoft Support. http://support.microsoft.com/kb/140418/, (accessed 20.12.10).
[4] File Times (Windows), Microsoft Developer Network (MSDN). http://msdn.microsoft.com/en-us/library/ms724290, (accessed 20.12.10).
[5] How to Use NTFS Alternate Data Streams, Microsoft Support. http://support.microsoft.com/kb/105763, (accessed 20.12.10).
[6] ListDataStreams.pl Perl Script, Dave Roth's Web site. http://www.roth.net/perl/scripts/db/code/LISTDATASTREAMS.PL, (accessed 20.12.10).
[7] Comparison of File Systems, NTFS.com. http://www.ntfs.com/ntfs_vs_fat.htm, (accessed 20.12.10).
[8] B. Carrier, File System Forensic Analysis. Addison-Wesley Publishing, 2005, ISBN: 0-32-126817-2.

[9] Windows Registry Information for Advanced Users, Microsoft Support. http://support.microsoft.com/kb/256986, (accessed 20.12.10).

[10] H. Carvey, Windows Registry Forensics. Syngress Publishing, Inc., 2011, ISBN: 9781597495806.

[11] Event Log Structures, Microsoft Developer Network Site. http://msdn.microsoft.com/en-us/library/aa363659(=VS.85).aspx, (accessed 20.12.10).

[12] Windows Event Log Reference, Microsoft Developer Network Site. http://msdn.microsoft.com/en-us/library/aa385785(v=VS.85).aspx, (accessed 20.12.10).

[13] Microsoft Portable Executable and Common Object File Format Specification, Windows Hardware Developer Central site. http://www.microsoft.com/whdc/system/platform/firmware/pecoff.mspx, (accessed 20.12.10).

[14] ImageHlp Structures, Microsoft Developer Network Site. http://msdn.microsoft.com/en-us/library/ms680198(v=VS.85).aspx, (accessed 20.12.10).

[15] Pefile, Google Code. http://code.google.com/p/pefile/>, (accessed 20.12.10).

[16] M. Ligh, S. Adair, B. Hartstein, and M. Richard, Malware Analyst's Cookbook and DVD: Tools and Techniques for Fighting Malicious Code. Wiley Publishing, Inc., 2010, ISBN: 978-0-470-61301-0.

Linux Systems and Artifacts

INFORMATION IN THIS CHAPTER

- Linux File Systems
- Linux Boot Process and Services
- Linux System Organization and Artifacts
- User Accounts
- Home Directories
- Logs
- Scheduling Tasks

INTRODUCTION

Modern Linux systems have come a long way from their humble roots as a free Unix-like system for home computers. Over the past 20 years, Linux has found its way into everything—to children's toys and networking devices to the most powerful supercomputing clusters in the world. While we can't teach you everything you will need to know to examine a supercomputing cluster, we can get you started with an exploration of standard Linux file system artifacts, directory structures, and artifacts of system and user activity.

LINUX FILE SYSTEMS

At the time of this writing, most current Linux systems use the Ext3 file system. Ext3 is the successor of Ext2, which added journaling but retained Ext2's under-lying structure otherwise. In fact, an Ext3 volume will happily mount as Ext2 if the user issues the mount command appropriately. Many other file systems are available via the Linux kernel, including ReiserFS, XFS, and JFS. Because these file systems are not generally used in a default Linux installation, their presence may indicate a purpose-built system (as opposed to a general-use desktop system).

> **NOTE**
> **Other Linux File Systems**
> In addition to the Ext family of file systems, you may come across other, less commonly used Linux file systems. None of these are currently supported by The Sleuth Kit, but can be examined logically using native Linux file system support.
>
> **ReiserFS** is a file system developed by Namesys, which was at one point the default for new SuSE Linux installations. It is no longer in common use by any major distribution but is the default for a handful of distributions, including Xandros and Linspire.
>
> **XFS** is a file system created by Silicon Graphics for the IRIX operating system. Its key strengths lie in the handling of very large files and very high throughput. This makes it a popular choice for streaming media applications.
>
> **JFS** is a file system originally created by IBM for the AIX operating system. That said, the JFS found in the Linux kernel is not compatible with the JFS used in AIX. Like XFS, JFS handles very large files and high throughput very well and has found use in similar applications as XFS.
>
> **YAFFS2** and **JFFS2** are file systems designed for use on flash and other embedded storage devices, such as network devices, media players, and telephones running specialized Linux distributions.

This section explores some of the Ext2 and 3 specific structures and forensically interesting information available, using the file system abstraction model described in Chapter 3 as a framework.

> **NOTE**
> **EXT4**
> Ext4 is the modern replacement for Ext3, which is beginning to appear as the default install option for many Linux distributions. Currently, the Sleuth Kit does not have proper Ext4 support, but some tasks do work. For example, running *ils* against a specific inode will still return expected results, but *fls* will exhibit inconsistent behavior. This is because the metadata structures have remained consistent with those found in an Ext2/Ext3 file system, but the data unit layer has changed quite dramatically.

File System Layer

Ext file systems have two major components that make up their file system layer structures: the *superblock* and the *group descriptor tables*. The superblock is a data structure found 1024 bytes from the start of an Ext file system. It contains information about the layout of the file system and includes block and inode allocation information, and metadata indicating the last time the file system was mounted or read. The group descriptor table is found in the block immediately following the superblock. This table contains allocation status information for each block group found on the file system [1]. The fsstat tool in the Sleuth Kit can be used to parse the content of these data structures and display information about the file system.

To demonstrate, we will create a small 10-Megabyte Ext2 file system. First we need to generate a 10-Megabyte file to act as the container for our file system.

```
user@ubuntu:~/images$ dd if=/dev/zero of=testimage.img bs=1024
  count=10000
10000+0 records in
10000+0 records out
10240000 bytes (10 MB) copied, 0.033177 s, 309 MB/s
```

Next, we can build the file system using the mke2fs command.

```
user@ubuntu:~/images$ mke2fs testimage.img
mke2fs 1.41.11 (14-Mar-2010)
testimage.img is not a block special device.
Proceed anyway? (y,n) y
Filesystem label=
OS type: Linux
Block size=1024 (log=0)
Fragment size=1024 (log=0)
Stride=0 blocks, Stripe width=0 blocks
2512 inodes, 10000 blocks
500 blocks (5.00%) reserved for the super user
First data block=1
Maximum filesystem blocks=10485760
2 block groups
8192 blocks per group, 8192 fragments per group
1256 inodes per group
Superblock backups stored on blocks:
  8193
Writing superblocks and filesystem accounting information: done
This filesystem will be automatically checked every 21 mounts or
180 days, whichever comes first. Use tune2fs -c or -i to override.
```

Running the fsstat command against our newly created file system yields the following output:

```
user@ubuntu:~/images$ fsstat testimage.img
FILE SYSTEM INFORMATION
--------------------------------------------
File System Type: Ext2
Volume Name:
Volume ID: 1c0806ef7431d187bb4c63d11ab0842e
Last Written at: Tue Oct 19 16:24:39 2010
Last Checked at: Tue Oct 19 16:24:39 2010
Last Mounted at: empty
Unmounted properly
Last mounted on:
Source OS: Linux
Dynamic Structure
Compat Features: Ext Attributes, Resize Inode, Dir Index
InCompat Features: Filetype,
Read Only Compat Features: Sparse Super,
  ...
```

Of particular interest in the previous section is the "Last Mounted At:" and "Last Mounted On:" displaying null/empty results. Because this file system has just been created, this is to be expected. For a heavily used file system, this would indicate an error or possibly intentional tampering.

Continuing with the `fsstat` output, we begin to see the information the file system layer has about lower layers.

```
METADATA INFORMATION
--------------------------------------------
Inode Range: 1 - 2513
Root Directory: 2
Free Inodes: 2501
```

The "Root Directory" entry provides the inode number of the root directory—this is the value the `fls` command uses by default. The next section of output details the layout of the blocks of the file system.

```
CONTENT INFORMATION
--------------------------------------------
Block Range: 0 - 9999
Block Size: 1024
Reserved Blocks Before Block Groups: 1
Free Blocks: 9585
BLOCK GROUP INFORMATION
--------------------------------------------
Number of Block Groups: 2
Inodes per group: 1256
Blocks per group: 8192
Group: 0:
  Inode Range: 1 - 1256
  Block Range: 1 - 8192
  Layout:
    Super Block: 1 - 1
    Group Descriptor Table: 2 - 2
    Data bitmap: 42 - 42
    Inode bitmap: 43 - 43
    Inode Table: 44 - 200
    Data Blocks: 201 - 8192
  Free Inodes: 1245 (99%)
  Free Blocks: 7978 (97%)
  Total Directories: 2
Group: 1:
  Inode Range: 1257 - 2512
  Block Range: 8193 - 9999
  Layout:
    Super Block: 8193 - 8193
    Group Descriptor Table: 8194 - 8194
    Data bitmap: 8234 - 8234
```

```
    Inode bitmap: 8235 - 8235
    Inode Table: 8236 - 8392
    Data Blocks: 8393 - 9999
 Free Inodes: 1256 (100%)
 Free Blocks: 1607 (88%)
 Total Directories: 0
```

In this output we have the majority of the information needed to extract raw data from the file system. We know that the file system is divided into two block groups, each with 8192 1024-byte blocks. We know which inodes are associated with which block groups, information that can be of use when recovering deleted data. We also know the location of the backup superblock, which can be used for sanity checking in the case of a corrupted or inconsistent primary superblock.

TIP

DebugFS

If you are using Linux as your examination platform, you can also use the included debugfs utility to gather much of this file system information. This is useful if you need to confirm an item you discovered using a forensic utility or wish to further investigate unusual data. Please reference the debugfs man page for usage information.

File Name Layer

File names in Ext file systems are stored as directory entries. These entries are stored in directories, which are simply blocks filled with directory entries. Each directory entry contains the file name, the address of the inode associated with the file, and a flag indicating whether the name refers to a directory or a normal file.

Ext file systems allow multiple file names to point to the same file—these additional names are known as hard links. A hard link is an additional directory entry that points to the same inode. Each hard link increments the inode's link count by one.

To demonstrate this, we can create a simple file, add some text to it, and examine the file.

```
user@ubuntu:~$ touch file1
user@ubuntu:~$ echo "i am file1" > file1
user@ubuntu:~$ cat file1
i am file1
user@ubuntu:~$ stat file1
  File: 'file1'
  Size: 11          Blocks: 8        IO Block: 4096   regular file
Device: 801h/2049d  Inode: 452126   Links: 1
Access: (0644/-rw-r--r--) Uid: ( 1000/ user) Gid: ( 1000/ user)
Access: 2010-10-19 21:06:36.534649312 -0700
Modify: 2010-10-19 21:06:34.798639051 -0700
Change: 2010-10-19 21:06:46.694615623 -0700
```

Here we have created "file1" and added some identifying text. We can use the `stat` command to display the file's inode information. Next, we use the `ln` command to create a "hard link" to file1.

```
user@ubuntu:~$ ln file1 file2
user@ubuntu:~$ stat file2
  File: 'file2'
  Size: 11          Blocks: 8      IO Block: 4096 regular file
Device: 801h/2049d Inode: 452126   Links: 2
Access: (0644/-rw-r--r--) Uid: ( 1000/ user) Gid: ( 1000/ user)
Access: 2010-10-19 21:06:36.534649312 -0700
Modify: 2010-10-19 21:06:34.798639051 -0700
Change: 2010-10-19 21:06:46.694615623 -0700
```

Note that file2 has the exact same inode number shown in the stat output of file1. Also note that the "Links" value is incremented.

```
user@ubuntu:~$ cat file2
i am file1
user@ubuntu:~$ stat file1
  File: 'file1'
  Size: 11          Blocks: 8      IO Block: 4096 regular file
Device: 801h/2049d Inode: 452126   Links: 2
Access: (0644/-rw-r--r--) Uid: ( 1000/ user) Gid: ( 1000/ user)
Access: 2010-10-19 21:06:56.798612306 -0700
Modify: 2010-10-19 21:06:34.798639051 -0700
Change: 2010-10-19 21:06:46.694615623 -0700
```

Dumping the content of file2 and reviewing the stat output of file1 one more time reinforce that these are effectively the same "file." file1 and file2 are both simply file names that reference the same inode.

A second type of link exists on Ext file systems—soft links. A soft link is a special file that has a path to another file in place of the block pointers in its inode. The soft link then serves as an indirect reference to the actual file.

We can add a soft link to our link chain by using the `-s` flag to the `ln` command.

```
user@ubuntu:~$ ln -s file1 file3
user@ubuntu:~$ stat file1
  File: 'file1'
  Size: 11          Blocks: 8      IO Block: 4096 regular file
Device: 801h/2049d Inode: 452126   Links: 2
Access: (0644/-rw-r--r--) Uid: ( 1000/ user) Gid: ( 1000/ user)
Access: 2010-10-19 21:06:56.798612306 -0700
Modify: 2010-10-19 21:06:34.798639051 -0700
Change: 2010-10-19 21:06:46.694615623 -0700
```

Note that the stat information for file1 has remained unchanged—file1 is "unaware" that it is also "file3."

```
user@ubuntu:~$ stat file3
  File: 'file3' -> 'file1'
  Size: 5          Blocks: 0      IO Block: 4096 symbolic link
Device: 801h/2049d Inode: 452127    Links: 1
Access: (0777/lrwxrwxrwx) Uid: ( 1000/ user) Gid: ( 1000/ user)
Access: 2010-10-19 21:07:33.382618755 -0700
Modify: 2010-10-19 21:07:33.382618755 -0700
Change: 2010-10-19 21:07:33.382618755 -0700
```

By running stat against file3 we can get a better idea of what is occurring. The "Size" value is the number of bytes in the target file name (five). As a soft link, file3 has no data allocated so the "Blocks" value is zero. In addition, because file3 has its own inode, it gets it own independent set of time stamps.

NOTE

Device Files

In addition to standard "files" and "directories," Linux has a few special device files that you will likely encounter when examining a Linux system.

A *character device* is a special file that transmits data one character at a time. Devices in this category include user input devices such as mice, keyboards, and serial devices such as serial ports and modems. Character devices generally stream their data—that is to say they do not support random access.

A *block device* is a special file that transmits data one *block* at a time, where a block is a specified amount of data. The canonical example of this is a hard drive device, which transmits data in blocks of 512 bytes at a time. Block device input and output can usually be buffered for speed and their data can be accessed nonsequentially.

Note that on a dead file system these files will not have much meaning but that you should be aware of their significance when reviewing links to them or scripts that reference them.

Metadata Layer

Metadata for files on Ext file systems are stored in inodes. Forensically interesting items contained in Ext inodes include the file's size and allocated blocks, ownership and permissions information, and time stamps associated with the file. In addition, an inode will contain a flag indicating whether it belongs to a directory or a regular file. As mentioned previously, each inode also has a link count, which is the number of file names that refer to this inode.

Ownership information includes User Identifier (UID) and Group Identifier (GID) values, which can be of importance in many different examinations. We will discuss more about mapping numeric UIDs and GIDs into their human-readable equivalent later.

Ext inodes store four time stamps, commonly referred to as MAC times.

- The **(M)odified** time stamp is updated when the content of the file or directory is written. So, if a file is edited or entries are added to or removed from a directory, this time stamp will update.

- The **(A)ccessed** time stamp is updated when the content of the file or directory is read. Any activity that opens a file for reading or lists the contents of a directory will cause this time stamp to be updated.
- The **(C)hanged** time stamp is updated when the inode is modified. Any permission changes or changes that cause the Modified time stamp to update will cause this time stamp to update as well.
- The **(D)eleted** time stamp is updated only when the file is deleted.

WARNING

Preventing A-Time Updates

Note that Ext systems can be mounted with the `noatime` option, which will prevent all Accessed time stamp values on that volume from being updated. If file system access time stamps don't match up with what secondary time sources such as network traffic captures or log files are indicating, a `noatime` mount is a more likely culprit than time travel.
For now...

It is important to note that altering the modification or access time is quite simple using the `touch` command. Items from the `touch` command's usage output that can be used to set specific time values can be seen in bold in the output that follows.

```
Usage: touch [OPTION]... FILE...
Update the access and modification times of each FILE to the
  current time.
A FILE argument that does not exist is created empty.
....
  -a                    change only the access time
  -c, --no-create       do not create any files
  -d, --date=STRING     parse STRING and use it instead of current
    time
...
  -m                    change only the modification time
  -r, --reference=FILE use this file's times instead of current
    time
  -t STAMP              use [[CC]YY]MMDDhhmm[.ss] instead of
    current time
  --time=WORD           change the specified time:
                        WORD is access, atime, or use: equivalent to -a
                        WORD is modify or mtime: equivalent to -m
  ...
```

While this is trivial to do, it is important to note that altering the C-time (inode change time) is *not* possible to do using the `touch` command—in fact, the C-time will be updated to record the time any time stamp alteration occurred! In a case where time stamps appear to have been modified, the C-time can end up being the "truest" time stamp available.

The inode also contains pointers to blocks allocated to the file. The inode can store the addresses of the first 12 blocks of a file; however, if more than 12 pointers are required, a block is allocated and used to store them. These are called indirect block pointers. Note that this indirection can occur two more times if the number of block addresses requires creating double and triple indirect block pointers.

Data Unit Layer

Data units in Ext file systems are called blocks. Blocks are 1, 2, or 4K in size as denoted in the superblock. Each block has an address and is part of a block allocation group as described in the block descriptor table. Block addresses and groups start from 0 at the beginning of the file system and increment. As noted in the Metadata section, pointers to the blocks allocated to a file are stored in the inode. When writing data into a block, current Linux kernels will fill the block slack space with zeroes, so no "file slack" should be present. Note that the allocation strategy used by the Linux kernel places blocks in the same group as the inode to which they are allocated.

Journal Tools

The core functional difference between Ext2 and Ext3 is the journal present in Ext3. Current Ext3 journal implementations only record metadata changes and are recorded at the block level. The journal is transaction based, and each transaction recorded has a sequence number. The transaction begins with a descriptor block, followed by one or more file system commit blocks, and is finalized with a commit block. See the `jcat` output that follows for an example of a simple metadata update excerpt.

```
...
4060: Allocated Descriptor Block (seq: 10968)
4061: Allocated FS Block 65578
4062: Allocated Commit Block (seq: 10968)
...
```

The usefulness of the information extracted from the journal is going to be highly dependent on the nature of your specific investigation, including the amount of time that has passed since the event of interest and the amount of file system activity that has occurred in the meantime. It is possible that old inode data may be present in the journal, which can provide a transaction log of old time stamps or old ownership information. Additionally, old inode information recovered from the journal may contain block pointers that have subsequently been wiped from a deleted inode.

Deleted Data

As demonstrated earlier, for each directory entry that points to a given inode, that inode's link count is incremented by one. When directory entries pointing to a given inode are removed, the inode's link count is subsequently decremented by one. When all directory entries pointing to a given inode are removed, the inode has a link count of zero and is considered "deleted." On Ext2 systems, this is where the process stops, so recovery in this case is fairly easy. On Ext3 systems, when the link count of an inode hits zero, the block pointers are also zeroed out. While the content is still present in the freed blocks (until these are reallocated and overwritten), the link between metadata and data has been scrubbed.

In *Forensic Discovery*, Dan Farmer and Wietse Venema make many interesting observations with regard to deletion of data. One item of note is the fact that deleting a block or inode effectively "freezes" that item until it is reused. If an attacker places their malware in a relatively low-use area of the file system and then later deletes it, it is quite possible that the deleted blocks and inode will remain preserved in digital amber, Jurassic Park–style, for quite some time [2].

This idea has some effect on data recovery. For example, if you are attempting to recover data that existed previously in the /usr/share/ directory and all files in that directory have blocks allocated in block group 45, restricting your carving attempts to unallocated blocks from group 45 may prove a time (and sanity) saver.

Linux Logical Volume Manager

Some Linux systems may have one or more partitions allocated to the Logical Volume Manager (LVM). This system combines one or more partitions across one or more disks into Volume Groups and then divides these Volume Groups into Logical Volumes. The presence of an LVM-configured disk can be detected by looking for partition type **8e**, which is identified as "Linux_LVM" in the fdisk command output shown here:

```
# fdisk -l
Disk /dev/sda: 8589 MB, 8589934592 bytes
255 heads, 63 sectors/track, 1044 cylinders
Units = cylinders of 16065 * 512 = 8225280 bytes
Disk identifier: 0x0006159f
   Device Boot     Start   End    Blocks Id System
/dev/sda1 *          1     25  200781 83 Linux
/dev/sda2           26   1044   8185117+ 8e Linux LVM
```

To gain access to actual file systems contained inside of the LVM, we will need to first identify and activate the volume group(s) and then process any discovered logical volume(s). As LVMs are a Linux-specific technology, this can only be performed from a Linux system.

First, we will need to scan all disks and display the name associated with the LVM as shown here for a volume group named "VolGroup00."

```
# pvscan
  PV /dev/sda2 VG VolGroup00 lvm2 [7.78 GB / 32.00 MB free]
  Total: 1 [7.78 GB] / in use: 1 [7.78 GB] / in no VG: 0 [0 ]
```

In order to access logical volumes contained within this Volume Group, it is necessary to activate VolumeGroup00 as shown here:

```
# vgchange -a y VolGroup00
2 logical volume(s) in volume group VolGroup00 now active.
# lvs
LV VG Attr Lsize Origin Snap% Move Log Copy%
LogVol00 VolGroup00 -wi-a- 7.25G
LogVol01 VolGroup00 -wi-a- 512.00M
```

At this point we can image each logical volume directly as if it were a normal volume on a physical disk.

```
# dd if=/dev/VolGroup00/LogVol00 bs=4k of=/mnt/images/
  LogVol00.dd
# dd if=/dev/VolGroup00/LogVol01 bs=4k of=/mnt/images/
  LogVol01.dd
```

LINUX BOOT PROCESS AND SERVICES

Understanding the Linux boot process is important when performing an investigation of a Linux system. Knowledge of the files user during system startup can help the examiner determine which version of the operating system was running and when it was installed. Additionally, because of its open nature, a sufficiently privileged user can alter many aspects of the boot process so you need to know where to look for malicious modification. A complete review of the Linux boot process is outside the scope of this book, but a brief description of the process follows.

The first step of the Linux boot process is execution of the boot loader, which locates and loads the kernel. The kernel is the core of the operating system and is generally found in the /boot directory. Next, the initial ramdisk (initrd) is loaded. The initrd file contains device drivers, file system modules, logical volume modules, and other items required for boot but not built directly into the kernel.

Once the kernel and initial ramdisk are loaded, the kernel proceeds to initialize the system hardware. After this, the kernel begins executing what we recognize as the operating system, starting the /sbin/init process. Once init starts, there are two primary methods by which it will proceed to bring up a Linux operating system—System V style and BSD style. Linux distributions generally follow System V examples for most things, including init's tasks and processing runlevels.

System V

The System V init system is the most common init style across Linux distributions. Under System V, the init process reads the /etc/inittab file to determine the default "runlevel." A runlevel is a numeric description for the set of scripts a machine will execute for a given state. For example, on most Linux distributions, runlevel 3 will provide a full multiuser console environment, while runlevel 5 will produce a graphical environment.

> **WARNING**
> **Modern Startup Methods**
> Modern desktop-focused Linux distributions are replacing antiquated init systems with backward-compatible, event-driven daemons. The most popular of these is "upstart," currently used by Ubuntu and Fedora. However, due to upstart being backward compatible with init, the inittab/runlevel paradigm will still be present on disk for the forseeable future.

Note that each entry in a runlevel directory is actually a soft link to a script in /etc/init.d/, which will be started or stopped depending on the name of the link. Links named starting with "S" indicate the startup order, and links starting with "K" indicate the "kill" order. Each script can contain many variables and actions that will be taken to start or stop the service gracefully.

```
/etc/rc3.duser@ubuntu:/etc/rc3.d$ ls -l
total 4
-rw-r--r-- 1 root root 677 2010-03-30 00:17 README
lrwxrwxrwx 1 root root 20 2010-07-21 20:17 S20fancontrol -> ../
    init.d/fancontrol
lrwxrwxrwx 1 root root 20 2010-07-21 20:17 S20kerneloops -> ../
    init.d/kerneloops
lrwxrwxrwx 1 root root 27 2010-07-21 20:17 S20speech-dispatcher
    -> ../init.d/speech-dispatcher
lrwxrwxrwx 1 root root 24 2010-08-21 00:57 S20virtualbox-ose ->
    ../init.d/virtualbox-ose
lrwxrwxrwx 1 root root 19 2010-07-21 20:17 S25bluetooth -> ../
    init.d/bluetooth
lrwxrwxrwx 1 root root 17 2010-08-21 08:28 S30vboxadd -> ../
    init.d/vboxadd
lrwxrwxrwx 1 root root 21 2010-08-21 08:32 S30vboxadd-x11 -> ../
    init.d/vboxadd-x11
lrwxrwxrwx 1 root root 25 2010-08-21 08:32 S35vboxadd-service ->
    ../init.d/vboxadd-service
lrwxrwxrwx 1 root root 14 2010-07-21 20:17 S50cups -> ../init.d/
    cups
lrwxrwxrwx 1 root root 20 2010-07-21 20:17 S50pulseaudio -> ../
    init.d/pulseaudio
lrwxrwxrwx 1 root root 15 2010-07-21 20:17 S50rsync -> ../
    init.d/rsync
lrwxrwxrwx 1 root root 15 2010-07-21 20:17 S50saned -> ../
    init.d/saned
lrwxrwxrwx 1 root root 19 2010-07-21 20:17 S70dns-clean -> ../
    init.d/dns-clean
lrwxrwxrwx 1 root root 18 2010-07-21 20:17 S70pppd-dns -> ../
    init.d/pppd-dns
lrwxrwxrwx 1 root root 24 2010-07-21 20:17 S90binfmt-support ->
    ../init.d/binfmt-support
```

```
lrwxrwxrwx 1 root root 22 2010-07-21 20:17 S99acpi-support ->
  ../init.d/acpi-support
lrwxrwxrwx 1 root root 21 2010-07-21 20:17 S99grub-common -> ../
  init.d/grub-common
lrwxrwxrwx 1 root root 18 2010-07-21 20:17 S99ondemand -> ../
  init.d/ondemand
lrwxrwxrwx 1 root root 18 2010-07-21 20:17 S99rc.local -> ../
  init.d/rc.local
```

As you can see there are numerous places an intruder can set up a script to help them maintain persistent access to a compromised system. Careful review of all scripts involved in the boot process is suggested in an intrusion investigation.

BSD

The BSD-style init process is a bit less complex. BSD init reads the script at /etc/rc to determine what system services are to be run, configuration information is read from /etc/rc.conf, and additional services to run from /etc/rc.local. In some cases, this is the extent of init configuration, but other implementations may also read additional startup scripts from the /etc/rc.d/ directory. BSD style init is currently used by Slackware and Arch Linux, among others.

LINUX SYSTEM ORGANIZATION AND ARTIFACTS

To be able to locate and identify Linux system artifacts, you will need to understand how a typical Linux system is structured. This section discusses how directories and files are organized in the file system, how users are managed, and the meaning of file metadata being examined.

Partitioning

Linux file systems operate from a single, unified namespace. Remember, everything is a file, and all files exist under the root directory, "/". File systems on different local disks, removable media, and even remote servers will all appear underneath a single directory hierarchy, beginning from the root.

Filesystem Hierarchy

The standard directory structure Linux systems should adhere to is defined in the *Filesystem Hierarchy Standard* (FHS). This standard describes proper organization and use of the various directories found on Linux systems. The FHS is not enforced per se, but most Linux distributions adhere to it as best practice. The main directories found on a Linux system and the contents you should expect to find in them are shown in Table 5.1.

Table 5.1 Standard Linux Directories	
/bin	essential command binaries (for all users)
/boot	files needed for the system bootloader
/dev	device files
/etc	system configuration files
/home	user home directories
/lib	essential shared libraries and kernel modules
/media	mount points for removable media (usually for automounts)
/mnt	temporary mount points (usually mounted manually)
/opt	add-on application packages (outside of system package manager)
/root	root user's home directory
/sbin	system binaries
/tmp	temporary files

WARNING

/ vs /root

In traditional Unix nomenclature, "/" is referred to as "root," as it is the root of the entire directory structure for the system. Unfortunately, this leads to confusion with the subdirectory "/root" found on many Linux systems. This is referred to as "slash root" or "root's home."

Ownership and Permissions

Understanding file ownership and permission information is key to performing a successful examination of a Linux system. Ownership refers to the user and/or group that a file or directory belongs to, whereas permissions refer to the things these (and other) users can do with or to the file or directory. Access to files and directories on Linux systems are controlled by these two concepts. To examine this, we will refer back to the test "file1" created earlier in the chapter.

```
user@ubuntu:~$ stat file1
  File: 'file1'
  Size: 11        Blocks: 8      IO Block: 4096 regular file
Device: 801h/2049d Inode: 452126    Links: 1
Access: (0644/-rw-r--r--) Uid: ( 1000/ user) Gid: ( 1000/ user)
Access: 2010-10-19 21:06:36.534649312 -0700
Modify: 2010-10-19 21:06:34.798639051 -0700
Change: 2010-10-19 21:06:34.798639051 -0700
```

The fifth line contains the information of interest—the "Access: (0644/-rw-r—r--)" item are the permissions, and the rest of the line is the ownership information. This file is owned by User ID 1000 as well as Group ID 1000. We will discuss users and groups in detail later in the chapter.

Linux permissions are divided among three groups, and three tasks. Files and directories can be *read*, *written*, and *executed*. Permissions to perform these tasks can be assigned based to the *owner*, the *group*, or the *world* (aka anyone with access to the system). This file has the default permissions a file is assigned upon creation. Reading from left to right, the owner (UID 1000) can read and write to the file, anyone with a GID of 1000 can read it, and anyone with an account on the system can also read the file.

File Attributes

In addition to standard read/write/execute permissions, Ext file systems support "attributes." These attributes are stored in a special "attribute block" referenced by the inode. On a Linux system, these can be viewed using the `lsattr` command. Attributes that may be of investigative interest include

- (A)—no atime updates
- (a)—append only
- (i)—immutable
- (j)—data journaling enabled

Remember that we are working outside of file system-imposed restrictions when we use forensic tools and techniques so these attributes do not impact our examination of data in question. The presence of specific attributes may be of investigative interest, however.

Hidden Files

On Linux systems, files are "hidden" from normal view by beginning the file name with a dot (.). These files are known as dotfiles and will not be displayed by default in most graphical applications and command line utilities. Hidden files and directories are a very rudimentary way to hide data and should not be considered overtly suspicious, as many applications use them to store their nonuser-serviceable bits.

/tmp

/tmp is the virtual dumping ground of a Linux system—it is a shared scratch space, and as such all users have write permissions to this directory. It is typically used for system-wide lock files and nonuser-specific temporary files. One example of a service that uses /tmp to store lock files is the X Window Server, which provides the back end used by Linux graphical user interfaces. The fact that all users and processes can write here means that the /tmp directory is a great choice for a staging or initial entry point for an attacker to place data on the system. As an added bonus, most users never examine /tmp and would not know which random files or directories are to be expected and which are not.

Another item to note with regard to the /tmp directory can be seen in the following directory listing:

```
drwxrwxrwt 13 root root 4.0K 2010-10-15 13:38 tmp
```

Note that the directory itself is world readable, writable, and executable, but the last permission entry is a "t," not an "x" as we would expect. This indicates that the directory has the "sticky bit" set. Files under a directory with the sticky bit set can only be deleted by the user that owns them (or the root user), even if they are world or group writable. In effect, stickiness overrules other permissions.

> **NOTE**
> **Sticky History**
> Decades ago, the sticky bit was placed on program files to indicate that their executable instructions should be kept in swap once the program exited. This would speed up subsequent executions for commonly used programs. While some Unix-like systems still support this behavior, it was never used for this purpose on Linux systems.

USER ACCOUNTS

The first place to begin looking for information related to user accounts is the "/etc/passwd" file. It contains a list of users and the full path of their home directories. The passwords for user accounts are generally stored in the "/etc/shadow" file.

> **NOTE**
> **/etc/passwd doesn't have... passwords?**
> The name "passwd" seems to indicate that the file will contain passwords, but it doesn't—password hashes are in "shadow." What gives?
> Once upon a time, "passwd" *did* hold the password hashes. Unfortunately, this represents a pretty big security risk since the "passwd" file is necessarily readable by all users on the system. Any sufficiently motivated user could then harvest and crack all the local passwords. Modern systems store the password hashes in "shadow" to limit the scope of attacks like this.

A typical entry in the "/etc/passwd" file is shown here with a description of each field: forensics:x:500:500::/home/forensics:/bin/bash

1. username
2. hashed password field (deprecated)
3. user ID
4. primary group ID
5. The "GECOS" comment field. This is generally used for the user's full name or a more descriptive name for a service account
6. The path of the user's home directory
7. The program to run upon initial login (normally the user's default shell)

The "/etc/passwd" file will usually be fairly lengthy, even on a single user system. A fairly old trick that is still occasionally seen in compromises in the wild is to add an additional "UID 0" user somewhere in the middle of these default accounts in an attempt to fade into the noise.

> **NOTE**
> **The Zero Effect**
> Because Linux permissions are granted by the numeric UID and GID and not the account name, any user account with UID 0 is the functional equivalent of root.

The "/etc/group" file has a format similar to /etc/passwd, but with fewer fields. Examples of typical entries can be seen here:

```
root:x:0:root
bin:x:1:root,bin,daemon
daemon:x:2:root,bin,daemon
wheel:x:10:root
```

The first field is the group name, second is the hash of the group password (password-protected groups are not typically used), the third is the group ID, and the fourth is a comma-separated list of members of the group. Additional unauthorized users in the root or wheel groups may be suspicious and warrant further investigation.

> **NOTE**
> **Wheel in the Sky**
> The wheel group is a holdover from the early days of Unix and refers to a "big wheel"— someone important. Modern Linux systems have carried over this tradition; in many cases, users in the wheel group have some set of administrative powers, generally including the ability to execute sudo commands.

The "/etc/shadow" file is the third item required for basic Linux authentication. It contains hashed user passwords and password-related information.

```
root:$1$gsGAI2/j$jWMnLcOzHFtlBDveRqw3i/:13977:0:99999:7:::
bin:*:13826:0:99999:7:::
...
gdm:!!:13826:0:99999:7:::
user:$1$xSS1eCUL$jrGLlZPGmD7ia61kIdrTV.:13978:0:99999:7:::
```

The fields of the shadow file are as follows:

1. Username
2. Encrypted password
3. Number of days since the Unix epoch (1 Jan 1970) that the password was last changed
4. Minimum days between password changes

5. Maximum time password is valid
6. Number of days prior to expiration to warn users
7. Absolute expiration date
8. Reserved for future use

One item to note is that the "*" and the "!!" in the password fields for daemon accounts "bin" and "gdm" indicate that these accounts do not have encrypted passwords. Because these are not user accounts, they have a null or invalid password field to prevent them from being used for an interactive login. Any nonuser accounts that do have encrypted password fields should be investigated.

TIP

Passwd Backups

Some Linux distributions generate backup copies of the user management files (passwd, shadow, and groups) when a user or group is added or modified. These files will have a minus or dash sign (–) appended to their name. This can be convenient in an intrusion investigation where a user has been added to the system. We can use the `diff` command to compare current and backup passwd files to look for any intruder user accounts.

```
user@ubuntu:~/images$ ls /etc/passwd*
/etc/passwd /etc/passwd-
user@ubuntu:~/images$ diff /etc/passwd /etc/passwd-
diff: /etc/passwd-: Permission denied
user@ubuntu:~/images$ sudo diff /etc/passwd /etc/passwd-
37d36
< hacker:x:1001:1001::/home/hacker:/bin/sh
```

HOME DIRECTORIES

On a Linux system, user home directories serve pretty much the same purpose they do on any other operating system—they provide users a location to store data specific to them. Well-behaved processes and services specific to an individual user will also store automatically created data in subdirectories. These are the standard visible subdirectories found on a Linux system using the GNOME desktop environment:

- **Desktop**—The user's Dektop directory. Any files present in this directory should be visible on the user's desktop in interactive graphical sessions.
- **Documents**—The default directory for office-type document files—text, spreadsheets, presentations, and the like.
- **Downloads**—Default directory for files downloaded from remote hosts; GNOME-aware Web browsers, file-sharing clients, and the like should deposit their data here.

- **Music**—Default location for music files.
- **Pictures**—Default location for pictures. Note that scanned images or images from attached imaging devices (webcams, cameras) will likely end up here unless otherwise directed.
- **Public**—Files to be shared with others.
- **Templates**—Holds document templates. New files can be generated from a given template via a right click in GNOME. Note that this directory is empty by default so any additions may indicate a frequently used file type.
- **Videos**—Default location for videos. Locally recorded or generated video should end up in this directory unless redirected by the user.

In addition to these "user-accessible" directories, various hidden directories and files are present. Some of these can contain valuable forensic data generated automatically or as a secondary effect of a user's activity.

TIP

You Can Go home Again

When a user account is deleted from a Unix system, the home directory may be left behind. If your examination warrants, it can be useful to look in the "/home" directory for additional directories that may contain old user data.

Shell History

The default command shell on most Linux distributions is the Bourne Again Shell, aka "BASH." Commands typed in any shell sessions will usually be stored in a file in the user's home directory called ".bash_history." Shell sessions include direct virtual terminals, GUI terminal application windows, or logging in remotely via SSH. Unfortunately, the bash shell records history as a simple list of commands that have been executed, with no time stamps or other indication of when the commands were entered. Correlation of history entries and file system or log file time information will be important if the time a specific command was executed is important to your investigation.

ssh

The .ssh directory contains files related to the use of the Secure Shell (ssh) client. SSH is used frequently on Linux and Unix-like systems to connect to a remote system via a text console. SSH also offers file transfer, connection tunneling, and proxying capabilities. There may be client configuration files present, which can indicate a particular use case for SSH.

When a user connects to a remote host using the ssh program, the remote host's hostname or IP address and the host's public key are recorded in the

".ssh/known_hosts" file. Entries in this file can be correlated with server logs to tie suspect activity to a specific machine. A traditional known_hosts entry looks like the following:

```
$ cat .ssh/known_hosts
192.168.0.106 ssh-rsaAAAAB3NzaC1yc2EAAAADAQABAAABAQDRtd74Cp19P044
zRDUdMkOEmkuD/d4WAefzPaf55L5Dh5CO6Sq+xG543sw0i1LjMN7C
IJbz+AnSd967aX/BZZimUchHk8gm2BzoAEbpOEPIJ+G2vLOrc+faM
1NZhDDzGuoFV7tMnQQLOrqD9/4PfC1yLGVlIJ9obd+6BR78yeBRdq
HVjYsKUtJ146aKoVwV60dafVlEfbOjh1/ZKhhliKAaYlLhXALnp8/
18EBj5CDqsTKCcGQbhkSPgYgxuDg8qD7ngLpB9oUvV9QSDZkmROR937MYi
IpUYPqdK5opLVnKn81B1r+TsTxiI7RJ7M53pOcvx8nNfjwAuNzWTLJz6zr
```

Some distributions enable the hashing of entries in the known_hosts file—a hashed entry for the same host looks like this:

```
|1|rjAWXFqldZmjmgJnaw7HJO4KtAg=|qfrtMVerwngkTaWC7mdEF3HNx/o=
ssh-rsaAAAAB3NzaC1yc2EAAAADAQABAAABAQDRtd74Cp19P044zRDUdMkOEm
kuD/d4WAefzPaf55L5Dh5CO6Sq+xG543sw0i1LjMN7CIJbz+AnSd967aX/BZZ
imUchHk8gm2BzoAEbpOEPIJ+G2vLOrc+faM1NZhDDzGuoFV7tMnQQLOrqD9/4
PfC1yLGVlIJ9obd+6BR78yeBRdqHVjYsKUtJ146aKoVwV60dafVlEfbOjh1/
ZKhhliKAaYlLhXALnp8/18EBj5CDqsTKCcGQbhkSPgYgxuDg8qD7ngLpB9oUv
V9QSDZkmROR937MYiIpUYPqdK5opLVnKn81B1r+TsTxiI7RJ7M53pOcvx8nNfjwA
uNzWTLJz6zr
```

Note that in both cases the stored public key is identical, indicating that the hashed host |1| is the same machine as host 192.168.0.106 from the first known_hosts file.

GNOME Windows Manager Artifacts

Because each Linux system can be quite different from any other Linux system, attempting to create an exhaustive list of possible user artifacts would be an exercise in futility. That said, some additional files generated by user activity on a default GNOME desktop installation are worth exploring. Because these artifacts are usually plain text, no special tools are needed to process them. Simply looking in the right location and being able to understand the significance of a given artifact is all that is required for many Linux artifacts. We will discuss a few of these artifacts in this section.

The hidden ".gconf" directory contains various GNOME application configuration files under a logical directory structure. Of particular interest in this structure is ".gconf/apps/nautilus/desktop-metadata/," which will contain subdirectories for any media handled by the GNOME automounter. If an icon for the volume appears on the user's desktop, an entry will be present in this directory. Each volume directory will contain a "%gconf.xml" file. An example of the content found inside this file is shown here:

```
user@ubuntu:~$ cat .gconf/apps/nautilus/desktop-metadata/
  EXTDISK@46@volume/\%gconf.xml
<?xml version="1.0"?>
```

```
<gconf>
    <entry name="nautilus-icon-position" mtime="1287452747"
      type="string">
          <stringvalue>64,222</stringvalue>
    </entry>
</gconf>
```

The "C-time" of the %gconf.xml file should correspond to the first time the volume was connected to the system in question. In the case of this file, the embedded icon-position "mtime" value also matches this time, as the icon was never respositioned.

```
File: '.gconf/apps/nautilus/desktop-metadata/EXTDISK@46@
   volume/%gconf.xml'
Size: 157         Blocks: 8         IO Block: 8192    regular file
Device: 1ch/28d   Inode: 23498767   Links: 1
Access: (0600/-rw-------) Uid: (1000/ user) Gid: ( 1000/ user)
Access: 2010-12-28 16:24:06.276887000 -0800
Modify: 2010-10-18 18:45:50.283574000 -0700
Change: 2010-10-18 18:45:50.324528000 -0700
```

The ".gnome2" subdirectory contains additional GNOME application-related artifacts. One of the items of interest here is ".gnome2/evince/ev-metadata.xml," which stores recently opened file information for items viewed with "evince," GNOME's native file viewer. This can provide information about files viewed on external media or inside of encrypted volumes. A similar file that may be present is ".gnome2/gedit-metadata.xml," which stores similar information for files opened in GNOME's native text editor "gedit."

The .recently-used.xbel file in the user's home is yet another cache of recently accessed files. An XML entry is added each time the user opens a file using a GTK application, and it does not appear that this file is ever purged automatically. On a heavily used system this file may grow quite large. An example entry is shown here:

```
<bookmark href="file:///tmp/HOWTO-BootingAcquiredWindows.pdf"
   added="2010-04-16T18:04:35Z" modified="2010-04-16T18:04:35Z"
   visited="2010-04-16T19:51:34Z">
 <info>
  <metadata owner="http://freedesktop.org">
   <mime:mime-type type="application/pdf"/>
   <bookmark:applications>
    <bookmark:application name="Evince Document Viewer"
       exec="&apos;evince %u&apos;" timestamp="1271441075"
       count="1"/>
   </bookmark:applications>
  </metadata>
 </info>
</bookmark>
```

Linux applications can cache various bits of data in the user's home under the appropriately named directory ".cache." One item of note in this directory is the Ubuntu/GNOME on-screen display notification log, which contains a time-stamped history of items displayed to the user via the notify-osd daemon. This can include items such as network connections and disconnections, which can be useful to determine if a laptop system was moved from one location to another.

```
user@ubuntu:~$ cat .cache/notify-osd.log
[2010-10-15T02:36:54-00:00, NetworkManager ] Wired network
Disconnected
[2010-10-15T02:37:30-00:00, NetworkManager ] Wired network
Disconnected
[2010-10-15T13:38:15-00:00, NetworkManager ] Wired network
Disconnected - you are now offline
[2010-10-15T13:39:03-00:00, NetworkManager ] Wired network
Disconnected - you are now offline
```

The ".gtk-bookmarks" file in the user's home directory is used by the GNOME file manager (Nautilus) to generate the "Places" drop-down list of locations. The default values are shown here:

```
-rw-r--r-- 1 user user 132 2010-10-13 18:21 .gtk-bookmarks
file:///home/user/Documents
file:///home/user/Music
file:///home/user/Pictures
file:///home/user/Videos
file:///home/user/Downloads
```

Any additional or altered values in this file may indicate a user-created shortcut to a frequently accessed directory. Additionally, this file may contain links to external or portable volumes that may not be immediately apparent or that exist inside of encrypted containers.

LOGS

Log analysis on Linux is generally quite straightforward. Most logs are stored in clear text, with a single line per event. Identifying which logs contain data you are after may be challenging, but processing these logs once you've found them is usually less involved than on Windows systems. Unfortunately, the amount of log information and the ease of access cuts both ways—logs on Linux systems tend to "roll over" after 28–30 days by default, and deleting or modifying logs is one of the most basic tasks an attacker may perform.

We will examine two types of logs: logs generated by or track user activity and logs generated by system activity.

User Activity Logs

We discussed shell history files previously—these are a great source of information about user activity. Unfortunately, because they usually do not contain any time information, their usefulness may be limited. There are additional logs that hold information about user access to the system that do record time stamps, however. Direct records of user activity on a Linux system are stored in three primary files: "/var/run/utmp," "/var/log/wtmp," and "/var/log/lastlog."

The "utmp" and "wtmp" files record user logons and logoffs in a binary format. The major difference between these files is that "utmp" only holds information about active system logons, whereas "wtmp" stores logon information long term (per the system log rotation period). These files can both be accessed via the last command using the -f flag.

```
user@ubuntu:~$ last -f wtmp.1
user    pts/2    :0.0         Thu Oct 14 19:40 still logged in
user    pts/0    :0.0         Wed Oct 13 18:36 still logged in
user    pts/0    cory-macbookpro. Wed Oct 13 18:22 - 18:35
   (00:12)
user    tty7     :0           Wed Oct 13 18:21 still logged in
reboot system boot 2.6.32-24-generi Wed Oct 13 18:17 - 21:49
   (12+03:32)
user    pts/0    :0.0         Wed Oct 13 18:05 - 18:05 (00:00)
user    tty7     :0           Wed Oct 13 18:04 - crash (00:13)
reboot system boot 2.6.32-24-generi Wed Oct 13 18:01 - 21:49
   (12+03:48)
user    tty7     :0           Sat Aug 21 09:46 - crash (53+08:15)
reboot system boot 2.6.32-24-generi Sat Aug 21 08:46 - 21:49
   (65+13:03)
user    pts/0    :0.0         Sat Aug 21 08:23 - 08:44 (00:21)
user    tty7     :0           Sat Aug 21 08:21 - down (00:22)
wtmp.1 begins Sat Aug 21 08:21:52 2010
```

The "lastlog" is a binary log file that stores the last logon time and remote host for each user on the system. On a live system, this file is processed via the lastlog command. Simple Perl scripts exist for parsing the file offline [3], but these scripts need to be modified to match the format definition of "lastlog" for the given system. The structures for "utmp," "wtmp," and "lastlog" are all defined in the "/usr/include/bits/utmp.h" header file on Linux distributions.

Syslog

The bulk of system logs on a Linux system are stored under the "/var/log" directory, either in the root of this directory or in various subdirectories specific to the application generating the logs. Syslog operates on client/server model, which enables events to be recorded to a remote, dedicated syslog server.

However, on a standalone Linux system, events are usually written directly to the files on the local host.

Syslog uses a "facility/priority" system to classify logged events. The "facility" is the application or class of application that generated the event. The defined syslog facilities are listed in Table 5.2.

Table 5.2 Syslog Facilities

auth	Authentication activity
authpriv	Authentication and PAM messages
cron	Cron/At/Task Scheduler messages
daemon	Daemons/service messages
kern	Kernel messages
Lpr	Printing services
mail	Email (imap, pop, smtp) messages
news	Usenet News Server messages
syslog	Messages from syslog
user	User program messages
Local*	Locally defined

Table 5.3 Syslog Severities

Emerg or panic	System is unusable
Alert	Action must be taken immediately
Crit	Critical conditions
Err	Error conditions
Warning	Warning conditions
Notice	Normal but significant conditions
Info	Informational messages
Debug	Debugging level messages, very noisy
None	Used to override (*) wildcard
*	All levels except none

Syslog levels indicate the severity of the issue being reported. The available levels and the urgency they are intended to relay are displayed in Table 5.3.

Syslog events are a single line containing made up of five fields:

1. Date of message creation
2. Time of message creation
3. Host name of the system creating the log entry
4. Process name creating the log entry
5. Text of the log entry

> **WARNING**
>
> **Remote Syslog Caveats**
>
> Syslog can be configured to log to a remote server, either entirely replacing or simply supplementing local logging. This is noted in the syslog configuration file with "*.* @hostname" as the syslog destination. The syslog protocol is clear text and is transmitted over the connectionless UDP protocol. Because message sources are not authenticated and messages are not signed, it is possible for an attacker to spoof syslog remote messages. A much more mundane threat is the silent dropping of logs if the syslog server fails to receive the UDP datagram for any reason.

Table 5.4 Common Log Files of Interest	
/var/log/messages	Catch-all, nonspecified logs
/var/log/auth.log	User authentication successes/failures
/var/log/secure	
/var/log/sulog	"su" attempts/success
/var/log/httpd/*	Apache Web Server
/var/log/samba/smbd.log	Samba (Windows File Sharing)
/var/log/samba/nmbd.log	
/var/log/audit/audit.log	Auditd/SELinux
/var/log/maillog	Mail servers (sendmail/postfix)
/var/log/cups/access_log	CUPS Printer Services
/var/log/cron	Anacron/cron
/var/log/xferlog	FTP servers

This uniform logging format makes searching for log entries of note on a Linux system relatively easy. It is important to note that most Linux systems implement some level of log rotation. For example, a default Ubuntu Linux desktop installation rotates logs every month, compressing the older log file with GZip for archival. Server systems will likely archive logs more rapidly and are more likely to delete logs from active systems after a shorter retention period.

Table 5.4 contains the default paths of some common logs of interest in many Linux examinations.

Command Line Log Processing

Linux system administrators are generally quite familiar with processing system log files using command line tools. Because Linux system logs are by and large plain text, this is done quite easily by chaining together a handful of text-processing and searching tools. The primary tools used for log file processing on Linux systems are sed, awk, and grep.

Sed is a **stream ed**itor. It is designed to take an input stream, edit the content, and output the altered result. It reads input line by line and performs specified actions based on matching criteria—usually line numbers or patterns to match. Sed operators are passed as single characters. Basic sed operators are:

- **p:** print
- **d:** delete
- **s:** substitute
- **y:** transform
- **!:** inverts the pattern match

For purposes of log analysis, sed is generally used to quickly eliminate log lines that are not of interest. For example, to delete all log lines containing the word "DEBUG," we would use the following sed command:

```
sed /DEBUG/d logfile.txt
```

Awk is a more robust text processing utility, but this additional power is wrapped in additional complexity. Sed and awk are used together frequently in Linux and Unix shell scripts to perform text transformations. While sed is line based, awk can perform field operations, so it is useful when you want to compare multiple text fields in a single log line. The default field separator in awk is any white space, but this can be changed to any character using the -F argument. So, to print the fifth field from every line in a log file, you would use:

```
awk '{print $5}' logfile.txt
```

To print the third field from every line in a comma-separated log file, you would use:

```
awk -F\, '{print $3}' logfile.txt
```

The grep command is a powerful text-searching utility. For log analysis, this is generally used to return lines that match specific criteria. Pattern matching in grep is handled by *regular expressions* (see the Regular Expressions sidebar for more information). For basic use, though, simply supplying a literal string to match is effective enough.

TIP

Regular Expressions

To become truly proficient with grep, an examiner must become familiar with "regular expressions," which may also be referred to as a "regex." In short, a regular expression is a shorthand value that describes a range of text to be selected. The syntax used to create a regex can appear quite arcane, and even seasoned Linux veterans will have to refer to a regex cookbook from time to time. A good online guide to begin exploring regular expressions can be found at http://www.regular-expressions.info/quickstart.html.

Using these three commands together can be quite effective. Let's say you have a SSH brute force login attack that may have been successful. A fast or long-lived SSH brute force attack can generate thousands to hundreds of thousands of log lines. Using these utilities we can whittle our log down to relevant entries very quickly. First, we will use sed to eliminate all lines that aren't generated by the SSH daemon (sshd). Next, we will use grep to extract only lines pertaining to accepted connections. Finally, we will use awk to reduce some of the extraneous fields in the log line.

```
user@ubuntu:/var/log$ sudo sed '/sshd/!d' auth.log | grep
  Accepted | awk '{print $1, $2, $3, $9, $11}'
Dec 17 13:50:51 root 192.168.7.81
Dec 18 12:55:09 root 192.168.7.81
```

> **TIP**
>
> **Log Statistics**
>
> If you need to generate simple statistics about the content of a log file or log files, several command line utilities can be used for this purpose:
>
> - `uniq` can be used with the "-c" flag to collapse repeating lines of data to a single line, preceded by the total number of lines "uniqued" together. `Uniq` only works on sorted data, so unsorted data should be preprocessed using the *sort* command. This can be useful when trying to determine "top talkers" from a file containing IP addresses or for finding the most (or least) commonly returned status codes from a Web server log.
> - `wc` can be used to count characters, words, or lines from input data. This can be useful when trying to determine the number of results returned for a specific `grep` query.

SCHEDULING TASKS

On Linux systems there are two main mechanisms for scheduling a job to be run in the future: `at` and `cron`. The at command is used to run a task once, at a specific point in the future. At jobs can be found under "/var/spool/cron." The cron process is used to schedule repeating tasks—processes to be run every night, once a week, every other week, and so on. There are two locations where cron jobs will be stored. System cron jobs are found in a set of directories defined in the "/etc/crontab" file and are typically in the aptly named directories "/etc/cron.hourly," "/etc/cron.daily," "/etc/cron.weekly," and "/etc/cron.monthly." Any scheduled tasks added by users will be found in "/var/spool/cron," such as jobs added by the at command. As you can surmise, cron jobs are a terrific way for an attacker to maintain persistence on a compromised system, so verifying these jobs will be critical in an intrusion investigation.

SUMMARY

While the adoption of Linux as a desktop is still fairly sparse, many of the skills involved in processing a Linux system are applicable to other Unix-like systems, to include Mac OS X, which is discussed in Chapter 6. While it is not taking the desktop world by storm, Linux is becoming more and more popular on embedded devices such as mobile phones and tablet computers. Examiners capable of exploiting these data sources for artifacts of interest will be in high demand in the years to come.

References

[1] Rémy Card, Blaise Pascal, Theodore Ts'o, Stephen Tweedie, Design and Implementation of the Second Extended Filesystem. http://web.mit.edu/tytso/www/linux/ext2intro.html, (accessed 9.10.10).

[2] D. Farmer, W. Venema, Forensic Discovery, Addison-Wesley, Upper Saddle River, NJ, 2005.

[3] Formatting and Printing Lastlog. http://www.hcidata.info/lastlog.htm, (accessed 9.11.10).

Mac OS X Systems and Artifacts

INFORMATION IN THIS CHAPTER

- OS X File System Artifacts
- OS X System Artifacts
- User Artifacts

INTRODUCTION

The first version of Mac OS X was released 10 years ago, and in the subsequent 10 years Apple has seen its fortune rise considerably. While not nearly as prevalent as Windows desktops and laptops, it is important that an examiner be prepared to deal with an OS X system if necessary. This chapter introduces the file system used by OS X, explains the layout of files and directories on the file system, and analyzes artifacts related to user and system activity.

OS X FILE SYSTEM ARTIFACTS

The file system used by OS X is called *HFS Plus* or *Mac OS Extended*. HFS+ is the successor to the Hierarchical File System (HFS) used on pre-OS X Mac operating systems. There are currently two variant HFS+ formats used to support journaling (*HFSJ*) and case-sensitive file names (*HFSX*). Beyond these extended capabilities, because these variants don't alter the function or artifacts available to the examiner, we will treat them all as "HFS+" throughout this chapter. The best source of information available about HFS+ is an Apple technical document entitled "Technical Note TN1150: HFS Plus Volume Format [1]."

HFS+ Structures

The volume header is one of the core structures of an HFS+ volume. It stores data about the file system, including the allocation blocks size, the volume creation time stamp, and the location of the special files required for HFS+ operation, discussed later in the chapter. The volume header is always located 1024 bytes from the start of the volume, with a backup copy located 1024 bytes before the end of the volume.

HFS+ uses *allocation blocks* as data units. The size of a single allocation block is defined in the volume header, but 4K bytes is a common value. Allocation blocks can be further grouped into *clumps*, which are somewhat similar to the block allocation groups found in Ext file systems under Linux. A file's data are addressed in terms of *extents*. An HFS+ extent is simply a 4-byte pointer to a starting allocation block and a 4-byte value indicating the length of the extent.

HFS+ files may have any number of data streams called *forks* associated with it. The two primary forks are the *data fork* and the *resource fork*. Generally the data fork holds the actual file content, while the resource fork will be empty or contain nonessential supporting information about the file. Additional forks may be created for a file for application specific purposes.

We can use the fsstat command from the Sleuth Kit to read information about the file system from the volume header. We will use the *nps-2009-hfsjtest1/img.gen1.dmg* file from the Digital Corpora as our test image while examining basic file system data.

```
FILE SYSTEM INFORMATION
--------------------------------------------
File System Type: HFS+
File System Version: HFS+
Volume Name: image
Volume Identifier: 9bee54da586b82f5
Last Mounted By: Mac OS X, Journaled
Volume Unmounted Properly
Mount Count: 11
Creation Date: Thu Jan 29 09:33:30 2009
Last Written Date: Thu Jan 29 09:33:42 2009
Last Backup Date: Wed Dec 31 16:00:00 1969
Last Checked Date: Thu Jan 29 09:33:30 2009
Journal Info Block: 2
METADATA INFORMATION
--------------------------------------------
Range: 2 - 28
Bootable Folder ID: 0
Startup App ID: 0
Startup Open Folder ID: 0
Mac OS 8/9 Blessed System Folder ID: 0
Mac OS X Blessed System Folder ID: 0
Number of files: 7
Number of folders: 4
CONTENT INFORMATION
--------------------------------------------
Block Range: 0 - 2559
Allocation Block Size: 4096
Number of Free Blocks: 443
```

From this output we can confirm the 4K allocation block size, some relevant time information associated with access to the volume, and a couple other pieces of OS

X operating system-specific startup metadata that aren't relevant on a nonsystem volume and are thus displayed as "0". These include the two Startup items and the "Blessed" System Folder lines. These would point to items in the /System/Library/CoreServices directory on an OS X boot volume.

NOTE

Sleuth Kit and HFS+

While the Sleuth Kit does support HFS+, at the time of this writing there are some limitations. Currently, the Sleuth Kit does not display deleted files and cannot process the HFS+ journal. Additionally, Sleuth Kit tools have no understanding of nondata forks, extended attributes, or HFS+ hard links. That said, the HFS+ analysis capabilities currently present in the Sleuth Kit should allow an examiner to perform a thorough examination in many types of cases.

In addition to various Sleuth Kit tools, we can also use *HFSExplorer* from Catacombae. HFSExplorer is an open source cross-platform application that can be used to open and examine HFS, HFS+, and HFSX volumes. In addition, individual files can be extracted for detailed examination. See Figure 6.1 for the HFSExplorer display of the file system information from the Digital Corpora test image.

We can continue our examination using fls from the Sleuth Kit.

```
forensics:~$ fls nps-2009-hfsjtest1/image.gen1.dmg
r/r 3: $ExtentsFile
r/r 4: $CatalogFile
r/r 5: $BadBlockFile
r/r 6: $AllocationFile
r/r 7: $StartupFile
r/r 8: $AttributesFile
d/d 21:        .fseventsd
d/d 19:        .HFS+ Private Directory Data^
r/r 16: .journal
r/r 17: .journal_info_block
d/d 20:        .Trashes
r/r 24: file1.txt
r/r 25: file2.txt
d/d 18:        ^^^^HFS+ Private Data
```

The "dollar" files are HFS+ special files used as the backbone of the HFS+ file system.

HFS+ Special Files

The bulk of the structures that an HFS+ relies upon for proper function are stored in the volume as hidden files, much like the MFT and associated files on an NTFS volume. An HFS+ volume has five such files, which are not directly accessible using standard file system utilities:

1. **The allocation file** is a bitmap that tracks the allocation status of each block of the volume.
2. **The catalog file** contains records for each file and directory on the volume. It serves many of the same functions that the Master File Table serves on an

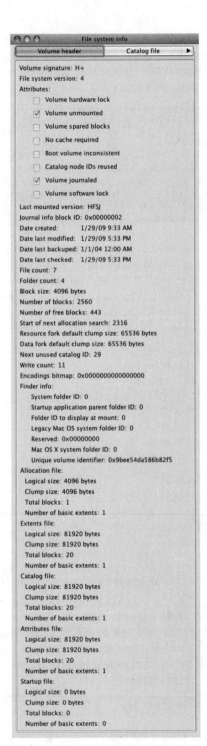

FIGURE 6.1

File system information in
HFSExplorer.

NTFS file system. By necessity, the location of the first extent of the catalog file is stored in the volume header. The location of all other files is stored in catalog records. HFS+ catalog records are 8K in length and include the catalog node ID (CNID) of the file or folder, the parent CNID, time stamp metadata, and information about the data and resource forks of the file.

3. **The extents overflow file** contains records for forks that have more than eight extents allocated to them. This file should be fairly sparse, as having more than eight extents indicates fairly severe fragmentation on an HFS+ file system.

4. **The startup file** is used to hold information used when booting from a system that doesn't have knowledge of HFS+.

5. **The attributes file** can be used to store extended attributes for files. The attributes file is used in the per-file compression found in OS X 10.6.

One important item to note is that the allocation strategy for CNIDs is interesting from an analysis perspective. CNIDs are 32-bit values allocated sequentially starting from 16. They are not reused until all 32-bit integers (minus the reserved CNIDs) have been assigned. This allows the CNID to serve as a relative time marker. Files with higher CNID values are newer than files with lower CNID values, despite what any time stamp information would indicate. Additionally, missing CNID values indicate that a file was once present and has been subsequently deleted. See Chapter 9 for more information on relative time values and extended time analysis.

Next, we will examine metadata for a single regular file in detail using istat.

```
forensics:~$ istat nps-2009-hfsjtest1/image.gen1.dmg 24
Catalog Record: 24
Allocated
Type: File
Mode: rrw-r--r--
Size: 28
uid / gid: 501 / 501
Link count:    1
Admin flags:   0
Owner flags:   0
File type:     0000
File creator:  0000
Text encoding:     0
Resource fork size: 0
Times:
Created:    Thu Jan 29 09:33:35 2009
Content Modified:    Thu Jan 29 09:33:42 2009
Attributes Modified: Thu Jan 29 09:33:42 2009
Accessed:   Thu Jan 29 09:33:35 2009
Backed Up: Wed Dec 31 16:00:00 1969
Data Fork Blocks:
2315
```

As you can see from the output just given, a Catalog Record supports five time stamps; however, only the first four are in active use on current HFS+ implementations.

Created: Updated when the file is created.
Content Modified: Updated when the file content is modified.
Attributes Modified: Updated when attributes (metadata) associated with the file are modified. This is similar to the inoded/metadata change time on Linux file systems.
Accessed: Updated when the file content is accessed.
Backed Up: Field is deprecated and usually null (as seen earlier).

Finally, to extract the file content we can use two different methods. First, the indirect method using icat.

```
forensics:~$ icat nps-2009-hfsjtest1/image.gen1.dmg 24
New file 1 contents - snarf
```

Alternatively, we can dump the allocation block directly using blkcat. We can see the block value in the istat output shown earlier under "Data Fork Blocks":

```
forensics:~$ blkcat nps-2009-hfsjtest1/image.gen1.dmg 2315
New file 1 contents - snarf
```

Note that HFS+ volumes are capable of maintaining a journal; however, currently there are no open source forensic utilities capable of processing the journal for artifacts.

TIP

DMG/UDIF Containers

The majority of OS X software is distributed as "DMG" files. DMG files are standalone disk-like images in the Universal Disk Image Format (UDIF). UDIF is the native image file format for OS X and, as expected, these image files will generally contain a HFS+ file system. UDIF images can be compressed, sparse, or encrypted. UDIF/DMG images can be examined using HFSExplorer.

Deleted Data

Unfortunately, recovery of deleted files from HFS+ volumes is quite difficult. Because of the constant rebalancing of the B-Tree structures inside of the Catalog File, file metadata information is usually overwritten soon after a file is deleted from the file system. This leaves the examiner in much the same boat as on Linux—data recovery is sometimes possible via data carving, but associating recovered content with file names or dates will not be straightforward. Many data formats will contain extractable secondary identifying information or time information, however. Extraction of these data is covered in Chapter 8.

Ownership/Permissions

OS X uses POSIX standard permissions as default. These are described in Chapter 5. In addition to POSIX permissions, OS X 10.4 and newer supported extended ACLs for more finely grained control to files. This should not affect the forensic examiner's ability to view file system content as we are viewing a dead file system outside of operating system restrictions. More information about the use and implementation of OS X extended ACLs is available at the Apple Developer Library [2].

OS X SYSTEM ARTIFACTS

Like Linux systems, OS X places all volumes under a single unified namespace below the root directory "/". Immediately beneath the root directory are the following directories:

Applications—This directory is the standard location for all installed OS X applications. Generally this directory will hold applications designed to be launched interactively via the OS X GUI.

Library—Library directories hold supporting data that may need to be modified during execution of a program. This generally includes things such as preferences, recent items, and other similar data. The root Library directory contains system-wide configuration data. User-specific data are stored under user Library directories.

Network—Directory for items in the Network domain; generally empty.

System—This directory contains operating system-specific data, somewhat analogous to contents of the system32 directory on a Windows system.

Users—The parent directory for user home directories.

Volumes—The parent directory for mounted volumes; similar to /mnt or /media on Linux systems.

bin and **sbin**—These directories contain command-line utilities included in the OS X system.

private—This directory contains (among other things) OS X versions of **/var**, **/tmp**, and **/etc.**

Property Lists

Many artifacts of interest on an OS X system are stored as *property lists* or *.plist* files. There are two types of property lists: plain text, XML property lists and binary property lists. Plain text plist files can be examined directly or viewed in any XML display program. Binary plists need to be converted to plain text prior to analysis. Due to being more compact than their plain text equivalent, binary plists are becoming used more and more commonly. A typical OS X install will have thousands of plist files, so knowing which will be relevant to your examination is key.

Many OS X-native, closed source utilities interact with plist files, including a basic command line utility called `plutil`. Fortunately, Pete M. Wilson has developed a Perl script that can convert binary plist files to their plain text equivalent [3]. His script, `plutil.pl`, is quite simple to use. When provided with the name of a binary plist file, `plutil.pl` parses the file and outputs a plain text version in the same directory.

Bundles

On an OS X system, the "applications" users generally interact with are not monolithic files at all, but are in fact special directories known as *bundles*. Bundles are directories that have their contents hidden from the end user's view by the operating system. Opening or double-clicking on an application bundle is enough to execute the application, but the actual executable code is several directories down from the bundle itself. Drilling down into the bundle via the OS X GUI can be performed via the right-click menu as shown in Figure 6.2.

FIGURE 6.2

"Show Package Contents" in OS X.

When examining an OS X system via the Sleuth Kit, the bundle will just be treated as a standard directory. Application bundles can be identified in a file listing by the ".app" extension in the directory name, and a set of subdirectories similar to the following:

```
Contents
Contents/Info.plist
Contents/MacOS
Contents/PkgInfo
Contents/Resources
Contents/Versions
```

The actual executable code is normally stored in the MacOS directory, with the other directories holding supporting data such as icons, text files, and the like.

System Startup and Services

On system boot, the bootloader boots the OS X kernel (*/mach_kernel*), which then runs the *launchd* process. Launchd serves as a replacement for *init* and the init

Table 6.1 Standard Startup Locations

/Library/LaunchAgents	Per-user agents provided by the administrator
/Library/LaunchDaemons	System-wide daemons provided by the administrator
/System/Library/LaunchAgents	Per-user agents provided by Mac OS X
/System/Library/Launch-Daemons	System-wide daemons provided by Mac OS X

scripts process found on Linux systems. The launchd takes its tasking from four directories. System tasks that run in the background are read from */System/Library/LaunchDaemons* and */Library/LaunchDaemons*, while user-interactive launch tasks are read from */System/Library/LaunchAgents* and */Library/LaunchAgents*. Launchd will read and process plists in these directories, launching the appropriate applications. Note that all of the plist files in these directories should be in the plain XML format and thus do not require conversion before examination. Per Apple's documentation [4], the division of startup tasks is shown in Table 6.1.

Kexts

OS X has the capability to load additional functionality into the kernel via *kernel extensions*. Kernel extensions are bundles with the extension *kext* and can be found in the /System/Library/Extensions directory. There are many Apple-provided kernel extensions in this directory, and there may be extensions for third-party hardware devices or programs that require low-level access, such as disk encryption software.

Network Configuration

The bulk of local system network configuration information on an OS X system is stored in various plist files under /Library/Preferences/SystemConfiguration. The *preferences.plist* file contains general settings for all the network interfaces on the system, as well as location-specific network profile information if this feature is in use. In addition, this file also shows the hostname of the computer, which may be important in a network-related examination.

```
<dict>
        <key>ComputerName</key>
        <string>forensic-macpro</string>
        <key>ComputerNameEncoding</key>
        <integer>1536</integer>
</dict>
```

The *com.apple.network.identification.plist* file is a rich source of historic network information. Among other data, this file contains a running list of previously assigned network addresses with time stamps. This information is obviously invaluable during investigation of a mobile laptop. For a relevant excerpt, see the following section.

```
            <dict>
                <key>Identifier</key>
<string>IPv4.Router=172.17.9.254;IPv4.RouterHardwareAddress=00:
    16:46:44:9a:43</string>
                <key>Services</key>
                <array>
                    <dict>
                        ...
                        <key>IPv4</key>
                        <dict>
                            <key>Addresses</key>
                            <array>
                                <string>172.17.9.47</string>
                            </array>
                            <key>InterfaceName</key>
                            <string>en0</string>
                            ...
                <key>Timestamp</key>
                <date>2010-03-30T20:15:59Z</date>
            </dict>
```

Note that because this file does not appear to expire results or roll over, it is possible that historic network data could be stored indefinitely.

The *com.apple.Bluetooth.plist* file contains a list of all Bluetooth devices that have ever been paired with the system, including time stamps.

```
            <key>LastInquiryUpdate</key>
            <date>2010-04-07T23:36:07Z</date>
            <key>LastNameUpdate</key>
            <date>2010-04-08T01:01:10Z</date>
            <key>LastServicesUpdate</key>
            <date>2010-04-08T01:01:11Z</date>
            <key>Manufacturer</key>
            <integer>15</integer>
            <key>Name</key>
            <string>forensic-iphone</string>
            <key>PageScanMode</key>
```

Hidden Directories

In addition to special bundle directory types that hide their contents from the user by default, OS X honors traditional Unix-style "dotfile" hiding. Files and directories named with a leading dot will be hidden from the user's view by default. There are not as many of these hidden files on OS X systems as there are on a standard Linux installation but some are present, including a couple significant examples we will examine shortly.

Installed Applications

/Library/Receipts contains information about applications installed via the OS X Installer system. This directory contains various "pkg" bundles, which contain information about the installed package. The creation times of these directories should correspond with the date that the software was installed.

Swap and Hibernation dataData

OS X stores swap files and hibernation data under the /private/var/vm directory. Depending on how heavily used (and short on resources) the system is, there will be anywhere from 1 to 10 numbered *swapfile* items in this directory. These contain paged out sections of memory and can persist on disk for some time. Additionally, if hibernation is enabled, a *sleepimage* file will be present. This file will be the same size as the available RAM on the system and will contain a copy of memory as it existed the last time the system was put to sleep. Any techniques used for processing unstructured data streams are applicable to these files, including string extraction and file carving.

System Logs

OS X shares many logs with other Unix-like operating systems, such as Linux. In general, BSD and Linux-derived applications for OS X will store logs under /private/var/log. OS X will generally have a syslog daemon running and will generate many of the same logs (including syslog-derived logs) that a standard Linux system does. For detailed information on syslog and Linux logging, please see Chapter 5. Of the most interest to the examiner are the logfiles shown in Table 6.2, all found under /private/var/log.

System-wide software created specifically for OS X will generally store logs under /Library/Logs. Examples include the "*Software Update.log*" file, which tracks when system software updates are applied, and the *CrashReporter, HangReporter,* and *PanicReporter* logs, which record application and kernel errors and make contain system state information related to the time they were generated.

Table 6.2 System Logs of Interest	
fsck_hfs.log	Record of all HFS/HFS+/HFSX volumes attached to the system
system.log	A catch-all log file, equivalent to messages on Linux
secure.log	Records all system authentication, including screensaver unlocks and SSH access.

USER ARTIFACTS

Each user on the system will have a plist stored under /private/var/db/dslocal/nodes/ Default/users/ that corresponds to their short username. This contains basic user information similar to /etc/passwd entries on Linux systems, including the path to the user's default shell, the user's long displayed name, and the user's UID. Group information is stored in /private/var/db/dslocal/nodes/Default/groups/ and is in a similar format. Of particular importance is the *admin.plist* file in the groups directory. Examining this file will help you determine if a given user has administrative or "root" privileges on this system. In the excerpt shown here, "root" and "user1" are both Administrators.

```
<array>
        <string>Administrators</string>
</array>
<key>users</key>
<array>
        <string>root</string>
        <string>user1</string>
</array>
```

The */Library/Preferences/com.apple.loginwindow.plist* file contains, among other items, information about the last user that logged into the system. This can be important during examination of a shared system.

```
<key>lastUser</key>
<string>loggedIn</string>
<key>lastUserName</key>
<string>forensic-user</string>
```

Home Directories

OS X systems are generally fairly "tidy." As such, a user's home directory is where most of the artifacts generated directly and indirectly by a user will be found. While certain user activities will generate artifacts in system areas (e.g., logging on and off), nearly all postauthentication user activity will be confined to items and residual data in their own home directory.

A standard user home directory will contain the default directories shown in Table 6.3.

Of all these directories, the one that contains the largest number of OS X-specific user artifacts is Library.

User's Library

A user's library contains a large number of indirect artifacts related to user activity. These include log files, preference settings, application artifacts, and artifacts generated from connecting to other devices or systems. It is an incredibly rich source of information exposing user activity on the system for several reasons. First, the Library is not a directory the user would ever explore under normal circumstances. Next, nearly all the artifacts present here are generated via interactive user activity,

Table 6.3 Standard Subdirectories in a User's Home
Desktop—all files saved to/displayed on the user's desktop are stored here
Documents—intended for text/office documents
Downloads—Internet (Web browser) downloads
Library—a per-user version of the Library directories discussed previously
Movies—intended for video files
Music—intended for music files
Pictures—intended for image files
Public—acts as a public drop box/world-readable
Sites—used to store files for the user's personal Web site

not automatic system processes. Finally, artifacts in the user's Library will generally persist indefinitely unless purged actively. The Library contains a handful of subdirectories, each of which is intended to store specific classes of data. This section discusses some of the forensically interesting content of each of these directories.

Preferences

Library/Preferences/ contains preference data for applications installed on the system. This generally includes items such as recently opened files or network locations and any configuration changes the user may have customized. Among items of interest in Preferences is *com.apple.quicktimeplayer.plist*, which contains a list of video files that were opened using QuickTime, including the full path to the file. The following excerpt is from one of the author's systems.

```
<dict>
        <key>altname</key>
        <string>IMG_1288.MOV - .../Downloads/IMG_1288.
          MOV</string>
        <key>dataRef</key>
        <data>
```

AAAAAAEeAAIAAAtNYWNpbnRvc2hIRAAAAAAAAAAAAAAAAAAADH

KHhBSCsAAAFJR2oMSU1HXzEyODguTU9WAAAAAAAAAAAAAAAAAA

AAAAAAAAAAAAAAAAAAAAAAAAAAAAAAAAAAAAAAAAAAAAAAAdr1

7cj4mD4AAAAAAAAAP////8AAEkgAAAAAAAAAAAAAAAABAACAAA

xyjowQAAABEACAAAyPj6rgAAAA4AGgAMAEkATQBHAF8AMQAyADgA

OAAuAE0ATwBWAAA8AGAALAE0AYQBjAGkAbgB0AG8AcwBoAEgARAAS
```
        ACFVc2Vycy9jb3J5L0Rvd25sb2Fkcy9JTUdfMTI4OC5NT1YAABMA
        AS8AABUAAgAL//8AAA==
        </data>
        <key>dataRefType</key>
        <string>alis</string>
        <key>name</key>
        <string>IMG_1288.MOV</string>
</dict>
```

Note that the "name" key is simply the bare file name, whereas the "altname" key is a relative path. The absolute path is embedded in the "dataRef" value. This is a base64-encoded value, which can be decoded any number of ways. The author prefers to use the decoding capabilities of openssl, as the openssl binary is generally present on any Unix-like system. There are many standalone base64 decoders for every imaginable operating system. To decode data, simply copy data out and save it to a file (1288-base64.data in this example) and run the following command:

```
forensics:~ user$ openssl enc -d -base64 -in 1288-base64.data
  -out decoded.bin
```

The full path can then be extracted using the strings command or by any hex dumping utility, such as xxd.

```
...
00000b0: 001a 000c 0049 004d 0047 005f 0031 0032  .....I.M.G._.1.2
00000c0: 0038 0038 002e 004d 004f 0056 000f 0018  .8.8...M.O.V....
00000d0: 000b 004d 0061 0063 0069 006e 0074 006f  ...M.a.c.i.n.t.o
00000e0: 0073 0068 0048 0044 0012 0021 5573 6572  .s.h.H.D...!User
00000f0: 732f 636f 7279 2f44 6f77 6e6c 6f61 6473  s/cory/Downloads
0000100: 2f49 4d47 5f31 3238 382e 4d4f 5600 0013  /IMG_1288.MOV...
0000110: 0001 2f00 0015 0002 000b ffff 0000  ../..........
```

As the name implies, the *com.apple.recentitems.plist* contains numerous related to recently opened files and recently accessed file servers. Unfortunately, these entries are not time stamped so correlation with outside time sources (e.g., file system metadata) will be necessary to build a complete picture of use. The section that follows contains an excerpt displaying the last three Windows file share hosts this system contacted.

```
<key>Hosts</key>
<dict>
        <key>Controller</key>
        <string>CustomListItems</string>
        <key>CustomListItems</key>
        <array>
                <dict>
                        <key>Name</key>
                        <string>forensics-2</string>
                        <key>URL</key>
                        <string>smb://forensics-2</string>
                </dict>
```

```
<dict>
        <key>Name</key>
        <string>unicron</string>
        <key>URL</key>
        <string>smb://unicron</string>
</dict>
<dict>
        <key>Name</key>
        <string>parabola</string>
        <key>URL</key>
        <string>smb://parabola</string>
</dict>
</array>
<key>MaxAmount</key>
<integer>10</integer>
</dict>
```

The *com.apple.DiskUtility.plist* contains a key named "*DUSavedDiskImageList*," which is used to populate the sidebar of the Disk Utility application. Items listed under this key display the full path for disk images that have been opened on the system. Note that this key can contain files that have been deleted from the system.

```
<key>DUSavedDiskImageList</key>
<array>
        <string>/Users/forensic/Downloads/ntfs-3g-2010.1.
           16-macosx.dmg</string>
        <string>/Users/forensic/Downloads/wxPython2.8-osx-
           unicode-2.8.9.1-universal-py2.4.dmg</string>
        <string>/Users/forensic/Downloads/HFSDebug-Lite-4.33.
           dmg</string>
        <string>/Users/forensic/Downloads/python-2.5-macosx.dmg
           </string>
        <string>/Users/forensic/Downloads/notecase-1.9.8.dmg
           </string>
        <string>/Users/forensic/Downloads/VirtualBox-3.2.
           10-66523-OSX.dmg</string>
</array>
```

The *com.apple.finder.plist* file is the main preference file for the Finder application, which is the graphical file explorer on OS X systems. This file contains numerous entries, but a few are of the most interest to an examiner. The "*FXConnectToLastURL*" key contains the full URL of the last server the system connected to via the Finder.

```
<key>FXConnectToLastURL</key>
<string>smb://my-server-1/c$</string>
```

Entries under the "*FXDesktopVolumePositions*" key correspond to the mount points and volume names of volumes that have been mounted on the system previously.

```
<key>FXDesktopVolumePositions</key>
<dict>
        <key>/Volumes/1GB</key>
        <dict>
                . . .
        </dict>
        <key>/Volumes/BT4</key>
        <dict>

                . . .
```

Finally, the "*FXRecentFolders*" key contains the user's most recently viewed directories.

```
<key>FXRecentFolders</key>
<array>
        <dict>
                <key>file-data</key>
                . . .
                <key>name</key>
                <string>Downloads</string>
        </dict>
```

As many Mac users also use iPods, iPhones, or iPads, examining the *com.apple. iPod.plist* may be an important part of an OS X investigation. This file contains data about any of these devices that have been attached to the system, including a wealth of identifying information (which has been redacted in the output here).

```
                <key>Connected</key>
                <date>2010-11-06T00:15:58Z</date>
                <key>Device Class</key>
                <string>iPhone</string>
                <key>Family ID</key>
                <integer>10004</integer>
                <key>Firmware Version</key>
                <integer>256</integer>
                <key>Firmware Version String</key>
                <string>4.1</string>
                <key>ID</key>
                <string>[REDACTED]</string>
                <key>IMEI</key>
                <string>[REDACTED]</string>
                <key>Serial Number</key>
                <string>[REDACTED]</string>
                <key>Updater Family ID</key>
                <integer>10004</integer>
                <key>Use Count</key>
                <integer>15</integer>
```

Application Support
The Application Support directory contains data supporting the operation of various programs installed on the system. This is generally used for data altered frequently

and/or stored for long periods. Examples include Address Book application data, iPod syncing information, and profile data for the Firefox browser. Firefox browser data analysis is covered in detail in Chapter 7. Removing an application from the system will not usually remove any Application Support data so this can be a rich source of archival data.

Data synced from an iPod, iPhone, or iPad can be found in the Library/Application Support/MobileSync/Backup directory. This directory will contain one or more subdirectories that appear to be a long string of random digits. This is the device's Unique Device Identifier (UDID). Multiple UDID directories may be present if multiple devices are synced to the machine or if multiple backups have occurred. The newest backup directory will be the "bare" UDID directory, and older backups will have the time and date they were created appended to the directory path (i.e., UDID-20101010-120000).

In each backup directory there will be (among the numerous files) an *Info.plist* file. This file contains information about the device that was backed up.

```
<key>Build Version</key>
<string>8A293</string>
<key>Device Name</key>
<string>Forensic iPhone</string>
<key>Display Name</key>
<string>Forensic iPhone</string>
<key>GUID</key>
<string>[REDACTED]</string>
<key>ICCID</key>
<string>[REDACTED]</string>
<key>IMEI</key>
<string>[REDACTED]</string>
<key>Last Backup Date</key>
<date>2010-07-24T06:22:33Z</date>
<key>Phone Number</key>
<string>1 (650) 555-1212</string>
<key>Product Type</key>
<string>iPhone2,1</string>
<key>Product Version</key>
<string>4.0</string>
<key>Serial Number</key>
<string>[REDACTED]</string>
<key>Sync Settings</key>
<dict>
```

While the values are redacted in this output, keep in mind that you can correlate the IMEI and Serial Number values from this file with those found in the *com.apple. iPod.plist* file given previously.

Logs

In addition to the system logs discussed earlier, the user's Library/Logs/ directory holds many user-specific application logs. These will be almost universally plain text log files with a .log extension that can be viewed in any text editor or processed using similar techniques to those discussed in Chapter 5. In addition to user application-specific logs, the *DiskUtility.log* can be a valuable resource to determine if a performed any disk burning or other activities using the Disk Utility application (or applicable subsystems).

See the following segment for an excerpt from the *DiskUtility.log*. Note the time-stamped output, which can be correlated to access or modification times found in file system output.

```
2010-10-21 13:37:52 -0700:    Disk Utility started.
2010-10-21 13:37:57 -0700:    Burning Image "raptor20091026.iso"
2010-10-21 13:37:59 -0700:    Image name: "raptor20091026.iso"
2010-10-21 13:37:59 -0700:    Burn disc in: "HL-DT-ST DVD-RW GH41N"
2010-10-21 13:37:59 -0700:    Erase disc before burning: No
2010-10-21 13:37:59 -0700:    Leave disc appendable: No
2010-10-21 13:37:59 -0700:    Verify burned data after burning: Yes
2010-10-21 13:37:59 -0700:    Eject disc after burning
2010-10-21 13:37:59 -0700:
2010-10-21 13:37:59 -0700:    Preparing data for burn
2010-10-21 13:37:59 -0700:    Opening session
2010-10-21 13:37:59 -0700:    Opening track
2010-10-21 13:37:59 -0700:    Writing track
2010-10-21 13:40:52 -0700:    Closing track
2010-10-21 13:40:52 -0700:    Closing session
2010-10-21 13:40:56 -0700:    Finishing burn
2010-10-21 13:40:56 -0700:    Verifying burn...
2010-10-21 13:40:56 -0700:    Verifying
2010-10-21 13:44:28 -0700:    Burn completed successfully
```

Caches

The Cache directory is user-specific dumping ground for items intended to be temporary. Despite this, application data can persist in the Cache directory for a very long time, sometimes persisting even after the application that created data has been removed. As data stored in Cache directory are application specific, a detailed examination of the contents is outside of the scope of this chapter. An example of Cache content analysis can be found in Chapter 7.

.Trash

Each user directory should contain a hidden directory named ".Trash." Unsurprisingly, this location is used as temporary file storage when a file is "deleted" using the Finder application. In OS X 10.5 and previous versions, simply viewing contents was the extent of examination possible for this directory. These versions of OS X did not keep track of the original location of the file, nor did they maintain any other metadata about the file. This has changed in OS X 10.6, which now stores the original path of the deleted file in a hidden *.DS_Store* file in the .Trash directory. The original path can be determined easily by viewing the *.DS_Store* file with a hex editor [5].

> **TIP**
> **.DS_Store Parsing**
> .DS_Store files can be examined interactively using the *hachoir-urwid* program, which is discussed in Chapter 8.

Shell History

OS X uses the Bourne Again Shell (BASH) by default, so if a user has used the terminal their shell history should be present in the user's home directory in the ".bash_history" file. Because most OS X users will not use the Terminal at any point, the presence of entries in this file may be a sign that the user is a "power user" or is at least somewhat tech savvy. As on Linux, this file does not have time values associated with each entry, but through careful system examination, inferred times for listed activity may be deduced.

SUMMARY

As Mac OS X systems continue to gain popularity, the ability to process these systems will become increasingly important. Additionally, many of the artifacts generated by OS X on desktops and laptops are also found on the iOS used in Apple's line of mobile products—the iPod Touch, the iPhone, and the iPad. This chapter discussed analysis of the HFS+ file system used on OS X systems. It detailed the extraction of binary property list files, which are used to store the bulk of OS X's configuration details and subsequently contain many artifacts of interest.

References

[1] Technical Note TN1150: HFS Plus Volume Format. developer.apple.com/library/mac/technotes/tn/tn1150.html, (accessed 23.11.10).
[2] Access Control Lists. http://developer.apple.com/library/mac/#documentation/MacOSX/Conceptual/BPFileSystem/Articles/ACLs.html.
[3] System Startup Programming Topics: The Boot Process. http://developer.apple.com/library/mac/#documentation/MacOSX/Conceptual/BPSystemStartup/Articles/BootProcess.html.
[4] plutil.pl for Windows/Linux. http://scw.us/iPhone/plutil/.
[5] Snow Leopard Put Back (Undelete). http://www.appleexaminer.com/MacsAndOS/Analysis/SLPutBack/SLPutBack.html.

Internet Artifacts

INFORMATION IN THIS CHAPTER

- Browser Artifacts
- Mail Artifacts

INTRODUCTION

It can be argued that nothing demonstrates the concept of evidence dynamics better than Internet artifacts. On a modern end-user computer system, the bulk of the user's interaction with the system will likely be related to Internet communication of some sort. Every click of a link, every bookmark, and every search query can leave telltale traces on the user's system. This chapter examines the application-specific artifacts created by Web browsers and then moves on to delve into analysis of the contents of local mailbox formats.

BROWSER ARTIFACTS

If the bulk of a computer user's time is spent on the Internet, then it's like that nearly all (or at least a great deal) of that time is spent interacting with a Web browser. The modern Web browsing experience is much richer than the creators of the World Wide Web had envisioned. As an example, at the time of this writing Google has begun distributing netbook computer systems, which are nothing more than minimal laptop systems with a Linux kernel running the Chrome Browser. This device's utility is based on the assumption that everything the user does—create and edit documents, etc.—will all occur via the Web. Even in seemingly unexpected cases, the analysis of Web browser artifacts can be a key factor of digital forensic analysis. For example, the authors have examined various compromised servers where the built-in Web browser was used to load additional tools onto the compromised server or to submit stolen data to a file sharing site. Going forward, knowledge of the forensic analysis of Web browsers will be crucial.

Internet Explorer

Microsoft ships its operating systems with the Internet Explorer (IE) Web browser as part of the base installation. IE has two primary areas where data of primary interest to forensic analysts are stored: in the index.dat "database" used by the Web browser and in the browser cache. These index.dat files are structured in a manner that has become known as the "MS IE Cache File" (MSIECF) format. The index.dat file contains a record of accessed URLs, including search queries, Web mail accesses, and so on, and is often considered the primary source of forensic information when it comes to IE Web browser analysis.

Index.dat File Location

On Windows XP and 2003 systems, the index.dat file of primary interest to forensics examiners is found in the path "C:\Documents and Settings\user\Local Settings\Temporary Internet Files\Content.IE5" directory.

On Windows Vista and Windows 7 systems, the file is located in the "C:\Users\user\AppData\Local\Microsoft\Windows\Temporary Internet Files\Content.IE5" directory.

Index.dat

Various open source tools can be used to access and parse the contents of the index.dat file into a readable format. Perhaps one of the most well-known open source tools for parsing index.dat files is `pasco` from FoundStone (pasco can be downloaded from http://sourceforge.net/projects/fast/files/Pasco/). Note that Pasco has not been updated since 2004, but it is still widely used in many forensic live CD distributions. Joachim Metz has developed an updated library based on further reverse engineering of the MSIECF format, which is available at http://sourceforge.net/projects/libmsiecf/. The libmsiecf library contains two programs. `Msiecfinfo` displays basic information about parsed MSIECF files, and `msiecfexport`, extracts the entries contained within the MSIECF files. This software is currently in an alpha state and is only available for Unix-like systems.

In addition, the Win32::URLCache, written by Kenichi Ishigaki, can also be used to parse index.dat files. If you're using ActiveState's ActivePerl, the Perl Package Manager (ppm) command to install the module on an Internet-connected system is

```
C:\perl>ppm install win32-urlcache
```

This ppm command will install the module, as well as all dependencies. This same module can be installed on other platforms using Perl's CPAN functionality:

```
perl -MCPAN -e "install Win32::UrlCache"
```

Based on documentation provided along with the module, code used to parse an index.dat file might look like the following:

```
my $index = Win32::UrlCache->new($config{file});
foreach my $url ($index->urls) {
  my $epoch = getEpoch($url->last_accessed);
```

```
my $hdr = $url->headers;
$hdr =~ s/\r\n/ /g;
my $descr = $url->url.":".$url->filename.":".$hdr;
print $epoch."|URL|".$config{system}."|".$config{user}."|".$descr.
   "\n";
}
```

Note that the *getEpoch()* function mentioned in the aforementioned code is a user-defined function that converts the time value from the index.dat file into a 32-bit Unix-formatted time value so that it can be included in a timeline.

The module is also capable of parsing out LEAK records, which are created when a history item is marked for deletion but the actual cached file is locked [1].

TIP

Index.dat Artifacts
Internet Explorer's artifacts are not so much the result of the use of the application as they are the result of the use of the WinInet application programming interface (API). When a user browses the Web using IE, artifacts are created (index.dat entries added, files written to the cache, etc.) to the appropriate locations, in that user's context. Many times malware will make use of the same APIs in order to communicate and exfiltrate data off of an infected system. Often, malware is running with System level privileges, and as such, an analyst would expect to find entries in index.dat files for the "Default User" or "LocalService" accounts.

Favorites

IE Favorites can also contain information that may be interesting or essential to a forensic analyst. "Favorites" are the IE version of bookmarks, providing an indication of a user's movements across the Internet. A user's favorites can be found (on Windows XP) in the "C:\Documents and Settings\user\Favorites" directory. The user's Favorites appear in the Internet Explorer version 8 browser as illustrated in Figure 7.1.

When a user profile is created (i.e., the account is created and the user logs in for the first time), the profiles Favorite's folder is populated with certain defaults.

FIGURE 7.1

User's IE 8 Favorites.

As seen in Figure 7.1, the user has chosen to add the Google.com Web site as a Favorite site. These Favorites appear as URL shortcut files (filename.url); the Google URL shortcut contains the following text. Users can create folders in order to organize their Favorites into common groups or simply add Favorites to the default folder.

Contents of the Google.url Favorite appear as follow:

```
[DEFAULT]
BASEURL=http://www.google.com/
[InternetShortcut]
URL=http://www.google.com/
IDList=
IconFile=http://www.google.com/favicon.ico
IconIndex=1
[{000214A0-0000-0000-C000-000000000046}]
Prop3=19,2
```

Contents of the URL shortcut can be viewed easily in a text editor or output to the console using the "type" (Windows) or "cat" (Linux) commands.

In addition to the content of the Favorites file, an analyst may find value in the file MAC times, which will illustrate when the file was created and when the file was last accessed or modified. Depending on the type of examination being performed, this information may prove to be valuable.

Cookies

Internet Explorer cookies can be found in Documents and Settings\%username%\ Cookies on Windows XP systems and in Users\%username%\AppData\Roaming\ Microsoft\Windows\Cookies on Vista and Windows 7 systems. Because Internet Explorer stores user cookies as discrete, plain text files per issuing host, these can be inspected directly. See the following for an example:

```
SaneID
3A345581BB019948
geico.com/
1536
3378255872
30795568
4048194256
30118489
*
```

While the content is plain text, some of the fields need to be deciphered to be of value, in particular lines 5 and 6 (the cookie's expiration time) and 7 and 8 (the creation time). The open source tool galleta was developed for this task. Here is the same cookie, processed with galleta:

SITE	VARIABLE	VALUE	CREATION TIME	EXPIRE TIME	FLAGS
geico.com/	SaneID	3A345581BB019948	12/02/2010 11:48:50	02/19/2020 06:28:00	1536

Cache

The browser's cache contains files that are cached locally on the system as a result of a user's Web browsing activity. On XP systems, these files are located in Documents and Settings\%username%\Local Settings\Temporary Internet Files\Content.IE5. On Vista and Windows 7 systems they can be found in Users\%username%\AppData\Local\Microsoft\Windows\Temporary Internet Files\Content.IE5.

Files cached locally are stored in one of four randomly named subdirectories. The MSIE Cache File located in this directory has all the information needed to map any files of interest located in the cache subdirectories with the URL the file was retrieved from. For example, in the following output from `msiecfexport`, we can see that the file "favicon[1].ico" in the O2XMPJ7 directory was retrieved from "login.live.com."

```
Record type           : URL
Offset range          : 80000 - 80384 (384)
Location              : https://login.live.com/favicon.ico
Primary filetime      : Dec 04, 2010 04:12:53
Secondary filetime    : Jun 15, 2010 22:12:26
Filename              : favicon[1].ico
Cache directory index : 0 (0x00) (O2XM9PJ7)
```

For comparison's sake, here is the same item as viewed by `pasco`, which produces tabbed-separated output.

```
URL https://login.live.com/favicon.ico 06/15/2010 15:12:26    12/03/2010
   20:12:53    favicon[1].ico    O2XM9PJ7    HTTP/1.1 200 OK Content-Length:
   1150 Content-Type: image/x-icon ETag: "0411ed6d7ccb1:46b" PPServer:
   PPV: 30 H: BAYIDSLGN1J28 V: 0 ~U:user
```

Firefox

Mozilla's Firefox browser is the second most widely used browser in the world, after Internet Explorer. Like the tools discussed in this book, it is open source software, so it is used commonly on Linux desktops, but is used on OS X and Windows as well.

Firefox 3 stores history data in SQLite 3 database files, which are quite easy to process using open source tools. Firefox stores these along with a few other items of interest in a user-specific profile directory. Please reference Table 7.1 for a listing of the default location of the profile directory on different operating systems.

Table 7.1 Firefox Profile Locations

Operating System	Location
Windows XP	C:\Documents and Settings\%username\Local Settings\ Application Data\Mozilla\Firefox\Profiles
Windows Vista/7	C:\Users\%username%\AppData\Roaming\Mozilla\Firefox\Profiles
Linux	/home/$username/.mozilla/firefox/Profiles
OS X	/Users/$username/Library/Application Support/Firefox/Profiles/

In this directory you will find one or more folders and a file named profiles.ini. The content of this file will be similar to the following:

```
[General]
StartWithLastProfile=1
[Profile0]
Name=default
IsRelative=1
Path=Profiles/fenkfs6z.default
```

When Firefox is started it will use this file to determine which profile directory to read from. In a multiple profile environment, StartWithLastProfile=1 directs Firefox to skip asking the user which profile to select and use the last-used profile by default. The next section describes the first Firefox profile, which on this system is also the only profile. In most cases a single profile named «default» will be the only profile present, as shown earlier. In a multiple-profile Firefox environment, additional named profiles will be present, and the last-used profile will be indicated by a «Default=1» variable. The Path variable points to the directory where this profile's data are stored.

Inside of each profile directory you will find numerous files and subdirectories.

The most important files here will be.sqlite files, which are the previously mentioned SQLite 3 databases. We will be examining four of these databases in detail.

• Formhistory.sqlite: stores data about form submission inputs—search boxes, usernames, etc.
• Downloads.sqlite: stores data about downloaded files
• Cookies.sqlite: stores data about cookies
• Places.sqlite: stores the bulk of "Internet history" data

TIP

Introduction to SQLite

Because many Web browser artifacts are stored in SQLite databases, it is important that an examiner has a minimum level of understanding of commands available for processing these files. To open a sqlite database using the command-line sqlite3 client, simply type *sqlite3 {name of database file}*. You will be dropped to the **sqlite>** prompt, indicating that you have attached to the database successfully. In addition to standard data retrieval queries performed by the SELECT statement, there are a handful of special sqlite3 queries the examiner should be aware of

> **.headers on**: Adds column headers to output, which annotates the fields.
> **.tables**: Displays all tables in the database.
> **.schema {table name}**: Displays all fields in the table.
> **.output {filename}**: Writes output to the named file instead of the screen.

Additionally, the sqlite statement "select * from sqlite_master;" will query the database itself and will produce output showing all tables and fields in each table in one set of output.

There are numerous open source utilities for interacting with SQLite databases. We will use two in this chapter: the command line *sqlite3* tool and the graphical *sqliteman* program. The sqliteman program can be installed on Ubuntu using the following command:

```
sudo apt-get install sqliteman
```

Additional prebuilt packages are available for OS X and Windows.

After backing up the user's Firefox profile, choose Open from the File menu and browse to the copy of the profile directory. Next, select the database you would like to examine and click Open. From here, you can browse the database structure, execute SQL queries, and export findings. Most of these databases have simple schemas with one table of interest. For example, to view data held in the formhistory.sqlite database, you would execute the following command:

```
SELECT * FROM moz_formhistory;
```

An example of results from this query is shown in Figure 7.2.

WARNING

Copy Protection

Be aware that when using standard database tools to interact with SQLite databases, you can write data in addition to reading so take care to only use these tools on duplicate copies of data.

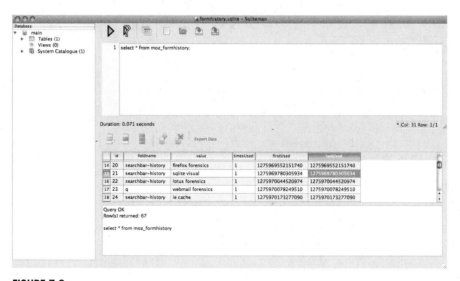

FIGURE 7.2

SQLite query for moz_formhistory.

The formhistory.sqlite database contains data that the user entered into forum submission fields. This includes items such as names, addresses, email addresses, phone numbers, Web mail subject lines, search queries, and usernames or "handlers" entered into forums.

The downloads.sqlite database contains records of the files downloaded by the user. Be aware that the files that show up in this database are those that are handled by the Firefox Download Manager. Multimedia files handled by browser plug-ins and other items that end up in the browser cache will not show up in this database. An important aspect of this particular database is that it allows the investigator to correlate items found on the file system to the URLs where they originated.

The cookies.sqlite database can produce information such as the last time the user visited a site that set or requested a specific cookie, whether or not the user was registered or logged in at a particular site, and other browser state information.

The places.sqlite database contains the most data related to user activity in the browser. In contrast to each of the previous databases examined, places.sqlite has a more complex multitable schema, which has been mapped in detail by Chris Cohen [2].

The two items of primary interest in most Web history examinations are the URL visited and the time of that visit. These two items are found in the url field in the moz_places table and in the visit_date in the moz_historyvisits table, respectively. The id field in the moz_places table corresponds to the places_id in the moz_historyvisits table. The visit_date is stored in «PRTime», which is a 64-bit integer counting the number of microseconds since the UNIX Epoch (January 1st, 1970 UTC). The following sqlite statement will retrieve these two values from their respective tables and convert the visit_date to a human-consumable format:

```
SELECT
datetime(moz_historyvisits.visit_date/1000000,'unixepoch'),
moz_places.url
FROM moz_places, moz_historyvisits
WHERE moz_places.id = moz_historyvisits.place_id
```

We will use the console sqlite3 client to perform this query.

```
forensics:~ forensics$ sqlite3 ~/Library/Application\ Support/
  Firefox/Profiles/fffffs6z.default/places.sqlite
sqlite> SELECT datetime(moz_historyvisits.visit_date/1000000,
  'unixepoch'), moz_places.url FROM moz_places, moz_historyvisits
  WHERE moz_places.id = moz_historyvisits.place_id;
...
2010-06-08 05:35:34|http://code.google.com/p/revealertoolkit/
2010-06-08 05:35:54|http://code.google.com/p/revealertoolkit/
  downloads/list
2010-06-08 05:35:58|http://code.google.com/p/revealertoolkit/
  downloads/detail?name=RVT_v0.2.1.zip&can=2&q=
2010-06-08 05:36:42|http://code.google.com/p/poorcase/
2010-06-08 05:36:46|http://code.google.com/p/poorcase/downloads/
  list
```

```
2010-06-08 05:36:46|http://code.google.com/p/poorcase/downloads/
   detail?name=poorcase.odp&can=2&q=
2010-06-08 05:36:50|http://code.google.com/p/poorcase/downloads/
   detail?name=poorcase_1.1.pl&can=2&q=
2010-06-08 05:37:12|http://liveview.sourceforge.net/
2010-06-08 05:37:12|http://sourceforge.net/project/showfiles.
   php?group_id=175252
2010-06-08 05:37:11|http://sourceforge.net/projects/liveview/
   files/
2010-06-08 05:37:35|http://www.google.com/search?q=system+combo+
   timeline&ie=utf-8&oe=utf-8&aq=t&rls=org.mozilla:
   en-US:official&client=firefox-a
2010-06-08 05:37:35|http://www.cutawaysecurity.com/blog/
   system-combo-timeline
2010-06-08 05:39:52|http://log2timeline.net/INSTALL.txt
2010-06-08 05:39:59|http://cdnetworks-us-2.dl.sourceforge.net/
   project/revit/revit07-alpha/revit07-alpha-20070804/revit07-
   alpha-20070804.tar.gz
...
```

Cache

In addition to browser history files, a user's browser cache may be of investigative importance. Table 7.2 contains the location of the Firefox cache on different operating systems. Examining this directory directly for viewing will usually yield a stream of numbered unidentifiable files along with one cache map file «_CACHE_MAP_» and three cache block files (_CACHE_001_ through _CACHE_003_). These are binary files that contain information regarding the URLs and filenames associated with cached data, as well as time stamp data.

Although there are free forensic applications for parsing these data, none of these tools are open source. These free tools are discussed in the Appendix.

Saved Session Data

If a Firefox session is not terminated properly, a file named sessionstore.js will be present in the user's profile directory. This file is used by Firefox to recover the browser session in case of a crash or other unexpected shutdown. If this file is present

Table 7.2 Firefox Cache Locations

Operating System	Location
Windows XP	C:\Documents and Settings\%username\Local Settings\ Application Data\Mozilla\Firefox\Profiles
Windows Vista/7	C:\Users\%username%\AppData\Roaming\Mozilla\Firefox\ Profiles
Linux	/home/$username/.mozilla/firefox/Profiles
OS X	/Users/$username/Library/Caches/Firefox/Profiles

upon start up, Firefox will use the contents to restore the browser windows and tabs the user last had open. The content is stored as a series of JavaScript Object Notation (JSON) objects and can be viewed using any text editor. JSON is structured data, however, and can be parsed and displayed in a more logical format using a JSON viewer or "pretty printer." One such open source application is the Adobe AIR-based *JSON Viewer* available at http://code.google.com/p/jsonviewer/. Figure 7.3 is a screenshot of an example sessionstore.js with structure viewed in JSON Viewer.

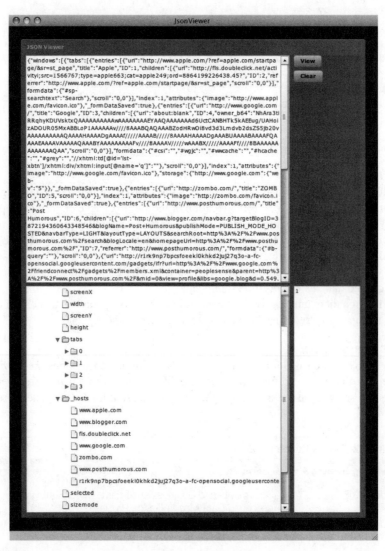

FIGURE 7.3

JSON Viewer.

Items of note in a sessionstore.js file include closed tabs and windows, saved form data, and temporary cookies.

Bookmarks and Bookmark Backups

Firefox stores Bookmarks in the places.sqlite database via combination of data in "moz_bookmarks," "moz_places," and "moz_items_annos" tables. Extraction of data from these tables has been documented thoroughly by Kristinn Gudjonsson [3]. Briefly, the SQL query Kristinn wrote to generate a simple list of stored bookmarks and associated dates is

```
SELECT moz_bookmarks.type,moz_bookmarks.title,moz_bookmarks.
  dateAdded,
moz_bookmarks.lastModified,moz_places.url,moz_places.title,
moz_places.rev_host,moz_places.visit_count
FROM moz_places, moz_bookmarks
WHERE
  moz_bookmarks.fk = moz_places.id
  AND moz_bookmarks.type <> 3
```

The moz_items_annos table may contain additional information relating to annotations the user has made to bookmarks, including the time the annotation was created and modified. In addition to direct SQLite queries, this time information can also be extracted using Kristinn's log2timeline tool, which is discussed in Chapter 9.

Firefox Bookmark Backups are found in the user's profile under the "bookmark-backups" directory. These are stored as a series of JSON objects and can be parsed using any number of JSON viewers, such as the previously mentioned *JSON Viewer*. Recorded artifacts include the date the bookmark was added, the title, and the URL of the bookmarked site.

Extensions

Firefox supports the installation of extensions, which can enhance or modify the behavior of the browser. A manifest of installed extensions can be found in the user's profile directory in the "extensions.rdf" file. This XML document describes the extensions installed for this user. Simply grepping for the strings "NS1:name" can provide a list of installed extensions:

```
NS1:name="Evernote Web Clipper"
NS1:name="XSS Me"
NS1:name="Google Feedback"
NS1:name="SQL Inject Me"
NS1:name="Redirect Remover"
NS1:name="1Password"
NS1:name="Tamper Data"
NS1:name="Access Me"
NS1:name="Google Toolbar for Firefox"
NS1:name="Default"
```

The code and supporting files that make up the extensions can be found in subdirectories of the *extensions* directory under the user's profile directory.

Chrome

Chrome is the open source Web browser developed by Google. In the two short years since its release Chrome has become the third most popular browser in the world and is the centerpiece of Chrome OS. Chrome is available for Windows, OS X, and Linux.

Like Firefox, Chrome utilizes a variety of SQLite databases to store user data. We can access these data using any SQLite client, but will use the base command line *sqlite3* program for most cases. Please reference Table 7.3 for a list of the storage locations for Chrome history on different operating systems.

"Cookies" is the SQLite database Chrome uses to store all cookies. Information stored in this database includes the creation time of the cookie, the last access time of the cookie, and the host the cookie is issued for.

The "History" SQLite database contains the majority of user activity data of interest, divided among numerous tables. Three tables are of particular interest:

downloads
urls
visits

The downloads table tracks downloaded files, in much the same manner as the Downloads.sqlite database does for Firefox. Items of interest include the local path of the saved file, the remote URL, and the time the download was initiated.

Together, urls and visits tables can be used to construct a good view of user browsing activity. Because the id field of the urls table maps to the url field of the visits table, the following SQL query will produce a report of browsing activity [4]:

```
SELECT urls.url, urls.title, urls.visit_count, urls.typed_count,
  urls.last_visit_time, urls.hidden, visits.visit_time, visits.
  from_visit
FROM urls, visits
WHERE
  urls.id = visits.url
```

Table 7.3 Chrome History Locations

Operating System	Location
Windows XP	C:\Documents and Settings\%username\Application Data\Google\Chrome\default
Windows Vista/7	C:\Users\%username%\AppData\Local\Google\Chrome\default
Linux	/home/$username/.config/google-chrome/Default
OS X	/Users/$username/Library/Application Support/Google/Chrome/Default/

The following section is an excerpt of the results produced by this query:

```
http://digitalcorpora.org/corpora/disk-images|Digital Corpora»
    Disk Images|1|0|12935304129883466|0|12935304129883466|76149
http://digitalcorpora.org/corp/images/nps/nps-2009-
    casper-rw|Index of /corp/images/nps/nps-2009-casper-
    rw|1|0|12935304152594759|0|12935304152594759|76150
http://digitalcorpora.org/corp/images/nps/nps-2009-
    casper-rw/|Index of /corp/images/nps/nps-2009-casper-
    rw|2|0|12935304190343005|0|12935304152594759|76151
http://digitalcorpora.org/corp/images/nps/nps-2009-
    casper-rw/|Index of /corp/images/nps/nps-2009-casper-
    rw|2|0|12935304190343005|0|12935304190343005|76150
http://digitalcorpora.org/corp/images/nps/nps-2009-casper-rw/
    narrative.txt||1|0|12935304181158875|0|12935304181158875|76152
```

Note that the visit_time value is stored in the "seconds since January 1, 1601 UTC" format used in many Chrome date fields

The "Login Data" SQLite database is used by Chrome to store saved login data. On Linux systems, this can include password data. On an OS X systems, native password storage systems are used.

"Web Data" is a SQLite database that contains data the user has opted to save for form auto-fill capabilities. This can include names, addresses, credit data, and more.

The "Thumbnails" SQLite database stores thumbnail images of visited sites. This can be useful for determining the content of sites of interest. Figure 7.4 shows a stored thumbnail binary blob as an image using SQLiteman's image preview functionality to view a particular thumbnail.

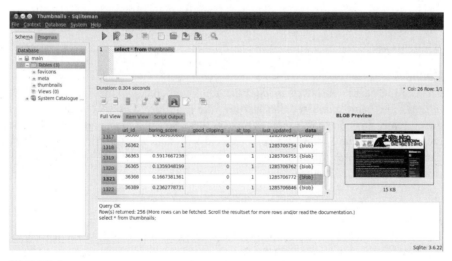

FIGURE 7.4

Site image embedded in "thumbnails" table.

The "url_id" field in this table maps to the "id" field in the "urls" table in the History database. This can be used to map a generated thumbnail to a particular visit at a specific time and date.

```
sqlite> select * from urls where id is 36368;
36368|http://blogs.sans.org/computer-forensics/|SANS Computer Forensic
    Investigations and Incident Response|3|0|12930180528625238|0|1413
```

Bookmarks

Chrome bookmarks are stored in "Bookmarks" file under the user's profile directory. This file contains a series of JSON objects and can be viewed with any JSON viewer or examined trivially as plain text. See the following section for an example of a bookmark entry:

```
{
  "date_added": "12924673772022388",
  "id": "108",
  "name": "Digital Corpora",
  "type": "url",
  "url": "http://digitalcorpora.org/"
},
```

Note that this date is also in the "seconds since January 1, 1601 UTC" format. A copy of the Bookmarks file named "Bookmarks.bak" will also be found in this directory.

Local State

The "Local State" file is used by Chrome to restore state after an unexpected shutdown. It is similar in function to the sessionstate.js file in Firefox and, like sessionstate.js, contains JSON objects. It can be viewed with any text editor or with the JSON Viewer we used to examine the sessionstate.js file in the previous section.

Cache

The Chrome cache consists of an *index* file, four numbered *data* files (*data_0* through *data_3*), and many numbered files starting with *f_* followed by six hex digits. There are currently no open source tools to process these files in a meaningful way, but the creation time of the f_ files can be correlated with data extracted from the History database. The f_ files can also be analyzed according to content. See Chapter 8 for a discussion of file artifact analysis.

Safari

Safari is the default browser included on Mac OS X. It is used almost exclusively by Mac OS X users, but is also available for Windows. Any examination of a Mac OS X system will likely require analysis of Safari artifacts. Please reference Table 7.4 for the location of Safari History files on Windows and OS X systems.

Table 7.4 Safari History Locations

Operating System	Location
Windows XP	C:\Documents and Settings\%username\Application Data\Apple Computer\Safari
Windows Vista/7	C:\Users\%username%\AppData\Roaming\Apple Computer\Safari
OS X	/Users/$username/Library/Safari

The main Safari history file is History.plist, which records the URL visited, the time and date of the previous visit, and the total number of times the site has been visited. Because this file is a plist, it can be processed using the plutil.pl script discussed in Chapter 6. The output from running this tool on a sample Safari History. plist can be seen here:

```
<?xml version="1.0" encoding="UTF-8"?>
<!DOCTYPE plist PUBLIC "-//Apple Computer//DTD PLIST 1.0//EN"
  "http://www.apple.com/DTDs/PropertyList-1.0.dtd">
<plist version="1.0">
<dict>
  <key>WebHistoryDates</key>
  <array>
    <dict>
      <key></key>
      <string>http://www.amazon.com/Digital-Forensics-Open-
        Source-Tools/dp/1597495867</string>
      <key>D</key>
      <array>
        <integer>1</integer>
      </array>
      <key>lastVisitedDate</key>
      <string>310529012.7</string>
      <key>title</key>
      <string>Amazon.com: Digital Forensics with Open Source
        Tools (9781597495868): Cory Altheide, Harlan Carvey: B
ooks</string>
      <key>visitCount</key>
      <integer>1</integer>
    </dict>
  ...
```

The time stamp just displayed is stored as a CFAbsoluteTime value (also known as *Mac Absolute Time*). This value is an offset representing the number of seconds since midnight January 1, 2001 GMT. Instead of converting these values manually, we can use *Safari Forensic Tools* (SFT), a set of command line tools designed for processing Safari's plist files.

> **TIP**
>
> **Compiling SFT**
>
> Jake Cunningham, the author of Safari Forensic Tools, has provided prebuilt binaries for Windows and Linux. If you plan to build them from source on Linux, you will need to install the GNUStep development environment. This can be accomplished on Ubuntu using apt-get:
>
> ```
> sudo apt-get install gnustep-devel
> ```

Safari maintains four main plist files of interest:

1. Downloads.plist
2. Bookmarks.plist
3. Cookies.plist
4. History.plist

The Safari Forensics Tools suite has individual utilities to parse and display the content of each plist.

Downloads.plist stores all files downloaded to the system. This does not include cached media, images, or any items handled by browser plugins. The Downloads. plist file can be processed by SFT tool safari_downloads. See the following for an example entry from this file:

```
DownloadEntryProgressBytesSoFar: 494185
DownloadEntryIdentifier: 6438149F-D8A0-4677-9D00-C46DFFEE96C2
DownloadEntryPath: ~/Downloads/gp_lin32_rc4_2.tar.bz2
DownloadEntryURL: http://cache.greenpois0n.com/dl/gp_lin32_
    rc4_2.tar.bz2
DownloadEntryProgressTotalToLoad: 494185
Status: Completed
```

This can be used to correlate web browsing history to files on disk.

Bookmarks.plist stores user bookmarks. Safari bookmarks are not as interesting artifact-wise as bookmarks for other browsers, as it does not store any time stamps related to the bookmark entry. This file can be processed using the SFT tool *safari_bm*.

```
Title: BookmarksMenu
        Windows NT Contains File System Tunneling Capabilities
            http://support.microsoft.com/kb/172190
```

As the name implies, *Cookies.plist* holds entries related to cookies. Artifacts of interest include the domain and path the cookie is issued for, the creation and expiration times, and the cookie content. The SFT tool safari_cookies can parse this file.

```
Path:        /
Expires:     2015-10-18 14:27:02 -0700
Domain:      .howstuffworks.com
Value:       [CS]v1|265F0693051D3BB9-40000104602169BD[CE]
Created:     2010-10-19 14:27:02 -0700 (309216422.496477)
Name:        s_vi
```

```
Path:      /
Expires:   2015-06-23 09:06:06 -0700
Domain:    .southwest.com
Value:     [CS]v1|2611C13705159919-40000173803F1B41[CE]
Created:   2010-06-24 09:06:06 -0700 (299088366.870542)
Name:      s_vi
```

The record of a user's visits to Web sites is stored in the *History.plist* file. The SFT tool `safari_hist` can be used to process this file into a tab-delimited format, listing the URL visited, the last visit date and time, the number of visits, and the title of the page in question. See the following excerpt for a sample.

```
URL  Last Visit Date/Time  Number of visits  Page Title
http://developer.apple.com/library/mac/#technotes/tn2006/tn2166.
   html  2010-11-08 11:15:11 -0800   1    Technical Note TN2166:
   Secrets of the GPT
http://developer.apple.com/library/mac/navigation/index.html
   #topic=Guides&section=Resource+Types    2010-11-06 22:25:33
   -0700   2   Mac OS X Developer Library
http://developer.apple.com/documentation/mac/files/Files-2.html
   2010-11-06 22:25:33 -0700 1 Guides
http://developer.apple.com/documentation/mac/files/Files-72.html
   2010-11-06 22:25:20 -0700 1 Guides
```

Cache

The Safari cache is stored in the Cache.db SQLite3 database. Cached data are stored primarily in two tables: cfurl_cache_response, which stores the URL and request metadata, and cfurl_cache_blob_data, which stores actual cached data [5]. In many cases, direct examination of the live database using sqlite queries will yield no results because the cache has been "emptied." However, unless the database has been vacuumed, the actual cached content will still be present in the database file and can be recovered using file carving techniques. This segment shows an excerpt of results of running `hachoir-subfile` against an "empty" Cache.db database.

```
forensics:~ $ hachoir-subfile Library/Caches/com.apple.Safari/
   Cache.db
[+] Start search on 78134272 bytes (74.5 MB)
[+] File at 32304 size=29913 (29.2 KB): JPEG picture
[err!] Unable to compute GifFile content size: Can't get field
   "image[0]" from /
[+] File at 73682: GIF picture
[+] File at 74468: JPEG picture
[+] File at 74498: TIFF picture
[+] File at 75280: JPEG picture
[+] File at 81604 size=1344 (1344 bytes): GIF picture
[+] File at 88754 size=16472 (16.1 KB): GIF picture
[+] File at 102814 size=93773 (91.6 KB): JPEG picture
```

```
[+] File at 203702: JPEG picture
[+] File at 204574: JPEG picture
[+] File at 209803: JPEG picture
[+] File at 215181 size=3709 (3709 bytes): JPEG picture
[+] File at 221369 size=3665 (3665 bytes): JPEG picture
[+] File at 226953 size=3201 (3201 bytes): JPEG picture
[+] File at 232104 size=2146 (2146 bytes): JPEG picture
[+] File at 236244 size=35133 (34.3 KB): GIF picture
[+] File at 237376: JPEG picture
[+] File at 249450: JPEG picture
[+] File at 252313 size=4365 (4365 bytes): JPEG picture
[+] File at 284855 size=1619 (1619 bytes): JPEG picture
[+] File at 288346 size=4272 (4272 bytes): JPEG picture
[+] File at 294697: JPEG picture
[+] File at 313240 size=596850 (582.9 KB): PNG picture:
    800x171x24
[+] File at 313779 size=3366 (3366 bytes): JPEG picture
[+] File at 319757 size=67069 (65.5 KB): JPEG picture
[+] File at 389267 size=4727 (4727 bytes): JPEG picture
[+] File at 399393: Macromedia Flash data: version 10,
    compressed
...
```

LastSession.plist

The LastSession.plist file is used by Safari to restore the browser state in case of an unexpected shutdown. This file can be parsed using the *plutil.pl* utility. Artifacts that can be extracted from this file are limited but, at a minimum, URLs and page titles can be recovered.

```
<key>BackForwardList</key>
<array>
  <dict>
    <key>Title</key>
    <string>Top Sites</string>
    <key>URL</key>
    <string>topsites://</string>
  </dict>
  <dict>
    <key>Title</key>
    <string>Technical Note TN2166: Secrets of the GPT
      </string>
    <key>URL</key>
    <string>http://developer.apple.com/library/
      mac/#technotes/tn2006/tn2166.html</string>
  </dict>
</array>
```

MAIL ARTIFACTS

For home users, local email storage may be falling by the wayside in favor of Web mail, but there are still many businesses using locally stored mail. This section covers extraction of content from the binary Microsoft Outlook format, as well as some methods to speed up analysis of plain text email formats used commonly on Linux systems.

Personal Storage Table

PST is the mail storage format used by Microsoft's Outlook email client. A user's PST file is not just for storage of email from their MSExchange server, but can also store email from POP3, IMAP, and even HTTP (such as Windows Live Hotmail) accounts. The PST file provides a data storage format for storing emails on the user's computer system. Users of OutLook email clients may also have an OST file, which is for offline storage of email. This file allows the user to continue reviewing the email that they do have, even while they are offline and cannot connect to their MSExchange server.

TIP

PST Formats

As of MSOffice 2003, a newer version of the PST file format, which is not backward compatible with earlier versions of the format, became available. This new format allows for greater storage capacity for emails and folders, in addition to supporting multilingual Unicode data.

　　Early in 2010, Microsoft released their Office document format publicly; PST file format documentation is available at the Microsoft Web site at http://msdn.microsoft.com/en-us/library/ff385210.aspx.

A user's PST file may be found in the "Local Settings\Application Data\Microsoft\Outlook" subfolder within their profile on Windows XP and 2003 systems; on Vista and Windows 7 systems, the user's PST file may be located in the "AppData\Roaming\Microsoft\Outlook" folder. However, PST files can be moved to any location within the file system, and an analyst may find several PST files on a system. PST files may contain considerable artifacts of user communications (as well as sharing files as attachments), and the value of the PST files will depend on the analyst's goals and the type of examination.

One of the first open source libraries for accessing the PST file format was libpst [6]. This library converts 32-bit, pre-OutLook 2003 PST files, as well as 64-bit Out-Look 2003 files, and is available as source RPMs, as well as .tar.gz files for download and installation. The library is also utilized by several of the utilities available at the referenced Web site, including `readpst` and `lspst`. In addition to the libpst library, the libpff library is also available [7] (the libpff library is available as a SourceForge.net project). As of November 11, 2010, the library is in alpha and is available as a .tar.gz file.

There may also be options available if you're interested in more of a cross-platform approach. In January 2010, Richard Johnson posted to his blog [8] that he'd developed an open-source Java library for accessing PST files using documentation available as part of the libpff project. According to his blog post, Richard had done this in order to be able to convert PST files to Gmail format in order to take advantage of the search capabilities afforded by Gmail; clearly, this may also be a capability of interest to forensic analysts. Richard made the open-source java-pst library available on Google Code [9]; in addition to the library, there is an alpha version of the pst2gmail conversion utility available on the Web at http://code.google.com/p/pst2gmail/.

> **NOTE**
>
> **Readpst.exe**
> Searches on Google for "readpst.exe" and "readpst.zip" reveal that there have been several efforts to produce a command-line executable version of the readpst utility associated with the libpst library, but for the Windows platform. Several of the available posts indicate that the utilities run in Wine, a free application for Linux systems that provide a compatibility layer for running Windows programs.

We can use the utilities provided by **libpff** to examine a sample PST file. The pffinfo tool will provide some basic information about the internals of a given PST.

```
user@ubuntu:~/pst$ pffinfo Outlook.pst
pffinfo 20101203
Personal Folder File information:
        File size:           7382016 bytes
        File content type: Personal Storage Tables (PST)
        File type:           64-bit
        Encryption type: compressible
Message store:
        Folders:             Subtree, Inbox, Outbox, Wastbox,
           Sentmail, Views, Common views, Finder
        Password checksum: N/A
```

To extract the email content, we will use pffexport. This tool has a variety of options that can be used to configure what is extracted and how it is represented. The most important of these is the -m option, which defines the export mode. By default only "allocated" messages are exported. Note that this includes items in the "Deleted Items" directory that have not been purged by the user. The -m all option tells pffexport to attempt to export messages recovered from the unallocated space of the PST structure.

```
user@ubuntu:~/pst$ pffexport -m all -t outlook-export Outlook.pst
```

Pffexport creates two directories when using these flags: one for exported allocated items and one for recovered deleted items. In this instance we did not encounter any recovered items. Inside the outlook-export.allocated/ directory is a directory named

"Top of Personal Folders." This contains a directory structure that will be familiar to anyone that has used Outlook:

```
Calendar  Deleted Items  Inbox    Junk E-mail Outbox Tasks
Contacts  Drafts         Journal  Notes       Sent Items
```

Messages stored in these directories are extracted into component pieces:

```
/home/user/pst/outlook-export.export/Top of Personal Folders/
   Sent Items/Message00066:
Attachments
Attachments/sample.xls
ConversationIndex.txt
Message.txt
OutlookHeaders.txt
Recipients.txt
```

As you can see, attachments are exported into an "Attachments" subdirectory. The "Message.txt" file is the actual mail content—the rest of the files are Outlook metadata.

For more information about internals of the PST format, please see Joachim Metz's extensive documentation at the **libpff** project page on SourceForge.net: http://sourceforge.net/projects/libpff/files/documentation/.

TIP

PST to mbox

The default operation of the `readpst` tool included in libpst is to read in a PST file and write the discovered directories out to individual mbox-formatted files. If the PST file you are working with can be parsed with `readpst`, this can be helpful as you can use the techniques described in the *mbox & maildir* section to search the mail content.

---

mbox and maildir

mbox and maildir are the two primary local mail storage formats used by Linux email clients. These formats are also supported by cross-platform mail clients, especially those with a Unix pedigree. Examples include Eudora, Thunderbird, and Apple's Mail.app. The older mbox format consists of a single flat file, containing numerous email entries, whereas the maildir format stores each email as a discreet file in a set of subdirectories.

Because both of these formats are plain text, searching for specific key words quickly can be performed without the need for a dedicated email forensics utility. We will demonstrate examination techniques using item 317398 from Digital Corpora, which is a large mail archive in mbox format. The file begins with the following lines:

```
From newville@cars.uchicago.edu Wed Feb 20 16:33:22 2002
Received: from localhost (newville@localhost)
   by millenia.cars.aps.anl.gov (8.11.6/8.11.2) with ESMTP id
   g1KMXMY05595
```

```
    for <ifeffit@millenia.cars.aps.anl.gov>; Wed, 20 Feb 2002
       16:33:22 -0600
X-Authentication-Warning: millenia.cars.aps.anl.gov: newville
   owned process doing -bs
Date: Wed, 20 Feb 2002 16:33:22 -0600 (CST)
From: Matt Newville <newville@cars.uchicago.edu>
X-X-Sender: newville@millenia.cars.aps.anl.gov
To: ifeffit@millenia.cars.aps.anl.gov
Message-ID: <Pine.LNX.4.43.0202201626470.5566-100000@millenia.
   cars.aps.anl.gov>
```

This mail entry continues with additional headers followed by the mail body. A new mail begins with another "From " line, which is the defined message delineator for the mbox format. Note that capitalization and the trailing space are intentional and required for new mail—this is known as the "From_" line.

We will use two different tools to examine this mailbox: `grepmail` and `mairix`. Both can be installed on Ubuntu systems using `apt-get`.

TIP

Mail Searching on Windows

`Grepmail` and `mairix` are also both available on Windows via the Cygwin installer program shown in Chapter 2.

Grepmail

`Grepmail` is a utility designed to search for individual mail entries that match a supplied set of criteria. `Grepmail` has knowledge of the mbox mail format and will return an entire message rather than a single matching line as is the case when using standard "grep." Although grepmail can only process mbox format mailboxes, it can parse compressed mailboxes and can search through a number of mailboxes at once. Selected `grepmail` options that may be of particular interest to examiners are listed here:

```
-b Search must match body
-d Specify a required date range
-h Search must match header
-H Print headers but not bodies of matching emails
-j Search must match status (A=answered, R=read, D=deleted,
O=old, F=flagged)
-Y Specify a header to search (implies -h)
```

In addition to header-specific searches, another feature of grepmail an examiner may find of value is its date searching capabilities. Grepmail understands dates entered in a number of nonstandard formats: "10/31/10," "4:08pm June eleventh," and "yesterday" are all valid date entries, for example. Additionally, date searches can be constrained by keywords such as "before," "since," or "between." Further discussion of extended time analysis in forensic examinations can be found in Chapter 9.

While `grepmail` certainly has interesting search capabilities, it does tend to slow down quite a bit dealing with very large (multiple gigabyte) mbox files. The grepmail program is better suited for queries against relatively small mailboxes and queries where a specific set of keywords, dates, and other search criteria are known in advance of the start of the examination and are unlikely to change. Many legal discovery examinations would fall into this category. For investigations that don't have a fixed set of examination criteria from the beginning or that involve large mailboxes, mairix may be a better utility.

Mairix

Mairix is a powerful mail searching utility that supports both maildir and mbox formats. The key difference between mairix and grepmail is that mairix first builds an index, which is subsequently queried as the examiner performs searches. Prior to searching, we need to provide a configuration file (mairixrc) that will tell mairix the location of our content to be indexed, where the index should go, and where any mail items that are returned in response to a query should be exported to.

We can build a minimal mairixrc file containing the following information:

```
base=.
mbox=input/mail.mbox
database=.database
mfolder=output
```

"Base" defines the base path that mairix will treat as its root. "mbox" points to the mbox file we will be examining. Note that this can be a colon-delimited set of mbox files if you need to index and examine multiple mailboxes. "Database" tells mairix where to store the index it will build. Finally, "mfolder "defines a directory where mairix will write the output from any subsequent queries. Search results are stored in maildir format by default.

Once the .mairixrc is written we can generate the index using:

```
mairix -v -f .mairixrc
...
Wrote 5283 messages (105660 bytes tables, 0 bytes text)
Wrote 1 mbox headers (16 bytes tables, 18 bytes paths)
Wrote 84528 bytes of mbox message checksums
To: Wrote 803 tokens (6424 bytes tables, 8158 bytes of text,
   53244 bytes of hit encoding)
Cc: Wrote 430 tokens (3440 bytes tables, 4187 bytes of text,
   4171 bytes of hit encoding)
From: Wrote 2074 tokens (16592 bytes tables, 22544 bytes of
   text, 38970 bytes of hit encoding)
Subject: Wrote 1875 tokens (15000 bytes tables, 13413 bytes of
   text, 39366 bytes of hit encoding)
Body: Wrote 165118 tokens (1320944 bytes tables, 1619831 bytes
   of text, 1488382 bytes of hit encoding)
Attachment Name: Wrote 385 tokens (3080 bytes tables, 6288 bytes
   of text, 1256 bytes of hit encoding)
(Threading): Wrote 5742 tokens (45936 bytes tables, 278816 bytes
   of text, 39685 bytes of hit encoding)
```

Note that adding the `-v` flag forces `mairix` to write status information to the console while indexing—omitting this flag will not harm anything but may give the indication of a hung program when indexing a very large mailbox.

Once the index has been generated we can begin issuing queries. Mairix supports a broad range of search operators, which we will not duplicate in their entirety here. Please review the `mairix` man page for a full list of search operators. The following search will return all messages with the word "vacation" in the body or subject.

```
user@ubuntu:~/mail$ mairix -f rcfile bs:vacation
Created directory ./output
Created directory ./output/cur
Created directory ./output/new
Created directory ./output/tmp
Matched 19 messages
```

The resulting mail files can be found in the "new" subdirectory under the folder defined as the "mfolder" in our .mairixrc file.

```
user@ubuntu:~/mail$ cd output/new/
user@ubuntu:~/mail/output/new$ ls
123456789.121.mairix 123456789.1663.mairix 123456789.1688.mairix
   123456789.2686.mairix 123456789.589.mairix
123456789.1616.mairix 123456789.1674.mairix 123456789.1691.
   mairix 123456789.2986.mairix 123456789.593.mairix
123456789.1618.mairix 123456789.1675.mairix 123456789.1692.
   mairix 123456789.579.mairix 123456789.619.mairix
123456789.1622.mairix 123456789.1677.mairix 123456789.2685.
   mairix 123456789.581.mairix
```

SUMMARY

This chapter identified and analyzed numerous artifacts generated by the top four browsers in use today. As deciphering a user's browser activity is becoming more and more relevant to a wider variety of investigations, being able to locate and process these data effectively is crucial. This chapter also extracted mail content and metadata from Outlook's binary format and discussed how to analyze locally stored mail in formats used commonly by Linux and OS X mail clients.

References

[1] The Meaning of LEAK Records. http://www.forensicblog.org/2009/09/10/the-meaning-of-leak-records/, (accessed 29.12.10).
[2] Firefox 3 Forensics—Research—Firefox Places Schema. http://www.firefoxforensics.com/research/firefox_places_schema.shtml.

[3] IR and forensic talk» Version 0.41 of log2timeline published. http://blog.kiddaland .net/2010/01/version-0-41-of-log2timeline-published/.

[4] SANS—Computer Forensics and Incident Response with Rob Lee. http://computer-forensics.sans.org/blog/2010/01/21/google-chrome-forensics/.

[5] Forensics from the sausage factory: Safari browser cache—Examination of Cache.db. http://forensicsfromthesausagefactory.blogspot.com/2010/06/safari-browser-cache-examination-of.html.

[6] libpst Utilities–Version 0.6.49. http://www.five-ten-sg.com/libpst/.

[7] libpff. http://sourceforge.net/projects/libpff/.

[8] java-libpst and pst2gmail. http://www.rjohnson.id.au/wordpress/2010/01/26/java-libpst-pst2gmail/, (accessed 26.01.10).

[9] java-libpst. http://code.google.com/p/java-libpst/.

File Analysis

INFORMATION IN THIS CHAPTER

- File Analysis Concepts
- Images
- Audio
- Video
- Archives
- Documents

FILE ANALYSIS CONCEPTS

To perform a comprehensive examination, we must understand the nature of the files we identify and extract. By understanding these files, we can more successfully uncover and exploit any higher order forensic artifacts that may be present within the files. This builds upon and complements the system and application analysis performed in previous chapters.

The analysis of individual files will be of key importance in many different examinations. A malicious document may be the initial entry point in a system compromise investigation. The validity of a critical document may be in question. The examiner may need to locate and identify illicit images or videos on the system. The presence of the same file on two different machines may tie those machines and users of the machines together. The fact that these files are intended to be self-contained and shared across systems is one of the key characteristics that makes them an interesting source of artifacts.

File analysis can be broken up into two distinct but complementary activities: *content identification* and *metadata extraction*. Content identification is the process of determining or verifying *what* a specific file *is*. Metadata extraction is the retrieval of any embedded metadata that may be present in a given file.

While we do cover the identification and subsequent artifact retrieval from various file types, this chapter is not intended to serve as a comprehensive work on digital content forensic analysis. Indeed, forensic analysis of any single digital media type (audio, video, or still images) is a complex topic that could fill volumes on its own. Instead, our focus is on retrieving and exploiting forensic artifacts as part of an examination of activities on a computer system or systems. Through analysis of the file content and any stored metadata, we can build a better narrative for our examination.

Throughout this chapter we will be using files retrieved from Digital Corpora (www.digitalcorpora.org), "a website of digital corpora for use in computer forensics research." In particular, we will examine files from the "Govdocs1" collection, which contains nearly one million files representing a wide variety of file types. This collection gives us the ability to demonstrate the use of various file analysis tools and techniques against files that are also freely available to the reader.

Content Identification

The goal of the content identification process is to confirm the content of a given file. Most computer users are familiar with the concept of *file extensions* as used on Windows systems to identify specific file types. The name of a file, though, isn't what makes a file. A medical doctor isn't a doctor because she puts "Dr." before her name—she is a doctor because of the years of schooling and medical training. Even without the title, she *is* a doctor. Similarly, a simple text file is a text file whether it is named "MyFile.txt" or "ThisIsAnEmptyFolder." The extension provides a hint to the Windows shell with regards to the content of the file—it is a convention of convenience, nothing more.

For many reasons, we as forensic examiners cannot simply accept this hint as ground truth and go on our way. First, it is conceivable that a user can change the file associations and default applications used to open specific files in an effort to conceal the nature of the files. For example, a user could change all AVI video files to have a .BIN extension and then associate this extension with a video player. Second, throughout the course of an examination it is not uncommon to discover files with no extension at all in a location of interest or with time stamps that place that file in a time period of interest. Generally, these will be temporary or cache files not meant for end-user consumption and may contain crucial investigation data.

To identify files based on their content properly, we use key structures inherent to specific file types to confirm or determine a given file's type. These are referred to as *magic numbers* or *magic values* and are generally specific hexadecimal values found at specific offsets from the beginning of a file.

The file command can be used to identify file types based on these magic values. By default, file will use the system "magic file," which is a long list of file magic number definitions. On Ubuntu, this file is located at "/usr/share/misc/magic" but local magic values may be defined in "/etc/magic" as well. Magic file test definitions can be fairly complex, but the most basic are of the form "look for this sequence of hex values at this offset into the file." For example, the most basic JPEG definition is as follows:

```
"0   beshort   0xffd8   JPEG image data"
```

The first column is the offset into the file to begin the test—right at the beginning in this test. The next column is the type of data to test. The "beshort" value in this column indicates "a two-byte value in big-endian byte order." The next column is test data. If the first two bytes of a file match the value in this column (FFD8 in hex) the test returns "true," and the file being tested will be reported to be "JPEG image data."

More complex test definitions are available in the magic format. The system magic file and the man page for the magic file are good references for the enterprising examiner.

Content Examination

Up to this point, the tools mentioned in this chapter have been relatively "automagic"—you point the tool at some content and it tells you (more or less) what that content is. This is certainly convenient, but it is imperative that an examiner understand how a tool operates and be able to confirm and validate correct operation (or, in some cases, confirm *incorrect* operation). To do so, we need to be able to view the raw content of file. The most basic method for doing so is via *hexadecimal dump* (or *hexdump*). A hexdump is simply a text representation of the underlying binary structure of the file in question. We'll use the program xxd (included as part of the vim editor, which is included by default on many Linux distributions) to view a hexdump of a sample PDF from Digital Corpora (997495.pdf).

```
0000000: 2550 4446 2d31 2e35 0d25 e2e3 cfd3 0d0a  %PDF-1.5.%......
0000010: 3435 2030 206f 626a 203c 3c2f 4c69 6e65  45 0 obj <</Line
0000020: 6172 697a 6564 2031 2f4c 2034 3538 3835  arized 1/L 45885
0000030: 2f4f 2034 392f 4520 3131 3138 342f 4e20  /O 49/E 11184/N
0000040: 3132 2f54 2034 3439 3338 2f48 205b 2036  12/T 44938/H [ 6
0000050: 3336 2032 3332 5d3e 3e0d 656e 646f 626a  36 232]>>.endobj
0000060: 0d20 2020 2020 2020 2020 2020 2020 2020  .
0000070: 2020 0d0a 7872 6566 0d0a 3435 2031 370d  ..xref..45 17.
0000080: 0a30 3030 3030 3030 3031 3620 3030 3030  .0000000016 0000
. . .
```

The first column is the byte count/offset in base 16. The second 8 columns are the hexadecimal representation of the file content. Each column represents 2 bytes. The rest of the line is the ASCII text rendition of the file. Nonprintable/non-ASCII characters are displayed as dots (.). While this is a quick method for viewing the content of a file, it is not ideal for extensive interaction and analysis. For more in-depth analysis, we can use a *hex editor*. As the name implies, hex editors are a class of software designed for editing binary files with no interpretation—reading and writing hexadecimal. Many simple hex editors are available that are nothing more than an interactive GUI version of the simple xxd tool we just used. For our purposes, we want to be able to view raw data of a file, but we also would like to be able to interactively interpret certain data structures we come across.

To examine binary files in a useful manner, we can use tools built around the *hachoir* framework. Hachoir is a Python library that parses and interprets a binary file bit by bit. In the author's own words, "Hachoir allows you to 'browse' any binary stream just like you browse directories and files." There are several tools that implement hachoir's binary parsing capability that will be of use as we examine various file formats throughout this chapter. On Ubuntu systems, installing Hachoir is quite simple. We can use a wildcard to `apt-get` to install all the available hachoir component packages.

```
user@forensics:~$ sudo apt-get install python-hachoir-*
Reading package lists... Done
Building dependency tree
Reading state information... Done
Note, selecting 'python-hachoir-regex' for regex 'python-hachoir-*'
Note, selecting 'python-hachoir-metadata' for regex 'python-hachoir-*'
Note, selecting 'python-hachoir-core' for regex 'python-hachoir-*'
Note, selecting 'python-hachoir-parser' for regex 'python-hachoir-*'
Note, selecting 'python-hachoir-urwid' for regex 'python-hachoir-*'
Note, selecting 'python-hachoir-subfile' for regex 'python-hachoir-*'
Note, selecting 'python-hachoir-wx' for regex 'python-hachoir-*'
...
```

> **TIP**
>
> **Getting the Latest Hachoir**
> The hachoir project is undergoing constant, rapid development. Versions of the various hachoir components provided by distribution package managers may be missing key features added to the source at any given time. To take advantage of the latest updates, you can check the development branch of hachoir out using mercurial:

```
hg clone https://bitbucket.org/haypo/hachoir
```

Throughout this chapter (and the rest of the book), we will discuss the use of three programs that use the hachoir library:

- `hachoir-metadata`, a tool that extracts and displays metadata from file formats recognized by hachoir-parser
- `hachoir-urwid`, a console GUI binary file browser
- `hachoir-subfile`, a tool for identifying and extracting identifiable files from inside binary streams

Metadata Extraction

As discussed in Chapter 3, metadata are *data about data*. In the context of a file system, metadata are additional information about content in blocks. In the context of file analysis, metadata are information stored within the file itself that provide some possibly interesting but otherwise nonessential information about the file.

Metadata are included to provide context or extended information that is outside of the scope of data itself, for example, author information, or time stamps beyond those on the local file system.

The value of metadata is highly dependent on the nature of a given examination and the types of files being examined. For a straightforward intrusion case, metadata may simply be a secondary source of data. In a litigation support examination, metadata may end up being the focal point of the entire case.

WARNING

Metadata Caveats

Not all file formats support metadata. In general, the *older* or *more simple* a particular file format is, the less likely it is to carry metadata at all and the less likely it is that any metadata present will be particularly interesting. Also, keep in mind that most metadata are not required for a file to serve its purpose—it is by definition peripheral.

Because of this, in most cases, metadata can be altered or eliminated without affecting the function of the content of the file. Depending on the investigation, though, the absence of metadata may be a forensic artifact in and of itself.

As metadata extraction is a relatively common task performed across a variety of disciplines, many generic metadata extraction tools have been developed. We will discuss two such tools: the `extract` tool that implements the *libextractor* library and `hachoir-metadata`, which build upon the *hachoir* library mentioned previously. Both tools are quite capable of extracting metadata from many files with minimal interaction. As we discuss specific file types, we will use these tools as well as more specialized tools designed to extract metadata from one (or a few) file types.

The `extract` tool can be installed easily on Ubuntu using the following command:

```
user@forensics:~$ sudo apt-get install extract
```

The `extract` tool has many flags and options that can be passed at execution time. Options that are most interesting to forensic analysis of file content are listed here.

```
Usage: extract [OPTIONS] [FILENAME]*
Extract metadata from files.
  -a, --all          do not remove any duplicates
  -d, --duplicates     remove duplicates only if types match
  -g, --grep-friendly   produce grep-friendly output (all
    results on one line per file)
  -H, --hash=ALGORITHM  compute hash using the given ALGORITHM
    (currently
                sha1 or md5)
  -L, --list         list all keyword types
  -p, --print=TYPE     print only keywords of the given TYPE
    (use -L to get a list)
  -r, --remove-duplicates remove duplicates even if keyword
    types do not match
  -V, --verbose       be verbose
  -x, --exclude=TYPE    do not print keywords of the given TYPE
```

In particular, depending on your specific use, removing duplicates *or* ensuring that no duplicates are removed may be important. See the following section for a sample of extract's output for a sample JPEG image file.

```
user@ubuntu:~$ extract /usr/share/pixmaps/faces/puppy.jpg
size - 96x96
resolution - 72x72 dots per inch?
mimetype - image/jpeg
```

Also, see the extract's output when reading a sample PDF.

```
user@ubuntu:~$ extract /usr/share/gnome/help/gnome-access-
   guide/C/gnome-access-guide.pdf
software - This is pdfTeX using libpoppler, Version 3.141592-
   1.40.3-2.2 (Web2C 7.5.6) kpathsea version 3.5.6
modification date - D:20090407113257-04'00'
creation date - 20090407113257-04'00'
keywords -
producer - pdfTeX-1.40.3
creator - LaTeX with hyperref package
subject -
title -
author -
format - PDF 1.4
mimetype - application/pdf
```

In both cases, data provided are fairly sparse, but extract supports a wide variety of file types.

Another utility that can be used to bulk extract metadata from files in a generic manner is hachoir-metadata. Hachoir-metadata uses the hachoir-parser library to retrieve metadata from many file formats, with a focus on music, video, and picture files. Note that hachoir-metadata does not currently support the wide range of exotic file types some of the other tools we will be using do, but it does provide more verbose data for the file types it does support. For instance, see the output from hachoir-metadata for the same test JPEG image used previously:

```
user@ubuntu:~$ hachoir-metadata /usr/share/pixmaps/faces/puppy.jpg
Metadata:
- Image width: 96 pixels
- Image height: 96 pixels
- Bits/pixel: 24
- Pixel format: YCbCr
- Compression rate: 9.0x
- Image DPI width: 72 DPI
- Image DPI height: 72 DPI
- Compression: JPEG (Baseline)
- Comment: JPEG quality: 85%
- Format version: JFIF 1.01
- MIME type: image/jpeg
- Endian: Big endian
```

A list of all parsers available in `hachoir-metadata` can be viewed using the `-parser-list` option. At the time of this writing, 35 different file types are supported. Note that an exhaustive examination of all forms of metadata and all document types would be futile and well outside the scope of this work. It is the authors' intention to explore forensically relevant and interesting document and metadata types.

Now that we understand the concepts related to file analysis, we can begin examining the various file types likely to be important in a variety of examinations. These files are broken down into five categories: *images*, *audio*, *video*, *archives*,and *documents*.

IMAGES

Images are a simple enough concept; these are files that contain data to be rendered as graphics. Many different image types are used for different purposes, but all have the goal of presenting image data to the viewer. In addition, most image file types are capable of carrying a variety of metadata, ranging from simple text comments to the latitude and longitude where the image was created. Depending on the investigation, the examiner may be interested in the content of the image (e.g., a photograph of a particular person) or metadata (information indicating that the image may have been altered in image editing software).

The `identify` utility included as part of the imagemagick package can be used to extract information from a wide variety of images. To get `identify` we will need to install imagemagick.

```
user@forensics:~$ sudo apt-get install imagemagick
```

Because the default output of `identify` is very sparse, we will include the "`-verbose`" flag to extract more information about the image. We will use the same test JPEG from before as reference.

```
user@ubuntu:~$ identify -verbose /usr/share/pixmaps/faces/puppy.jpg
Image: /usr/share/pixmaps/faces/puppy.jpg
  Format: JPEG (Joint Photographic Experts Group JFIF format)
  Class: DirectClass
  Geometry: 96x96+0+0
  Resolution: 72x72
  Print size: 1.33333x1.33333
  Units: PixelsPerInch
  Type: TrueColor
  Endianess: Undefined
  Colorspace: RGB
  Depth: 8-bit
```

```
Channel depth:
  red: 8-bit
  green: 8-bit
  blue: 8-bit
Channel statistics:
  red:
    min: 0 (0)
    max: 255 (1)
    mean: 117.579 (0.461094)
    standard deviation: 64.1817 (0.251693)
    kurtosis: -0.687544
    skewness: 0.430921
  green:
    min: 0 (0)
    max: 255 (1)
    mean: 121.92 (0.478116)
    standard deviation: 62.863 (0.246522)
    kurtosis: -0.66723
    skewness: 0.131649
  blue:
    min: 0 (0)
    max: 255 (1)
    mean: 76.2197 (0.298901)
    standard deviation: 74.8287 (0.293446)
    kurtosis: -0.643199
    skewness: 0.91572
Image statistics:
    Overall:
    min: 0 (0)
    max: 255 (1)
    mean: 78.9296 (0.309528)
    standard deviation: 76.239 (0.298976)
    kurtosis: -0.823781
    skewness: 0.630468
Rendering intent: Undefined
Interlace: None
Background color: white
Border color: rgb(223,223,223)
Matte color: grey74
Transparent color: black
Compose: Over
Page geometry: 96x96+0+0
Dispose: Undefined
Iterations: 0
Compression: JPEG
Quality: 85
Orientation: Undefined
```

```
Properties:
    date:create: 2010-07-24T15:03:19-07:00
    date:modify: 2010-06-18T02:04:48-07:00
jpeg:colorspace: 2
    jpeg:sampling-factor: 2x2,1x1,1x1
    signature: 54b2634b34b7359af479f233afd4ada15
        5af0e0413899929b6bbf8e8fef93ffd
Profiles:
    Profile-exif: 20 bytes
Artifacts:
    verbose: true
Tainted: False
Filesize: 3.38KiB
Number pixels: 9KiB
Pixels per second: 900KiB
User time: 0.010u
Elapsed time: 0:01.010
Version: ImageMagick 6.5.7-8 2009-11-26 Q16 http://www
    .imagemagick.org
```

This is an incredible amount of data for a 72 × 72 image that is under 4K in size! Note that the two dates listed here are from the **file system metadata**, not any embedded file metadata.

Identify is a good choice for extracting data from a wide variety of image files *en masse*, as the imagemagick library supports over 100 different image file formats. We will discuss a handful of the most common image file formats and the forensic artifacts they contain next.

There are three main types of image metadata in use today.

- **EXIF** (Exchangeable Image File Format) was developed to embed information about the device capturing the image (typically a camera) into the image itself. EXIF metadata consist of a series of Tags and Values, which can include things such as the make and model of the camera used to generate the image, the date and time the image was captured, and the geolocation information about the capturing device.
- **IPTC** refers to the "Information Interchange Model" developed by the International Press Telecommunications Council (IPTC). This standard, sometimes referred to as "IPTC Headers," was designed originally to embed information about images used by newspapers and news agencies. It is used primarily by photojournalists and other industries producing digital images for print.
- **XMP** is the XML-based "eXensible Metadata Platform" developed by Adobe in 2001. It largely supersedes the earlier metadata schemes and is open and extensible. While used most commonly for image metadata, its extensibility allows it to be used for other types of files as well.

For the specific image files discussed here, we will note which of these metadata formats are supported and additionally note any file-specific metadata an examiner may be able to extract.

JPEG

JPEG files are the predominant image type in general use today. JPEG is an acronym for "Joint Photographic Experts Group," which is the name of the committee that created the JPEG standard in 1992. JPEG images use a "lossy" compression format designed to minimize the size of photographs and other realistic image content while retaining the bulk of visual information.

JPEG image files can be rich with metadata. The "JPEG File Interchange Format (JFIF)" extended the JPEG format to include a minimal amount of metadata, including pixel density and aspect ratio, and optionally a small embedded thumbnail of the image to be used by gallery display applications.

In addition to JPEG-specific JFIF metadata, JPEG files may also contain EXIF, IPTC, or XMP metadata. Many programs are capable of reading these metadata types. We will examine three—`exiftool`, `exiv2`, and `hachoir-metadata`.

Using `exiftool` is straightforward. Simply pass a file name to the command and `exiftool` will read and parse all available metadata by default. We will use item 808913 from Digital Corpora as an example.

```
ExifTool Version Number        : 8.15
File Name                      : 808913.jpg
Directory                      : .
File Size                      : 1492 kB
File Modification Date/Time    : 2005:09:14 10:00:15-07:00
File Permissions               : r--r--r--
File Type                      : JPEG
MIME Type                      : image/jpeg
Exif Byte Order                : Big-endian (Motorola, MM)
Image Description              :
Make                           : NIKON CORPORATION
Camera Model Name              : NIKON D1X
X Resolution                   : 300
Y Resolution                   : 300
Resolution Unit                : inches
Software                       : Ver.5.01
Modify Date                    : 2005:08:31 21:44:15
Y Cb Cr Positioning            : Co-sited
Exposure Time                  : 1/500
F Number                       : 11.0
Exposure Program               : Program AE
Exif Version                   : 0220
Date/Time Original             : 2005:08:31 21:44:15
Create Date                    : 2005:08:31 21:44:15
Components Configuration       : Y, Cb, Cr, -
Compressed Bits Per Pixel      : 2
Exposure Compensation          : 0
```

```
Max Aperture Value            : 4.8
Metering Mode                 : Multi-segment
Flash                         : No Flash
Focal Length                  : 50.0 mm
Maker Note Version            : 2.00
ISO                           : 200
Color Mode                    : Color
Quality                       : Normal
White Balance                 : Auto
Focus Mode                    : AF-C
Flash Setting                 :
Flash Type                    :
White Balance Fine Tune       : 0
WB RB Levels                  : 2.125 1.24609375 1 1
Program Shift                 : 0
Exposure Difference           : 0
Compression                   : JPEG (old-style)
Preview Image Start           : 1646
Preview Image Length          : 25318
Tone Comp                     : Normal
Lens Type                     : G VR
Lens                          : 24-120mm f/3.5-5.6
Flash Mode                    : Did Not Fire
AF Area Mode                  : Dynamic Area
AF Point                      : Center
AF Points In Focus            : Lower-right
Shooting Mode                 : Single-Frame
Color Hue                     : Mode1
Light Source                  : Natural
Shot Info Version             : 0100
Hue Adjustment                : 3
Lens Data Version             : 0100
Lens ID Number                : 120
Lens F Stops                  : 5.33
Min Focal Length              : 24.5 mm
Max Focal Length              : 119.9 mm
Max Aperture At Min Focal     : 3.6
Max Aperture At Max Focal     : 5.7
MCU Version                   : 124
Sensor Pixel Size             : 5.9 x 5.9 um
User Comment                  :
Sub Sec Time                  : 03
Sub Sec Time Original         : 03
Sub Sec Time Digitized        : 03
Flashpix Version              : 0100
Color Space                   : sRGB
Exif Image Width              : 3008
Exif Image Height             : 1960
Interoperability Index        : R98 - DCF basic file (sRGB)
Interoperability Version      : 0100
Sensing Method                : One-chip color area
File Source                   : Digital Camera
Scene Type                    : Directly photographed
```

```
CFA Pattern                          : [Blue,Green][Green,Red]
Custom Rendered                      : Normal
Exposure Mode                        : Auto
Digital Zoom Ratio                   : 1
Focal Length In 35mm Format          : 75 mm
Scene Capture Type                   : Standard
Gain Control                         : None
Contrast                             : Normal
Saturation                           : Normal
Sharpness                            : Normal
Subject Distance Range               : Unknown
GPS Version ID                       : 2.2.0.0
GPS Latitude Ref                     : North
GPS Longitude Ref                    : West
GPS Altitude Ref                     : Above Sea Level
GPS Time Stamp                       : 21:43:35.84
GPS Satellites                       : 04
GPS Map Datum                        :
Thumbnail Offset                     : 27316
Thumbnail Length                     : 5452
Image Width                          : 3008
Image Height                         : 1960
Encoding Process                     : Baseline DCT, Huffman coding
Bits Per Sample                      : 8
Color Components                     : 3
Y Cb Cr Sub Sampling                 : YCbCr4:2:2 (2 1)
Aperture                             : 11.0
Blue Balance                         : 1.246094
GPS Altitude                         : 133 m Above Sea Level
GPS Latitude                         : 30 deg 14' 51.60" N
GPS Longitude                        : 89 deg 25' 3.60" W
GPS Position                         : 30 deg 14' 51.60" N, 89 deg 25'
                                       3.60" W

Image Size                           : 3008x1960
Lens ID                              : AF-S VR Zoom-Nikkor 24-120mm
                                       f/3.5-5.6G IF-ED

Lens                                 : 24-120mm f/3.5-5.6 G VR
Preview Image                        : (Binary data 25318 bytes, use -b
                                       option to extract)

Red Balance                          : 2.125
Scale Factor To 35 mm Equivalent     : 1.5
Shutter Speed                        : 1/500
Create Date                          : 2005:08:31 21:44:15.03
Date/Time Original                   : 2005:08:31 21:44:15.03
Modify Date                          : 2005:08:31 21:44:15.03
Thumbnail Image                      : (Binary data 5452 bytes, use -b
                                       option to extract)

Circle Of Confusion                  : 0.020 mm
Field Of View                        : 27.0 deg
Focal Length                         : 50.0 mm (35 mm equivalent: 75.0 mm)
Hyperfocal Distance                  : 11.35 m
Light Value                          : 14.9
```

There are several items of interest in this extensive output, including the make and model of the camera, the original image creation date, information about the lens and camera settings, and GPS data. We can plug these data into Google maps and see where the photograph was taken, as shown in Figure 8.1.

Viewing the image indicates that this is likely accurate GPS information (Figure 8.2).

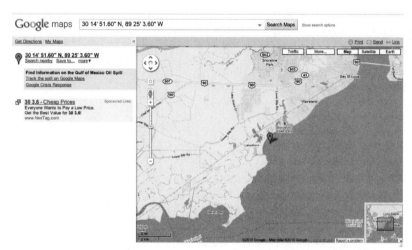

FIGURE 8.1

Google Maps View of extracted GPS coordinates.

FIGURE 8.2

Actual content of 808913.jpg.

We can also use the `exiv2` utility to recover metadata from this document.

```
File name          : 808913.jpg
File size          : 1527500 Bytes
MIME type          : image/jpeg
Image size         : 3008 x 1960
Camera make        : NIKON CORPORATION
Camera model       : NIKON D1X
Image timestamp    : 2005:08:31 21:44:15
Image number       :
Exposure time      : 1/500 s
Aperture           : F11
Exposure bias      : 0 EV
Flash              : No flash
Flash bias         :
Focal length       : 50.0 mm (35 mm equivalent: 75.0 mm)
Subject distance   :
ISO speed          : 200
Exposure mode      : Auto
Metering mode      : Multi-segment
Macro mode         :
Image quality      : NORMAL
Exif Resolution    : 3008 x 1960
White balance      : AUTO
Thumbnail          : image/jpeg, 5452 Bytes
Copyright          :
Exif comment       :
```

Note that the default output of `exiv2` is relatively sparse. Use the `-pa` flag to produce more verbose output similar to `exiftool`'s default output. Using `exiv2` in this manner also produces tag names that can be processed more easily by subsequent scripting. For example, the GPS information appears as follows in the verbose `exiv2` run:

```
Exif.GPSInfo.GPSVersionID     Byte      4 2.2.0.0
Exif.GPSInfo.GPSLatitudeRef   Ascii     2 North
Exif.GPSInfo.GPSLatitude      Rational  3 30deg 14.86000'
Exif.GPSInfo.GPSLongitudeRef  Ascii     2 West
Exif.GPSInfo.GPSLongitude     Rational  3 89deg 25.06000'
Exif.GPSInfo.GPSAltitudeRef   Byte      1 Above sea level
Exif.GPSInfo.GPSAltitude      Rational  1 133 m
Exif.GPSInfo.GPSTimeStamp     Rational  3 21:43:35.8
Exif.GPSInfo.GPSSatellites    Ascii     3 04
Exif.GPSInfo.GPSMapDatum      Ascii    10
```

This more clearly indicates the source of the information when compared to the same data retrieved by `exiftool`. Exiv2 also has the benefit of being orders of magnitude faster than `exiftool` for most tasks. This is beneficial when performing bulk processing of thousands or tens of thousands of images. The primary reason `exiftool` is so much slower may also be framed as an advantage—because it is written in Perl, it can be executed on any system with a Perl interpreter.

TIP

JPEG Quantization Tables

An interesting side effect of JPEG compression is that the method used to create or edit a JPEG may leave tell-tale markings in the *quantization tables* present in the JPEG content. These can serve as a tool mark indicating that the JPEG was likely generated by a specific make and model of digital camera [1].

`Hachoir-metadata` is not quite as full featured as the previous tools with respect to extracting JPEG metadata, but it does have the advantage of being innately read-only. It is also designed solely for the task of metadata extraction, which keeps its operation simple.

```
Metadata:
- Image width: 3008 pixels
- Image height: 1960 pixels
- Bits/pixel: 24
- Pixel format: YCbCr
- Compression rate: 11.8x
- Creation date: 2005-08-31 21:44:15
- Latitude: 30.2476666667
- Altitude: 133.0 meters
- Longitude: -89.4176666667
- Camera aperture: 4.5
- Camera focal: 11
- Camera exposure: 1/500
- Camera model: NIKON D1X
- Camera manufacturer: NIKON CORPORATION
- Compression: JPEG (Baseline)
- Producer: Ver.5.01
- Comment: JPEG quality: 95% (approximate)
- MIME type: image/jpeg
- Endianness: Big endian
```

GIF

Graphics Interchange Format (GIF) is an image format used primarily for icons and simple graphics. It uses lossless compression, which is well suited for dealing with large areas of solid color. The GIF format also supports transparency and animation. Because GIF files aren't generated by cameras or other imaging devices, there has never been a need for built-in metadata. Thus, GIF metadata are sparse to the point of near nonexistence. Generally, metadata in GIFs are limited to image information and sometimes a single simple comment field. GIF images can have XMP tags embedded in them but this is not common. Exiftool and hachoir-metadata can both process GIF metadata.

We will examine item 135900 from Digital Corpora, first using `exiftool`.

```
ExifTool Version Number       : 8.15
File Name                     : 135900.gif
Directory                     : 135
File Size                     : 15 kB
File Modification Date/Time   : 1997:04:26 11:08:49-07:00
File Permissions              : r--r--r--
File Type                     : GIF
MIME Type                     : image/gif
GIF Version                   : 89a
Image Width                   : 478
Image Height                  : 580
Has Color Map                 : Yes
Color Resolution Depth        : 8
Bits Per Pixel                : 4
Background Color              : 0
Comment                       : Image generated by Ghostscript
                                (device=ppmraw).
Image Size                    : 478x580
```

What follows is the same file as seen by `hachoir-metada`.

```
Metadata:
- Image width: 478 pixels
- Image height: 580 pixels
- Number of colors: 16
- Bits/pixel: 4
- Pixel format: Color index
- Compression: LZW
- Comment: Image generated by Ghostscript (device=ppmraw)
- Format version: GIF version 89a
- MIME type: image/gif
- Endianness: Little endian
```

PNG

Portable Network Graphics (PNG) is another format for the lossless compression of images. It is intended to provide a free and open replacement for GIF images and is suitable for many of the same uses as GIF. As such, embedded metadata present in PNG files are also relatively sparse and usually limited to image information and a single comment field. Like GIF images, PNGs can contain XMP tags but this is rare.

We can extract the (minimal) metadata from item 696048 in Digital Corpora using `hachoir-metadata`:

```
Metadata:
- Image width: 2160 pixels
- Image height: 1080 pixels
- Bits/pixel: 24
- Pixel format: RGB
- Compression rate: 6.8x
- Compression: deflate
- Producer: GraphicConverter
- Comment: DESCRIPTION: IDL TIFF file\nIgnored Tags: $010D
- MIME type: image/png
- Endianness: Big endian
```

TIFF

The Tagged Image File Format (TIFF) is an image file format used commonly in publishing and graphic design. It is the default file format for many applications on OS X, including the default screen capture utility Grab. TIFF was created originally as a unified format for scanned documents and is still common for fax and scanning applications to generate TIFF images. As the name suggests, TIFF image files support internal metadata tags. There are also extended versions of TIFF, such as Geo-TIFF (used to store geographical image data) and the Microsoft Document Imaging format used to store scanned or faxed documents. In addition, many of the "Raw" formats used as lossless storage by digital cameras are TIFF-based. Metadata from TIFF files can be processed using `exiftool`.

AUDIO

Audio files consist of data that impart sound when decoded properly. This could be music, voice mail messages, or any other sort of recorded audible material. If your case revolves around the identification and extraction of audio data, it is likely that the audio content will be of primary interest. However, audio formats can carry rich metadata that can help provide additional information relevant to your investigation.

WAV

The Waveform Audio File Format (WAV) is a standard for storing an audio bitstream originally developed by Microsoft and IBM for use on desktop PCs. WAV audio is stored as a series of tagged chunks inside of a Resource Interchange File Format (RIFF) container. The RIFF container format supports INFO chunks, which contain various metadata tags. In addition to these RIFF-specific tags, RIFF container files (like WAV audio) can contain XMP metadata.

```
user@ubuntu:~/Downloads$ hachoir-metadata mediaexample.wav
Common:
- Author: administrator
- Duration: 3 sec 299 ms
- Channel: mono
- Sample rate: 44.1 kHz
- Bits/sample: 16 bits
- Compression rate: 1.0x
- Creation date: 2005-09-26
- Compression: Microsoft Pulse Code Modulation (PCM)
- Bit rate: 705.6 Kbit/sec
- Producer: Sony Sound Forge 7.0
- MIME type: audio/x-wav
- Endian: Little endian
```

Here we can see possibly interesting metadata, such as the name of the application used to create the WAV file, as well as the "Author" and creation date.

MPEG-3/MP3

The venerable MP3 format is by and large the most popular format for digital music in use today. Originally published by the Moving Picture Experts Group (MPEG) in 1993, the MP3 format soon became the preferred format for the nascent file sharing networks such as Napster and Gnutella (formerly Kazaa). MP3 uses a lossy compression scheme based on the study of human hearing, which allows for a 1:10 compression ratio over raw digital audio data. This means a typical song will be around 5 to 6 megabytes in MP3 format. With 1990s network speeds, this reduction of file size enabled the quick transfer of songs and albums. Today, it allows even the smallest portable device to store many days worth of music.

MP3 files may contain metadata in two different formats: ID3v1 and ID3v2. ID3v1 tags are limited to an array of 128 bytes appended to the end of the MP3 file. Extended ID3v1 tags add an additional 227 bytes for use immediately prior to the ID3v1 tag. Because this provides a very limited amount of space in which to store metadata, in 1998 a replacement metadata format was created and named ID3v2. ID3v2 tags are not fixed size and may contain a much richer variety of metadata when compared to ID3v1 tags. In addition to expected metadata-like track title and artist information, ID3v2 tags can include embedded image data [2].

The `id3v2` program can be used to extract both types of ID3 tags. In addition, the `exiftool` and `hachoir-metadata` programs we have already used will also extract both forms of ID3 tags.

MPEG-4 Audio (AAC/M4A)

The Advanced Audio Coding (AAC) standard is the modern successor to the MP3 and is designed to serve a similar function. AAC files may be referred to as "MP4 Audio" or "M4A" files. AAC compressed audio is usually stored in an MPEG-4 container format. As the MP4 container can store audio, video, or both, the M4A naming and file extension is used to hint that this MP4 container holds solely audio information. MP4 video is discussed in the next section.

Examiners processing modern digital devices will very likely encounter AAC audio files. It is supported audio format on nearly every portable device in use today, from handheld game consoles to mobile phones.

AAC/M4A files may contain ID3 tags as seen in MP3 files, but may also contain a number of MP4-specific metadata tags. These tags can be retrieved using the AtomicParsley tool. While this tool can also be used to write metadata, the relevant options for metadata extraction are shown here.

```
user@forensics:~$ AtomicParsley
AtomicParlsey sets metadata into MPEG-4 files & derivatives supporting 3 tag
    schemes: iTunes-style, 3GPP assets & ISO defined copyright notifications.
AtomicParlsey quick help for setting iTunes-style metadata into MPEG-4 files.
General usage examples:
  AtomicParsley /path/to.mp4 -T 1
  AtomicParsley /path/to.mp4 -t +
  AtomicParsley /path/to.mp4 --artist "Me" --artwork /path/to/art.jpg
  Atomicparsley /path/to.mp4 --albumArtist "You" --podcastFlag true
  Atomicparsley /path/to.mp4 --stik "TV Show" --advisory explicit
Getting information about the file & tags:
  -T --test   Test file for mpeg4-ishness & print atom tree
  -t --textdata Prints tags embedded within the file
  -E --extractPix Extracts pix to the same folder as the mpeg-4 file
...
```

We will use the AtomicParsley tool to extract metadata from an archival audio file one of the authors created in 2004 using iTunes:

```
AtomicParsley Lateralus.m4a -tE
  Major Brand: M4A - version 0
  Compatible Brands: M4A mp42 isom
  Tagging schemes available:
  iTunes-style metadata allowed.
  ISO-copyright notices @ movie and/or track level allowed.
  uuid private user extension tags allowed.
---------------------------
  Track level ISO user data:
Track 1:
  No user data for this track.
---------------------------
  3GPP assets/ISO user data:
---------------------------
  iTunes-style metadata tags:
Atom "©nam" contains: Lateralus
Atom "©ART" contains: Tool
Atom "©wrt" contains: Tool
Atom "©alb" contains: Lateralus
```

```
Atom "gnre" contains: Metal
Atom "trkn" contains: 9 of 13
Atom "disk" contains: 1 of 1
Atom "@day" contains: 2001
Atom "cpil" contains: false
Atom "tmpo" contains: 0
Atom "@too" contains: iTunes v4.5
Atom "----" [iTunNORM] contains: 0000118C 000010C6 00008D88
  0000B033 0008023C 00076BA8 00007E8D 00007E8D 00013344 000280F2
Atom "----" [iTunes_CDDB_IDs] contains:
  13+6E36238CDD88E9432B0DEA4286C0B545+1295274
Atom "covr" contains: 1 piece of artwork
---------------------------
free atom space: 2048
padding available: 2048 bytes
user data space: 95707
media data space: 63408499
---------------------------
Extracted artwork to file: Lateralus_artwork_1.png
```

In addition to metadata tags and internal file structure information, we can see that using the file contained an embedded thumbnail image, which has been extracted as instructed with the `-E` argument.

> **TIP**
>
> **M4P and M4R**
> On systems where Apple's iTunes is used heavily you may find M4P and M4R files. M4P are AAC files protected by Apple's Fairplay DRM, which restricts playback on nonauthorized devices. M4R files are simply AAC files intended to be used as iPhone ringtones.

ASF/WMA

Advanced Systems Format (ASF) is Microsoft's container format designed for streaming media delivery. It is used to store Windows Media Audio (WMA) data in addition to Windows Media Video (WMV), which will be discussed in the next section. Both the ASF container and the WMA compression codecs are proprietary to Microsoft; however, both have been reverse engineered to the point where they can be played or converted using a *libavcodec*-based software such as *ffmpeg* or *Video LAN Client*. ASF containers may also hold metadata that can be extracted using `exiftool` and `hachoir-metadata`.

```
Common:
- Duration: 4 sec 878 ms
- Creation date: 2005-09-26
- Creation date: 2005-09-26 21:19:20
```

```
- Bit rate: 48.6 Kbit/sec (max)
- Comment: Engineer=administrator
- Comment: Is seekable
- MIME type: audio/x-ms-wma
- Endian: Little endian
Audio stream #1:
- Channel: mono
- Sample rate: 44.1 kHz
- Bits/sample: 16 bits
- Compression: Windows Media Audio V7 / V8 / V9
- Bit rate: 48.6 Kbit/sec
```

VIDEO

Video files contain (at the very least) data that decode into a sequence of moving images. The large majority of video files will also contain an audio component that will be synchronized to the video component. Given these two distinct components, video files are generally created in the form of a *container* file that contains one or more *streams*. The method used to compress and encode data in these streams is referred to as a *codec*. To play back the content successfully, the proper codec is required. We will discuss some specific codecs in their respective sections that follow.

Like many of the other file formats discussed, various video file formats can carry metadata with them. Example metadata can include relatively benign items such as the intended aspect ratio of the video content to more interesting information such as the date the file was created or the name of the program used to generate the file.

MPEG-1 and MPEG-2

MPEG-1 and MPEG-2 are standards for video and audio compression and transmission developed by the Moving Pictures Experts Group. MPEG-1 (sometimes simply referred to as MPG files) was used on video CDs (VCDs) in the 1990s. VCDs were popular in Asia but did not see widespread availability in the United States. MPEG-2 is the subsequent, higher quality video standard used on DVDs and digital cable and satellite transmissions. Neither of these formats carries any appreciable metadata.

MPEG-4 Video (MP4)

In addition to AAC audio, the MPEG-4 container is used to hold video content as well. MPEG-4 video files generally have an "MP4" extension. The MP4 Registration Authority maintains a list of registered codecs for streams within MP4 files. Most MP4 video files intended for playback on a variety of systems will have a video stream encoded using the MPEG-4 Advanced Video Codec (MPEG-4 AVC), which may also be referred to as H.264. The audio stream will normally be AAC, just as in MP4 audio files. Because the container is the same, metadata can be extracted from MP4 videos using `AtomicParsley` in the same manner as for MP4 audio.

AVI

Audio Video Interleave is a container format introduced in 1992 by Microsoft. Like WAV, AVI is a descendent of the RIFF format, which stores contents as "chunks" and can include an INFO chunk to store metadata. Additionally, XMP metadata can be embedded into an AVI.

An AVI file can contain video and audio streams compressed by numerous codecs. These codecs are identified using fixed sequences of four bytes called *FourCC* codes. Like the magic numbers mentioned earlier, these codes tell AVI player software the codecs necessary to decode the content properly.

As a RIFF-derived format, AVI containers can be parsed the same way as WAV files with respect to metadata extraction. For metadata extracted from a sample AVI downloaded from Microsoft's media example site, see the following.

```
Common:
- Artist: Microsoft
- Duration: 6 sec 333 ms
- Image width: 320 pixels
- Image height: 240 pixels
- Copyright: 2005 Microsoft
- Frame rate: 30.0 fps
- Bit rate: 3.7 Mbit/sec
- Comment: Has audio/video index (3176 bytes)
- MIME type: video/x-msvideo
- Endian: Little endian
Video stream:
- Duration: 6 sec 333 ms
- Image width: 320 pixels
- Image height: 240 pixels
- Bits/pixel: 24
- Compression: Radius Cinepak (fourcc:"cvid")
- Frame rate: 30.0 fps
Audio stream:
- Duration: 6 sec 333 ms
- Channel: stereo
- Sample rate: 48.0 kHz
- Bits/sample: 16 bits
- Compression rate: 1.0x
- Compression: Microsoft Pulse Code Modulation (PCM)
- Bit rate: 1.5 Mbit/sec
```

ASF/WMV

Like Windows Media Audio (WMA), Windows Media Video (WMV) is a proprietary Microsoft format for compressing video. It is stored in an ASF container and is generally accompanied by a synchronized WMA stream. Processing these files for metadata is exactly the same as processing ASF/WMV, except the output may contain some video-specific metadata.

```
Common:
- Title: support.microsoft.com
- Author: Microsoft
- Duration: 9 sec 858 ms
- Creation date: 2005-09-28 15:40:21
- Copyright: 2005 Microsoft
- Bit rate: 178.6 Kbit/sec (max)
- Comment: Is seekable
- MIME type: video/x-ms-wmv
- Endian: Little endian
Audio stream #1:
- Channel: mono
- Sample rate: 22.1 kHz
- Bits/sample: 16 bits
- Compression: 10
- Bit rate: 21.7 Kbit/sec
Video stream #1:
- Image width: 640 pixels
- Image height: 480 pixels
- Bits/pixel: 24
- Compression: Windows Media Video V9
- Bit rate: 156.8 Kbit/sec
```

MOV (Quicktime)

The QuickTime File Format is referred to more commonly by the file extension used by Apple QuickTime movies—.MOV. This format is largely superseded by the MPEG-4 format, but older QuickTime files may still be found during an investigation. QuickTime metadata can be extracted using qtinfo, part of the *quicktime-utils* package on Ubuntu. The qtinfo program implements functionality from *libquicktime*.

```
user@ubuntu:~/qt$ qtinfo sample_sorenson.mov
swScaler: Exactly one scaler algorithm must be chosen
Type: Quicktime
    copyright: © Apple Computer, Inc. 2001
    name:QuickTime Sample Movie
  1 audio tracks.
    2 channels, 16 bits, sample rate 22050, length 108544
      samples, compressor QDM2.
    Sample format: 16 bit signed.
    Channel setup: Not available
    Language: eng
    supported.
```

```
1 video tracks.
  190x240, depth 24
  rate 12.000000 [600:50] constant
  length 60 frames
  compressor SVQ1.
  Native colormodel: YUV 4:2:0 planar
  Interlace mode: None (Progressive)
  Chroma placement: MPEG-1/JPEG
  No timecodes available
  supported.
0 text tracks.
```

MKV

The Matroska Multimedia Container format is a relatively recently developed open standard, which can be used to carry audio, video, images, and subtitle tracks. Over the last half of the decade the MKV format gained widespread popularity among individuals involved in file sharing, especially file sharing of Japanese Animation videos, in part due to its ability to carry subtitles within the file.

The mkvtoolnix package contains various command line tools that can be used to manipulate, extract, and identify the streams inside a Matroska container, in addition to identifying and extracting metadata. Hachoir-metadata is aware of the MKV format and can parse out metadata as well. Like most video files, interesting information is usually limited to authorship and creation time.

Note that if you want to use GUI versions of the mkvtoolnix utilities you'll need to install the "mkvtoolnix-gui" package—the default package is console only.

ARCHIVES

Archive files are container files designed to hold other files. These containers can generally apply various compression algorithms to the contained files and may support encryption of their contents. Archive files may have a small amount of metadata, usually in the form of user-supplied notes. Many archives will retain some file system time stamps when adding files to a container. In addition, some archive types may retain information from their system of origin, including UID and GID information from Unix-like systems.

ZIP

The ZIP format is one of the older compression and archive formats still in current use. It is supported on any platform you are likely to use and doesn't appear to be in danger of fading away any time soon. ZIP archives can use numerous compression mechanisms and two forms of encryption—a weak password-based scheme defined in the original ZIP specification and the more current form, which uses AES. We can use the `unzip` command to retrieve information about the content of a ZIP archive without actually extracting. This can be good to examine file modification dates embedded in the archive.

```
user@ubuntu:~/Downloads$ unzip -v BiffView.zip
Archive: BiffView.zip
  Length Method Size Cmpr Date Time CRC-32 Name
-------- ------ ------- ---- ---------- ----- -------- ----
  2020 Defl:N 629 69% 2008-04-15 12:01 80bdeec9 xlsspec/1904.html
  477 Defl:N  306 36% 2008-06-30 15:12 f8438b88 xlsspec/404.html
  818 Defl:N  397 52% 2008-04-15 12:01 a4c4130d xlsspec/ADDIN.html
...lines removed...
  122880 Defl:N 40081 67% 2008-06-30 15:17 4c4cefa4 BiffView.exe
  16384 Defl:N 1782 89% 2008-06-30 15:16 7b4c3e2b DIaLOGIKa.
    b2xtranslator.CommonTranslatorLib.dll
  61440 Defl:N 19292 69% 2008-06-30 15:16 ca90a7d8 DIaLOGIKa.
    b2xtranslator.Spreadsheet.XlsFileFormat.dll
  36864 Defl:N 11199 70% 2008-06-30 15:16 8009c24d DIaLOGIKa.
    b2xtranslator.StructuredStorageReader.dll
  20480 Defl:N 4187 80% 2008-06-30 15:16 b33559d4 DIaLOGIKa.
    b2xtranslator.Tools.dll
--------------- ----------
  3779194  465706 88%  271 files
```

We can see here that the visible portion of the contents of this archive was last modified between April and June of 2008.

We can also examine the structure of the ZIP archive interactively with `hachoir-urwid`. For an expanded tree view showing the detail for a single entry in the archive, see Figure 8.3.

RAR

The Roshal Archive (RAR) format is a proprietary compression and archive format developed by Eugene Roshal. Key features of RAR are very good compression, archive repair and recovery capabilities, archive splitting, and in-built strong encryption. It is for all these reasons that RAR archives are the format of choice for piracy groups distributing content. RAR archives are also used frequently to exfiltrate data during computer intrusions.

We can examine the contents of RAR archives using the RAR plugin to 7zip, which can be installed on Ubuntu via the following command:

```
sudo apt-get install p7zip-rar
```

We can examine a hacking tool retrieved from packetstormsecurity.org. The "l" flag will tell `7z` to list the content of the archive.

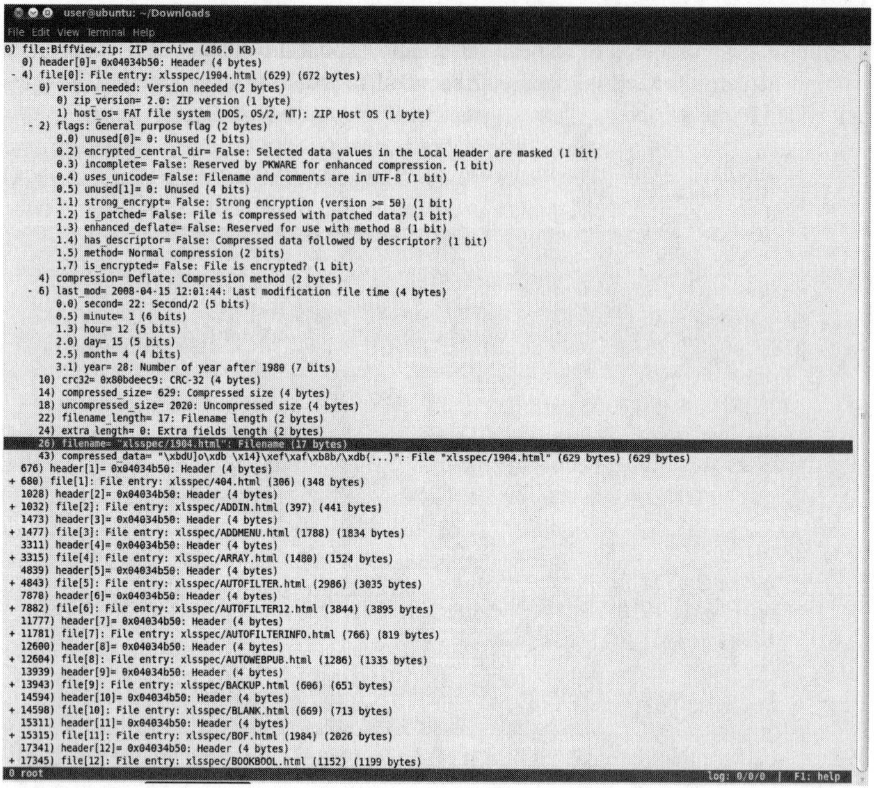

FIGURE 8.3

Hachoir-urwid examination of BiffView.zip.

```
user@ubuntu:~/Downloads$ 7z l PuttyHijackV1.0.rar
7-Zip 9.04 beta Copyright (c) 1999-2009 Igor Pavlov 2009-05-30
p7zip Version 9.04 (locale=en_US.utf8,Utf16=on,HugeFiles=on,1 CPU)
Listing archive: PuttyHijackV1.0.rar
----
Path = PuttyHijackV1.0.rar
Type = Rar
Solid = -
Blocks = 5
Multivolume = -
Volumes = 1

Date        Time Attr      Size    Compressed   Name
------------------- ----- ------------ ------------ ------------
2008-07-31  16:51:41 ....A    1775    852          PuttyHijack.txt
2008-06-20  12:51:14 ....A    9116    2908         HijackDLL.cpp
2008-06-20  12:51:46 ....A    32768   10973        HijackDLL.dll
```

```
2008-06-20  13:05:44  ....A    5221    2040      PuttyHijack.c
2008-06-20  13:05:45  ....A   32768   12578      PuttyHijack.exe
------------------- ----- ------------ ------------ ------------
                             81648   29351 5 files, 0 folders
```

We can see that the dates are all in the June/July 2008 time frame. One scenario where this information may be useful is in the case of time stamp manipulation—if this archive were found on a compromised system and the extracted copy of "PuttyHijack.exe" had a modification date in 2005, we would then have overt evidence of time stamp alteration.

Some RAR archives (especially those used to distribute pirated software) may contain comments, "NFO" files, or "greets" that can be displayed using this tool as well.

7-zip

The 7-zip (or 7z) format is an open archive and compression format that has become popular as a replacement for both ZIP and RAR's functions. It has highly efficient compression, supports strong AES encryption, and supports extremely large files. In addition, the 7-zip program is an open source and can be used to process many other archive formats on Linux, Windows, and OS X systems (among others). 7-zip can be installed on Ubuntu using the following command:

```
sudo apt-get install p7zip-full
```

7z archives generally do not hold a great deal of metadata, but they will retain the modification times of the files at the time they were archived.

TAR, GZIP, and BZIP2

On Linux systems "tarballs" are the standard method of archiving and compressing data. In true Unix spirit, archiving and compression steps are split among different tools. The tar command is used to concatenate selected files into a single, solid archive. This tar archive is then compressed, usually using the GZIP or BZIP2 compression utilities. This compressed archive is the "tarball." Modern versions of the tar command will accept flags indicating which compression to use at the time the archive is created, eliminating the need to manually compress after the fact.

One interesting artifact unique to tarballs is the fact that they retain the owner and group information from the system they were created on, in addition to the time stamp artifacts seen in other archive formats. Let's examine the "Turtle" FreeBSD rootkit as found on packetstormsecurity.org. To ensure that we don't lose any fidelity, we will unwrap the tarball in layers. First, we can look inside the compression layer at the tarball using the gunzip command:

```
user@ubuntu:~/Downloads$ gunzip --list --verbose Turtle.tar.gz
method crc date time        compressed  uncompressed ratio
  uncompressed_name
defla 9d77901e Sep 29 19:05 4403        20480 78.6% Turtle.tar
```

We can see that the tar archive was last modified on September 29th, but that is the only artifact of interest at this layer. We can now drill a step deeper, into the tar archive itself. As stated, we can pass flags to the `tar` command that indicate we need to decompress the archive prior to processing with `tar`:

```
user@ubuntu:~/Downloads$ tar --list --verbose --gunzip --file
    Turtle.tar.gz
drwxr-xr-x angelo/angelo 0 2010-09-29 15:20 turtle/
drwxr-xr-x angelo/angelo 0 2010-09-29 15:20 turtle/module/
-rw-r--r-- angelo/angelo 142 2010-09-29 09:47 turtle/README
-rwxr-xr-x angelo/angelo 321 2010-09-29 09:44 turtle/run.sh
-rwxr-xr-x root/angelo 5821 2010-09-29 15:18 turtle/module/
    turtle.ko
-rwxr-xr-x angelo/angelo 5718 2010-09-29 15:18 turtle/module/
    turtle.c
-rw-r--r-- angelo/angelo 97 2010-09-26 10:10 turtle/module/
    Makefile
```

Here we can see that files in the archive were owned by a user named "angelo," who did development work on this rootkit on at least two different dates (September 26th and 29th).

DOCUMENTS

"Document" is a relatively generic term; however, in the context of forensic file analysis, a "document" is a file type containing text, images, and rendering information. Various Microsoft Office file types and Adobe's Portable Document Format (PDF) are examples of "documents." This is the most extensive portion of the chapter because of the wide variety of document types that can be of interest during any given examination, and because of the richness of forensic data that can be retrieved from these files.

Nearly every document type carries with it some amount of metadata, ranging from authorship information and document revision histories to internal time stamps and information about the system(s) used to edit the file. During examinations performed in support of legal inquiries, these and other pieces of metadata may be crucial in authenticating a document as genuine (or not). In an intrusion-related examination, a document may contain an exploit allowing an attacker to gain control over the target system.

WARNING

Digital Trigger Discipline

When examining possibly hostile documents, treat them as you would any other piece of malicious code. The goal of a malicious document is to execute unwanted code on the system—don't let it be your examination system! Always work with hostile documents inside a virtual machine to reduce the risk of accidental compromise.

OLE Compound Files (Office Documents)

You may not be familiar with the name "OLE Compound File" but you are very likely familiar with the files that use this format. Documents created using the Microsoft Office 1997–2003 binary formats are OLE Compound files, for example, PowerPoint presentations, Word Documents (DOC), and Excel Spreadsheets (XLS). Other names for OLE compound files are "Compound Binary Files", "Compound Document Files", "Office Binary Files", or "COM Structured Storage Files".

OLE files are really tiny, dedicated, portable file systems. Like traditional file systems, they hold data in a structured manner and can also contain metadata. OLE files have two main storage concepts: *storage objects* and *stream objects*. A storage object performs the same functions as a directory on a standard file system; like a directory, it can contain additional storage objects that act as subdirectories. Stream objects are sequences of sectors allocated for a discrete piece of data. Thus, in the OLE "file system", streams take up the role of files.

An OLE file is made up of a root storage object (similar to the root directory on standard file systems) and *at least one* stream object representing the default data for the file. For example, in a Word 2003 document, this default stream object will contain the majority of the true file content. In addition to this stream object, the root storage object can contain any number of additional storage objects, each of which may contain one or more additional streams [3].

NOTE

BTK Foiled by Document Metadata

The BTK Killer claimed the lives of 10 victims from 1974 through 1991 and evaded capture for 30 years. In the end, it was metadata embedded in a Word document that led to his arrest.

"The BTK killer's last known communication with the media and police was a padded envelope which arrived at FOX affiliate KSAS-TV in Wichita on February 16, 2005. A purple, 1.44-MB Memorex floppy disk was enclosed in the package...Police found metadata embedded in a Microsoft Word document on the disk that pointed to Christ Lutheran Church, and the document was marked as last modified by "Dennis." A search of the church website turned up Dennis Rader as president of the congregation council. Police immediately began surveillance of Rader [4]."

OLE files can contain numerous pieces of metadata, including Authorship information, editorial comments, revision history, information about the amount of time spent editing a document, the username of the last user to open the document for writing, and various time stamps. We will examine a couple of tools available for extracting these data. First, we will examine the demo tools in *libforensics*. Libforensics is a Python 3.1 framework for developing computer forensics applications developed by Michael Murr. It is currently in prerelease but the demonstration tools for extracting OLE metadata are worth examining. To use libforensics, we will need to check out a current code snapshot using the *mercurial* source code control system. See the checkout request and results that follow.

```
user@ubuntu:~/source$ hg clone https://libforensics.googlecode
  .com/hg/ libforensics
requesting all changes
adding changesets
adding manifests
adding file changes
added 44 changesets with 648 changes to 423 files
updating to branch default
249 files updated, 0 files merged, 0 files removed, 0 files
  unresolved
```

We now have a copy of the libforensics source tree under our local directory "libforensics." The libforensics README says we need to copy the "lf" directory into our Python 3.1 path.

```
user@ubuntu:~/source$ cd libforensics/code
user@ubuntu:~/source/libforensics$ sudo cp -R lf /usr/lib/python3.1/
```

In the "demo" directory, numerous Python programs exist for processing different types of artifacts. We are only interested in OLE-related programs for the moment. If you recall the file system abstraction discussed in Chapter 3 and subsequent use of the Sleuth Kit utilities, the naming convention used by these utilities should be familiar. We will only be using olels.py, which lists the entries in an OLE file.

We can test this on "darknet5.doc," retrieved from Stanford University's Web site. We will execute oleps.py with the -lpr options to provide the greatest amount of information.

```
user@ubuntu:~/source/libforensics/demo$ python3.1 olels.py -lpr
  ~/Downloads/darknet5.doc
r/r 32: \x05SummaryInformation
  1601-01-01 00:00:00 1601-01-01 00:00:00 492
r/r 2: WordDocument
  1601-01-01 00:00:00 1601-01-01 00:00:00 79906
r/r 31: 1Table
  1601-01-01 00:00:00 1601-01-01 00:00:00 35816
r/r 1: Data
  1601-01-01 00:00:00 1601-01-01 00:00:00 109193
d/d 3: ObjectPool
  2002-10-16 06:30:18.586000 2002-10-16 06:30:17.845000 0
d/d 13: ObjectPool/_1089739458
  2002-10-16 06:30:17.855000 2002-10-16 06:30:17.855000 0
r/r 17: ObjectPool/_1089739458/\x03ObjInfo
  1601-01-01 00:00:00 1601-01-01 00:00:00 6
r/r 15: ObjectPool/_1089739458/\x03EPRINT
  1601-01-01 00:00:00 1601-01-01 00:00:00 114884
r/r 14: ObjectPool/_1089739458/\x0101e
  1601-01-01 00:00:00 1601-01-01 00:00:00 20
```

```
r/r 16: ObjectPool/_1089739458/\x01CompObj
   1601-01-01 00:00:00 1601-01-01 00:00:00 113
r/r 19: ObjectPool/_1089739458/VisioInformation
   1601-01-01 00:00:00 1601-01-01 00:00:00 28
r/r 18: ObjectPool/_1089739458/VisioDocument
   1601-01-01 00:00:00 1601-01-01 00:00:00 73699
r/r 20: ObjectPool/_1089739458/\x05SummaryInformation
   1601-01-01 00:00:00 1601-01-01 00:00:00 61544
r/r 21: ObjectPool/_1089739458/\x05DocumentSummaryInformation
   1601-01-01 00:00:00 1601-01-01 00:00:00 528
d/d 4: ObjectPool/_1089739296
   2002-10-16 06:30:17.855000 2002-10-16 06:30:17.845000 0
r/r 8: ObjectPool/_1089739296/\x03ObjInfo
   1601-01-01 00:00:00 1601-01-01 00:00:00 6
r/r 6: ObjectPool/_1089739296/\x03EPRINT
   1601-01-01 00:00:00 1601-01-01 00:00:00 265812
r/r 5: ObjectPool/_1089739296/\x01Ole
   1601-01-01 00:00:00 1601-01-01 00:00:00 20
r/r 7: ObjectPool/_1089739296/\x01CompObj
   1601-01-01 00:00:00 1601-01-01 00:00:00 113
r/r 10: ObjectPool/_1089739296/VisioInformation
   1601-01-01 00:00:00 1601-01-01 00:00:00 28
r/r 9: ObjectPool/_1089739296/VisioDocument
   1601-01-01 00:00:00 1601-01-01 00:00:00 101771
r/r 11: ObjectPool/_1089739296/\x05SummaryInformation
   1601-01-01 00:00:00 1601-01-01 00:00:00 61964
r/r 12: ObjectPool/_1089739296/\x05DocumentSummaryInformation
   1601-01-01 00:00:00 1601-01-01 00:00:00 504
d/d 22: ObjectPool/_1089739502
   2002-10-16 06:30:17.865000 2002-10-16 06:30:17.865000 0
r/r 26: ObjectPool/_1089739502/\x03ObjInfo
   1601-01-01 00:00:00 1601-01-01 00:00:00 6
r/r 24: ObjectPool/_1089739502/\x03EPRINT
   1601-01-01 00:00:00 1601-01-01 00:00:00 71232
r/r 23: ObjectPool/_1089739502/\x01Ole
   1601-01-01 00:00:00 1601-01-01 00:00:00 20
r/r 25: ObjectPool/_1089739502/\x01CompObj
   1601-01-01 00:00:00 1601-01-01 00:00:00 113
r/r 28: ObjectPool/_1089739502/VisioInformation
   1601-01-01 00:00:00 1601-01-01 00:00:00 28
r/r 27: ObjectPool/_1089739502/VisioDocument
   1601-01-01 00:00:00 1601-01-01 00:00:00 36441
r/r 29: ObjectPool/_1089739502/\x05SummaryInformation
   1601-01-01 00:00:00 1601-01-01 00:00:00 61828
r/r 30: ObjectPool/_1089739502/\x05DocumentSummaryInformation
   1601-01-01 00:00:00 1601-01-01 00:00:00 472
r/r 34: \x01CompObj 1601-01-01 00:00:00 1601-01-01 00:00:00 106
```

```
r/r 33: \x05DocumentSummaryInformation
  1601-01-01 00:00:00 1601-01-01 00:00:00 1912
v/v 36: $Header 0 0 0
v/v 37: $DIFAT 0 0 0
v/v 38: $FAT 0 0 0
v/v 39: $MiniFAT 0 0 0
```

Note that each stream has a date field displayed, but this information is only valid for Root and directory objects. We can see that this document was last modified October 16, 2002 at 6:30 am (UTC). We can also see that this document appears to have Visio objects embedded in it in addition to the default "WordDocument" stream, which contains the text of the document. Ole1s.py also supports generating output in the Sleuth Kit mactime format for processing into a timeline.

OLE metadata can be extracted using the wvSummary tool, which is part of the *wv* package.

```
user@ubuntu:~/Downloads$ wvSummary darknet5.doc
Metadata for darknet5.doc:
  Template = "Normal.dot"
  Security Level = 0
  Created = 2002-10-16T05:45:00Z
  Last Saved by = "paul england"
  Revision = "5"
  Last Printed = 2002-10-16T00:02:00Z
  Keywords = ""
  Subject = ""
  Generator = "Microsoft Word 10.0"
  Number of Characters = 44050
  Last Modified = 2002-10-16T06:30:00Z
  Creator = "Paul England"
  Number of Pages = 1
  msole:codepage = 1252
  Number of Words = 8067
  Description = ""
  Editing Duration = 2009-04-22T20:10:48Z
  Title = "The Darknet and the Future of Content Distribution"
  _EmailSubject = "DRM 2002 submission"
  _AuthorEmail = "pengland@exchange.microsoft.com"
  Links Dirty = FALSE
  Number of Lines = 734
  Document Parts = [(0, "The Darknet and the Future of Content
    Distribution")]
  Scale = FALSE
  Number of Paragraphs = 200
  Unknown6 = FALSE
```

```
Unknown7 = 659579
_AuthorEmailDisplayName = "Paul England"
Company = "Microsoft Corporation"
Document Pairs = [(0, "Title"), (1, 1)]
Unknown1 = 51917
_AdHocReviewCycleID = 985029792
Unknown3 = FALSE
msole:codepage = 1252
_PreviousAdHocReviewCycleID = 1239174308
```

As you can see, this document has a number of pieces of interesting metadata, including creation, modification, printing times, number of revisions, and the author's name and email address.

> **TIP**
>
> **Excel Binary Internal Structure**
> Excel binary spreadsheet files (XLS) have an additional layer of internal structure within the OLE-structured storage. The file format of the main Excel content streams is known as the "Binary Interchange File Format" or "BIFF" format. The "Book" or "Workbook" stream of an XLS will be stored in this BIFF format. The additional structures represented in the BIFF format can contain additional artifacts of forensic interest. These can be extracted and examined using `biffview`, an open source Excel-binary debugging utility, available here: http://b2xtranslator.sourceforge.net/download.html

Office Open XML

Office Open XML (OOXML) is one of two current competing open standards for editable documents (PDF, discussed later, is for fixed-layout documents). It is Microsoft's replacement for the binary, proprietary OLE compound format just discussed. Like the OLE compound format, an OOXML file is a container that holds a series of embedded files within it. The good news is, this container is the ubiquitous ZIP archive. This means that the examination techniques used against ZIP files will (for the most part) work here as well. Once we have identified and recorded the ZIP-related artifacts, we can extract the contents for examination.

We can extract the content using unzip and examine the individual pieces. To make examination of XML documents more pleasant, we will need a couple of tools out of the *xml-twig-tools* package— `xml_pp` (an XML pretty-printer) and `xml_grep` (an XML-aware grep-like tool).

```
sudo apt-get install xml-twig-tools
```

We will examine "blue_book.docx," retrieved from the Center For Disease Control's Web site (www.cdc.gov/traumaticbraininjury/pdf/blue_book.docx).

```
user@ubuntu:~/Downloads$ unzip -l blue_book.docx
Archive:  blue_book.docx
  Length      Date    Time    Name
  ------      ------   -----   ------
    2711   1980-01-01  00:00   [Content_Types].xml
     590   1980-01-01  00:00   _rels/.rels
    4112   1980-01-01  00:00   word/_rels/document.xml.rels
 2221742   1980-01-01  00:00   word/document.xml
     745   1980-01-01  00:00   word/header3.xml
     745   1980-01-01  00:00   word/header1.xml
     745   1980-01-01  00:00   word/footer3.xml
     947   1980-01-01  00:00   word/endnotes.xml
     745   1980-01-01  00:00   word/header2.xml
     745   1980-01-01  00:00   word/footer1.xml
     953   1980-01-01  00:00   word/footnotes.xml
    1720   1980-01-01  00:00   word/footer2.xml
   51676   1980-01-01  00:00   word/media/image12.emf
   12364   1980-01-01  00:00   word/media/image11.emf
   54344   1980-01-01  00:00   word/media/image10.emf
   53656   1980-01-01  00:00   word/media/image9.emf
   23756   1980-01-01  00:00   word/media/image7.emf
   32508   1980-01-01  00:00   word/media/image6.emf
    6992   1980-01-01  00:00   word/theme/theme1.xml
  152194   1980-01-01  00:00   word/media/image1.png
   53988   1980-01-01  00:00   word/media/image8.emf
   42788   1980-01-01  00:00   word/media/image2.emf
   53576   1980-01-01  00:00   word/media/image4.emf
  115076   1980-01-01  00:00   word/media/image5.png
   32108   1980-01-01  00:00   word/media/image3.emf
   13128   1980-01-01  00:00   word/settings.xml
   38445   1980-01-01  00:00   word/styles.xml
   11533   1980-01-01  00:00   word/numbering.xml
     296   1980-01-01  00:00   customXml/_rels/item1.xml.rels
     341   1980-01-01  00:00   customXml/itemProps1.xml
     218   1980-01-01  00:00   customXml/item1.xml
     836   1980-01-01  00:00   docProps/core.xml
    2675   1980-01-01  00:00   word/fontTable.xml
     260   1980-01-01  00:00   word/webSettings.xml
    2325   1980-01-01  00:00   docProps/app.xml
--------- --          -------
 2991583               35 files
```

Listing the content with unzip, we notice that the embedded time stamps are invalid. Although OOXML is using ZIP as its container, it does not store accurate time stamps for the component files because they are not needed for function of the document.

Main "metadata" are contained in "docProps/core.xml," but other artifacts may be scattered throughout the document.

```
user@ubuntu:~/Downloads/blueBook$ xml_pp docProps/core.xml
<?xml version="1.0" encoding="UTF-8" standalone="yes"?>
<cp:coreProperties xmlns:cp="http://schemas.openxmlformats.
   org/package/2006/metadata/core-properties" xmlns:dc="http://
   purl.org/dc/elements/1.1/" xmlns:dcmitype="http://purl.
   org/dc/dcmitype/" xmlns:dcterms="http://purl.org/dc/terms/"
   xmlns:xsi="http://www.w3.org/2001/XMLSchema-instance">
      <dc:title>TRAUMATIC BRAIN INJURY IN THE UNITED STATES</
         dc:title>
      <dc:subject>TBI</dc:subject>
      <dc:creator>CDC</dc:creator>
      <cp:keywords>TBI</cp:keywords>
      <dc:description></dc:description>
      <cp:lastModifiedBy>cut4</cp:lastModifiedBy>
      <cp:revision>4</cp:revision>
      <cp:lastPrinted>2010-02-03T20:19:00Z</cp:lastPrinted>
      <dcterms:created xsi:type="dcterms:W3CDTF">2010-03-
         17T15:18:00Z</dcterms:created>
      <dcterms:modified xsi:type="dcterms:W3CDTF">2010-03-
         17T15:23:00Z</dcterms:modified>
</cp:coreProperties>
```

Additional metadata may be found in the extended properties XML file, found in "docProps/app.xml." An excerpt of this file is show here:

```
user@ubuntu:~/Downloads/blueBook$ xml_pp docProps/app.xml
<?xml version="1.0" encoding="UTF-8" standalone="yes"?>
<Properties xmlns="http://schemas.openxmlformats.org/
   officeDocument/2006/extended-properties" xmlns:vt="http://
   schemas.openxmlformats.org/officeDocument/2006/docPropsVTypes">
      <Template>Normal.dotm</Template>
      <TotalTime>8</TotalTime>
      <Pages>74</Pages>
      <Words>14846</Words>
   <Characters>84623</Characters>
   <Application>Microsoft Office Word</Application>
   <DocSecurity>0</DocSecurity>
   <Lines>705</Lines>
   <Paragraphs>198</Paragraphs>
 ...
```

Be aware that any embedded files can retain any metadata you may expect to find—JPEGs can carry their EXIF information with them inside of the OOXML, for example.

OpenDocument Format

OpenDocument Format (ODF) is another open standard for editable documents similar to OOXML. It was originally developed by Sun Microsystems and is supported by a wide variety of open source programs. It is the native format of Sun's OpenOffice suite of programs. Like the OOXML format, the easiest way to examine the components that make up ODF files is to examine them as a zip archive, extract data, and examine the individual components. We can examine "open source 1-pager.odt," retrieved from the Whitehouse's Web site (http://www.whitehouse.gov/files/documents/ostp/opengov_inbox/open%20source%201-pager.odt).

The file has been renamed to "opensource.odt" on the local examination system for clarity.

```
user@ubuntu:~/Downloads$ unzip -l opensource.odt
Archive: openSource.odt
Length    Date        Time    Name
-------   ----------  -----   -----
     39   2009-04-08  19:06   mimetype
      0   2009-04-08  19:06   Configurations2/statusbar/
      0   2009-04-08  19:06   Configurations2/accelerator/current.xml
      0   2009-04-08  19:06   Configurations2/floater/
      0   2009-04-08  19:06   Configurations2/popupmenu/
      0   2009-04-08  19:06   Configurations2/progressbar/
      0   2009-04-08  19:06   Configurations2/menubar/
      0   2009-04-08  19:06   Configurations2/toolbar/
      0   2009-04-08  19:06   Configurations2/images/Bitmaps/
     22   2009-04-08  19:06   layout-cache
  18761   2009-04-08  19:06   content.xml
  23045   2009-04-08  19:06   styles.xml
   1107   2009-04-08  19:06   meta.xml
   6435   2009-04-08  19:06   Thumbnails/thumbnail.png
   7590   2009-04-08  19:06   settings.xml
   1965   2009-04-08  19:06   META-INF/manifest.xml
----------------  -----
  58964   16 files
```

Traditional metadata are found in "meta.xml," which we can view using xml_pp:

```
user@ubuntu:~/Downloads/openSourceDoc$ xml_pp meta.xml
<?xml version="1.0" encoding="UTF-8"?>
<office:document-meta office:version="1.1" xmlns:dc="http://purl.
   org/dc/elements/1.1/" xmlns:meta="urn:oasis:names:tc:opendocu
   ment:xmlns:meta:1.0" xmlns:office="urn:oasis:names:tc:opendoc
   ument:xmlns:office:1.0" xmlns:ooo="http://openoffice.org/2004/
   office" xmlns:xlink="http://www.w3.org/1999/xlink">
  <office:meta>
  <meta:generator>StarOffice/8$Solaris_Sparc OpenOffice.org_
     project/680m17$Build-9310</meta:generator>
```

```
    <meta:initial-creator>Christopher Hankin</meta:initial-creator>
    <meta:creation-date>2009-03-17T05:56:00</meta:creation-date>
    <meta:print-date>2009-03-17T09:30:38</meta:print-date>
    <meta:editing-cycles>0</meta:editing-cycles>
    <meta:editing-duration>PT7H0M0S</meta:editing-duration>
    <meta:user-defined meta:name="Info 1"/>
    <meta:user-defined meta:name="Info 2"/>
    <meta:user-defined meta:name="Info 3"/>
    <meta:user-defined meta:name="Info 4"/>
    <meta:document-statistic meta:character-count="5526"
      meta:image-count="0" meta:object-count="0" meta:page-
      count="2" meta:paragraph-count="37" meta:table-count="0"
      meta:word-count="851"/>
  </office:meta>
</office:document-meta>
```

One interesting item of note is that OpenDocument metadata include the exact build number of the application that generated the document, which could be used a secondary time signal in case of suspected backdating of a document.

Rich Text Format

Rich Text Format (RTF) is a document format developed by Microsoft intended to facilitate the transfer of documents across differing platforms. This is the native format for documents created in the Windows *Wordpad* utility and the *TextEdit* application on Mac OS X. The RTF format has been in use since 1987 and has received some significant updates as the years have progressed, including the addition of XML elements in the most recent revision. Take simple RTF document displayed in Figure 8.4 as an example.

RTF markup is fairly terse and is interspersed directly with the text being affected, so while simply viewing the raw RTF text is possible, it can be somewhat tedious for larger, more complex documents.

```
{\rtf1\ansi\ansicpg1252\cocoartf949\cocoasubrtf540
{\fonttbl\f0\fswiss\fcharset0 Helvetica;}
{\colortbl;\red255\green255\blue255;}
{\info
{\doccomm RTF comment}
{\author Ann Onymous}
{\*\copyright CC}}\margl1440\margr1440\vieww9000\viewh8400\
  viewkind0
\pard\tx720\tx1440\tx2160\tx2880\tx3600\tx4320\tx5040\tx5760\
  tx6480\tx7200\tx7920\tx8640\ql\qnatural\pardirnatural
\f0\fs24 \cf0 This is a
\b Rich
\b0
\i Text
\i0 \ul File\ulnone .}d
```

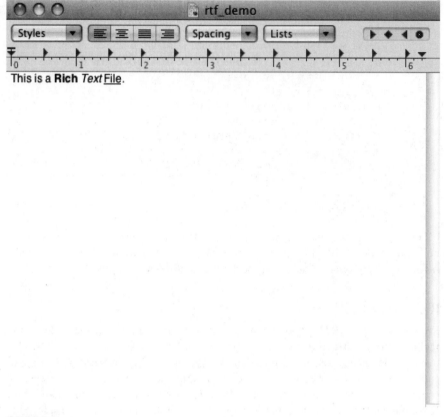

FIGURE 8.4

Simple RTF document.

In addition, because RTF natively stores its text in ASCII, non-ASCII characters are represented as escaped byte sequences in the raw RTF. This makes direct viewing of nonrendered, non-ASCII RTF files futile.

RTF metadata are contained in the body of the document itself and can be viewed directly with no additional tools.

PDF

Adobe's *Portable Document Format* is an open format designed to be a self-contained method for transmitting fixed-layout documents between systems. A PDF created on one system should present an identical rendered document on any system it is viewed upon without the user installing additional fonts, graphics libraries, or any software beyond a PDF viewer. Over the past decade, PDFs have become ubiquitous and are used for everything from standard government forms to digital magazines.

At its most basic, a PDF is container file that holds a sequence of PostScript layout instructions and embedded fonts and graphics. In addition to simply displaying document data, PDFs can contain interactive form fields, such as text input fields and checkboxes. This enables PDFs to be used in place of traditional paper forms used for clerical tasks. Over the years, the type of content that can be stored in a PDF has grown and now includes links to external content, JavaScript, and Flash movie objects. During the time period in which this book was written, malicious PDFs were one of the primary vectors for desktop system compromises.

PDFs can contain two different types of metadata. The *Document Information Directory* contains key/value pairs with authorship information, document title, and creation/modification time stamps. Modern PDFs support the *Extensible Metadata Platform* (XMP) method of storing metadata, which you may recall is also used to store metadata in some graphic file formats.

Exiftool can be used to extract metadata from PDF files. We will work with item 025835 from Digital Corpora in the following examples.

```
exiftool digitalcorpora/025/025835.pdf
ExifTool Version Number    : 8.15
File Name                  : 025835.pdf
Directory                  : digitalcorpora/025
File Size                  : 409 kB
File Modification Date/Time : 2008:12:29 10:50:01-08:00
File Permissions           : r--r--r--
File Type                  : PDF
MIME Type                  : application/pdf
PDF Version                : 1.6
XMP Toolkit                : Adobe XMP Core 4.0-c316 44.253921,
                             Sun Oct 01 2006 17:14:39
Metadata Date              : 2008:12:29 13:50:01-05:00
Creator Tool               : Adobe InDesign CS (3.0.1)
Format                     : application/pdf
Document ID                : uuid:c8670dad-5726-4376-a186-
                             3e33d82a2d90
Instance ID                : uuid:61f43463-8ce2-4f88-93b5-
                             605851bc842a
Page Count                 : 4
Create Date                : 2007:09:26 10:33:57-04:00
Creator                    : Adobe InDesign CS (3.0.1)
Producer                   : Adobe PDF Library 6.0
Modify Date                : 2008:12:29 13:50:01-05:00
Title                      : ASK28_Inside_24231e.indd
```

Of particular interest are the embedded dates and the Creator/Producer tags. Many malicious PDF files will be created with various command line tools that set the Creator/Producer tags to their name. An emailed PDF that purports to be a global trade report about emerging markets that has "pypdf" as the creator is *probably* not legitimate.

If a PDF is created via one of the interactive PDF creation utilities (such as Adobe InDesign), a history of changes to the document may be recorded. These changes can provide interesting data if extracted, including dates and times of changes. In addition, it may be possible to extract older versions of a PDF. This can be of interest when a document is redacted prior to publication—older versions of the document may contain the nonredacted information.

To examine a PDF for historical versions, we can use the `pdfresurrect` tool, which is installed easily on Ubuntu via `apt-get`. The tool accepts four flags:

- **-i** will display verbose historical information
- **-w** writes each recoverable version of the document out to disk
- **-q** displays the total number of versions present
- **-s** scrubs the historical data from the document

Again examining 025835 from Digital Corpora, we can determine if any older versions are present:

```
pdfresurrect -q 025835.pdf
025835.pdf: 8
```

We can list more information about these versions with `-i`. Because this is quite verbose, we will use `grep ModDate` to restrict output to just the modification dates of each revision.

```
pdfresurrect -i 025835.pdf | grep ModDate
ModDate: (D:20070926103434-04'00')
ModDate: (D:20081229134840-05'00')
ModDate: (D:20081229134904-05'00')
ModDate: (D:20081229134912-05'00')
ModDate: (D:20081229134925-05'00')
ModDate: (D:20081229134934-05'00')
ModDate: (D:20081229134947-05'00')
ModDate: (D:20081229135001-05'00')
```

Note the recorded change in relative time zone from the September 2007 creation to the December 2008 modifications. Further analysis could include extracting the revisions out and comparing the different versions visually.

To assist in the diagnosis and analysis of potentially malicious PDF files, Didier Stevens has created two Python utilities: `pdfid.py` and `pdf-parser.py`. `Pdfid.py` is a high-level scanner that looks for functionality used frequently in malicious PDFs, whereas `pdf-parser.py` will parse and display the building blocks of a PDF for further examination. A treatise on the analysis of malicious PDF documents is outside of the scope of this book, but Didier has produced an excellent guide, which is freely available at http://didierstevens.com/files/data/malicious-pdf-analysis-ebook.zip.

Origami is another set of useful utilities geared toward analyzing (and creating) malicious PDF documents. It has an optional graphical interface that can be used to explore the structure of a PDF document interactively.

Origami is written in Ruby and is currently hosted in a Mercurial repository on Google Project Hosting. We can check out the most recent revision of the code with the following command:

```
hg clone https://origami-pdf.googlecode.com/hg/ origami-pdf
```

The GUI interface is stored in the "walker" directory. Because the GUI is built around the GIMP Toolkit version 2 (GTK2), we need to install Ruby-GTK2 bindings. Additionally, the core origami libraries require OpenSSL bindings. We can install both using apt-get on an Ubuntu system.

```
sudo apt-get install libgtk2-ruby libopenssl-ruby
```

> **TIP**
> **Ruby Gems**
> The Ruby-GTK2 and OpenSSL bindings can also be installed using the Ruby gems package manager if you don't want to use the native system package manager or are attempting to install on a system without native package management.

Figure 8.5 examines one of the sample PDF documents included with the Origami suite, a cross-platform command launcher example (calc.pdf).

FIGURE 8.5

Examining malicious PDF sample with Origami.

SUMMARY

This chapter examined artifacts present in various image files, audio files, video containers, archives, and document formats. Because of the transient nature of these files, they have the capability of retaining information about the systems they are created or modified on even as they pass from host to host or volume to volume. Careful examination of artifacts contained within file formats can be the key that ties a remote user or system to the activity of interest.

References

[1] Multimedia: "Comparing JPEG Quantization Tables"—Computer Forensic Blog. http://computer.forensikblog.de/en/2007/12/comparing_jpeg_quantization_tables.html.

[2] History—ID3.org. http://www.id3.org/History.

[3] Microsoft Corporation (2007). Windows Compund Binary File Format Specification. [Document]. http://download.microsoft.com/download/0/B/E/0BE8BDD7-E5E8-422A-ABFD-4342ED7AD886/WindowsCompoundBinaryFileFormatSpecification.pdf.

[4] The BTK Killer—Wichita, Kansas—American Serial Killers. http://americanserialkillers.com/articles/the-btk-killer-wichita-kansas/, 2006.

Automating Analysis and Extending Capabilities

INFORMATION IN THIS CHAPTER

- Graphical Investigation Environments
- Automating Artifact Extraction
- Timelines

INTRODUCTION

If you have been working straight through this book, you should be able to perform a successful examination using only the tools and techniques discussed in the previous chapters. This chapter focuses on expanding your analytical capabilities in two distinct ways. First, we examine tools that build upon the programs and concepts from the previous chapters and, in doing so, provide additional benefit to the examiner. These benefits include a more integrated working environment, collaboration possibilities, extended searching and filtering capabilities, and automation. The second part of the chapter deals with extended concepts of temporal analysis. Because timeline generation and analysis are such an integral part of many forensic examinations, it is imperative to have a good understanding of how to extract more meaning from time data.

GRAPHICAL INVESTIGATION ENVIRONMENTS

Many of the tools examined in previous chapters are command line or console based, which can be a tremendous advantage in various scenarios and provide a great deal of flexibility. However, some workflows are better suited to a graphical environment. Advantages of using a graphical examination platform include integrated case management, built-in keyword searching, and greater continuity when examining between the various file system layers. The prime example of the open source graphical forensic environment is the venerable *Autopsy* browser, created by Brian Carrier as a visual front end to the Sleuth Kit tools. The Autopsy browser does not provide any capabilities above and beyond those provided by the command line Sleuth Kit tools but does provide a more comfortable environment for examiners who are primarily GUI users. The next two sections discuss two graphical investigation environments that do provide a host of additional examination capabilities: PyFLAG and the Digital Forensics Framework.

PyFLAG

PyFLAG is the Python-based Forensics and Log Analysis GUI created by Michael Cohen and David Collett to support unified examination of disparate data types often encountered in modern forensic examinations [1]. Because PyFLAG is a Web-based, database-backed application, a user generally just needs a Web browser to perform an examination. Being a Web/database application gives PyFLAG several advantages over more traditional forensic utilities, which tend to be single-user/single-computer bound. A PyFLAG instance can support multiple users on a single case or multiple users working on different cases in parallel. As any examiner can tell you, when it rains, it pours, so having the ability to scale up the number of examiners that can work on a given case at one time can be incredibly valuable. In addition to the server model, PyFLAG has some other features that make it an interesting tool for an examiner using open source tools.

Virtual File System

Much like the unified file system concept common to Unix and Linux systems (as discussed in Chapter 5), PyFLAG features a unified Virtual File System (VFS) for all objects under examination. PyFLAG refers to each of these items as *inodes*. Each item loaded into the PyFLAG database receives a PyFLAG inode, in addition to the internal file system metadata address it may already have. This means that any number of file system images, network traffic captures, standalone log files, and even streams of unstructured data may be loaded under the same virtual root and subsequently processed with PyFLAG.

Additionally, as an examination using PyFLAG proceeds it is not uncommon to discover nested files (such as files inside of archives, or files recovered via carving or extracted from a network packet capture). These nested files will be allocated a PyFLAG inode chained under their parent item. These chained inodes will be indicated by a pipe character (|).

Scanners

PyFLAG's scanners are discrete modules with a specific task. A scanner will run over objects loaded into the VFS and perform a function. For example, the PstFile.py scanner will run over inodes loaded into the VFS, determine if they are an Outlook PST, and process them accordingly. This processing populates the VFS with inodes referencing any discovered discrete items inside of the PST, which are then rescanned with any additional loaded scanners. Using discrete scanners coupled with the inode creation and nesting mentioned earlier can enable an examiner to fairly rapidly gain deep knowledge of the true contents of the file system in question.

SQL Queries

The bulk of the PyFLAG GUI is simply a front end to submitting SQL queries to the back-end database, and then formatting and displaying the results. One nice aspect of this division is that the database can be queried and manipulated directly, without the necessity of the browser. Indeed, many of the more advanced functions of PyFLAG require direct database interaction.

If you are not familiar with SQL queries, however, PyFLAG should still be usable and may, in fact, assist you in learning SQL. On each set of responses displayed by the PyFLAG GUI that are results of a SQL query, there will be a "SQL Used" Icon that resembles a hand holding some traditional database icons. Clicking this will display the SQL query the GUI issued to the database to generate the page in question.

Additionally, PyFLAG uses SQL to do all of its display filtering. In any of the filtering dialogues, you can enter SQL directly or you can use the provided "helper" functions that display available tables and operators.

Keyword Searching and Indexing

PyFLAG does not offer "on demand" keyword scanning. This isn't necessarily a shortcoming, as performing a full file system scan for each keyword is incredibly time-consuming on large file systems. Instead, PyFLAG offers indexed searching. PyFLAG builds an index based on a dictionary file, which allows for very fast searching. However, it only builds this index when a new source is loaded into a case. As the PyFLAG dictionary is empty after installation, this effectively means that unless the examiner takes steps to set up a dictionary, keyword searching won't be possible.

The PyFLAG FAQ contains a handy set of commands to populate the index with a large number of keywords sourced from the wordlist file included for spellcheck support on most Linux distributions:

```
~/pyflag$ grep -E ...+ /usr/share/dict/words > keywords.txt
~/pyflag$ pyflag_launch ./utilities/load_dictionary.py
   keywords.txt
```

This retrieves all three-letter or longer words and loads them into the PyFLAG database. Note that this technique can be extended to load any arbitrary set of keywords for indexing.

Carving and Advanced Carving

PyFLAG supports file carving in a fairly novel way, through use of the VFS. Using simple header/footer signature carving, PyFLAG carvers generate VFS inodes corresponding to the location and run length of the corresponding hit. The only overhead from carving is the time and cycles required to perform the carving rather than the heaps of disk space required for a standard carving operation. Additionally, PyFLAG carvers will run over all inodes present in the VFS, to include inodes generated by scanners. Given this, it is possible to extract embedded files from within archives without performing the intermediary extraction and decompression phases out to disk.

PyFLAG also supports a handful of advanced carvers that use built-in knowledge of the file structures they are carving. The three advanced carvers currently supplied with PyFLAG are for PDFs, JPEGs, and ZIP archives.

Log Analysis

As the name belies, PyFLAG is equally intended to be used for log analysis as well as file system forensic analysis. Because logs entries are stored in the PyFLAG database and are indexed in the same manner as all other content, keyword searches across the database will produce log results in addition to file system results. PyFLAG currently has native knowledge of the Windows binary event log format, IIS logs, Apache Logs, and Linux IPTables logs, but also supports generating log templates based on a source log file.

Network and Memory Forensics Support

While an exploration of these capabilities is outside the scope of this book, it is important to be aware that one of PyFLAG's greatest strengths is its ability to intelligently parse various application-layer networking protocols. Network protocols currently supported in PyFLAG include HTTP Web traffic, SMTP and POP mail transfer, IRC chat, and VOIP telephony.

PyFLAG also interfaces with the Volatility framework, an open source framework for performing forensic analysis memory images from Windows and Linux systems. Items recovered from network or memory captures will be populated into the VFS and can be processed further using any of the appropriate scanners.

An excellent walkthrough of performing a unified investigation using PyFlag is available in Michael Cohen and AAron Walters' write up from the 2008 Digital Forensics Research Workshop Forensics challenge [2]. To demonstrate basic usage of PyFLAG for file system forensic analysis, we will install the application and explore some of the features available using Lance Mueller's first Forensic Practical Image, available at http://www.lancemueller.com/blog/evidence/WinXP2.E01.

Installation

PyFLAG installation is a bit more involved than many of the other packages we have used up to this point. It has many components and is not currently included in any package management systems. In addition, the most recent version is only available via the *darcs* source code management system. We will need to start out by making sure we have all the dependencies required for PyFLAG's operation. The install document (available online at http://www.pyflag.net/pyflag/INSTALL or with the PyFLAG source) states the following packages are required and handily provides the Debian/Ubuntu package names:

- build environment (build-essential)
- python dev files (python-dev)
- libz (libz-dev)
- libmagic (libmagic-dev)

- MySQLdb (python-mysqldb)
- PIL (python-imaging)
- pexpect (python-pexpect)
- dateutil (python-dateutil)
- urwid (python-urwid)

Additionally, we will need the "mysql-server," "python-sqlite," and "python-pyparsing" packages. We have some of these already, but requesting them again will not hurt anything, so we can install all of these (and their dependencies, and so on) in one shot with the following command:

```
sudo apt-get install build-essential python-dev libz-dev
  libmagic-dev python-mysqldb python-imaging python-pexpect
  python-dateutil python-urwid mysql-server python-sqlite
  python-p6
```

PyFLAG can provide additional, optional functionality if the following packages are installed:

- geoip (libgeoip-dev) for Maxmind GeoIP support
- libjpeg (libjpeg62-dev) for Advanced JPEG Carving support
- afflib for AFF image support
- libewf for EWF (Encase E01) image support
- clamd (clamav-daemon) for Virus Scanning support

Because we installed AFFLIB and LibEWF from source in Chapter 2, we can skip these and only install the other packages using:

```
sudo apt-get install libgeoip-dev libjpeg62-dev clamav-daemon
```

With all the prerequisites installed, we can fetch the current development branch of the PyFLAG source code. PyFLAG uses `darcs` revision control software. If you don't have this installed, you can rectify this with `apt-get`. We can fetch a copy of the current source to work with using the following command:

```
darcs get --partial http://www.pyflag.net/pyflag
```

Once the command completes we will have a new directory named *pyflag* in our current directory. We will need to move into this directory and execute the included "`autogen.sh`," which will set up the build environment.

```
sh autogen.sh
```

This will create the configure script and associated files, so once this is completed a standard build will complete the process:

```
./configure
make
sudo make install
```

TIP

PyFLAG Windows Installation

The PyFLAG project provides a set of instructions on how to get PyFLAG up and running on Windows, as well as pointers to the requisite packages at the following URL: http://www.pyflag.net/cgi-bin/moin.cgi/PyFlagWindows.

The next step is to start up PyFLAG.

```
user@ubuntu:~/source/pyflag$ sudo pyflag
Checking schema for compliance
31172(Warning): Error: Unable to connects - does the DB Exist?:
  (1049, "Unknown database 'pyflag'")
31172(Warning): Error: Unable to connects - does the DB Exist?:
  (1049, "Unknown database 'pyflag'")
31172(Infomation): Serving PyFlag requests on
  http://127.0.0.1:8000
```

Note that the errors are completely normal—the "pyflag" database does not exist the first time you run PyFLAG. Setting this up is the first thing we have to do.

Once we open a Web browser and navigate to the provided URL, we will be prompted to initialize the database. If we check the "Upgrade the database?" box and click Submit, PyFLAG will build the "pyflag" database using the appropriate schema.

Before continuing further, we need to confirm (and possibly change) some PyFLAG configuration data. There are two primary configuration directives of concern: *uploaddir* and *resultdir*. These determine where PyFLAG looks for input files and where it places output files. Because PyFLAG will not be able to read or write to the file system outside of these directories, ensure that they exist and make sure to place any data you plan on analyzing with PyFLAG in the *uploaddir* directory.

TIP

PyFLAG Tuning

If you plan on using PyFLAG for processor and memory intensive tasks, you may find the default settings too restrictive. If you are running PyFLAG on a large machine, experiment with these values for performance increases.
- maximum_worker_memory
- workers
- job_queue
- job_queue_poll

Usage

Once the database is created and our configuration options are acceptable, the next step is to start a new case (Case Management -> New Case). Give your case a memorable name and click Submit.

Next, we will need to add an image file to process using PyFLAG. Select Load Data -> Load IO Data Source. You should see the screen shown in Figure 9.1.

Using our example image shown in Figure 9.1, we will select "EWF" as the IO Subsystem. After hitting Submit, we see the screen in Figure 9.2. Note that PyFLAG performs some preliminary analysis of the loaded data, hinting at the content in the red highlighted text.

Because this is a file system image, we will select "Sleuthkit" as the file system type. This tells PyFLAG what driver to use to analyze the structure of the data source we are loading. Before proceeding, we will need to provide a VFS Mount Point for the data source. This is like creating a mount point when mounting a volume on a Linux system. We can put whatever we would like here, but it is best to choose something relevant to the source material, such as "WinXP2."

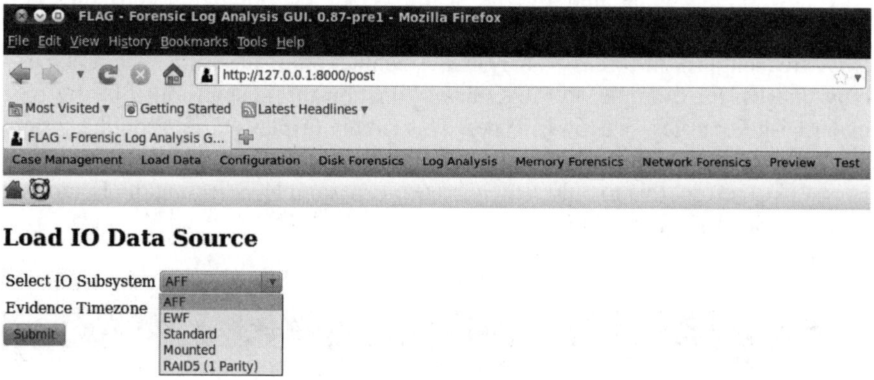

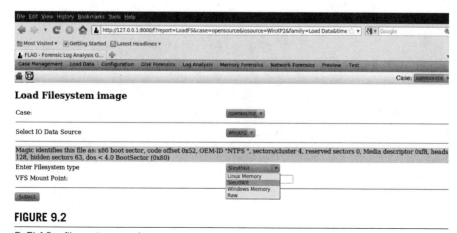

FIGURE 9.1

PyFLAG—adding an image file.

FIGURE 9.2

PyFLAG—file system parsing.

Once the file system driver loads, you should get a file browser view similar to Figure 9.3.

From here we can browse through the file system using the GUI, export files, and so on. Before we do that, though, we can exercise some of PyFLAG's more interesting capabilities. Selecting Load Data -> Scan Filesystem takes us to the screen shown in Figure 9.4.

This is the main configuration panel that determines which scanners are run against the VFS (or a subsection defined under the "Scan Files" entry). Each entry shown is a category, and clicking on the tool icon to the left of each lets an examiner drill down and enable or disable specific scanners. Once we are done setting which scanners we want, we can click "Submit" to kick off the scanning process. This yields the display seen in Figure 9.5.

After scanning is complete, you are returned to the file system browser. Any new inodes generated by the scanner will be populated into the VFS automatically.

A frequent task in forensic analysis is examination of files of a specific type—only images, for example. PyFLAG has a function that displays all files by type under Disk Forensics -> Browse Types. This simply displays all files on the system for which a type was able to be determined. We can utilize the filtering capabilities of PyFLAG to restrict this to only JPEG images, for example. Selecting the Filter icon brings up the page shown in Figure 9.6.

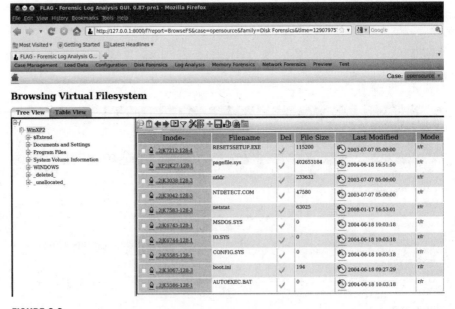

FIGURE 9.3

PyFLAG—file system browsing.

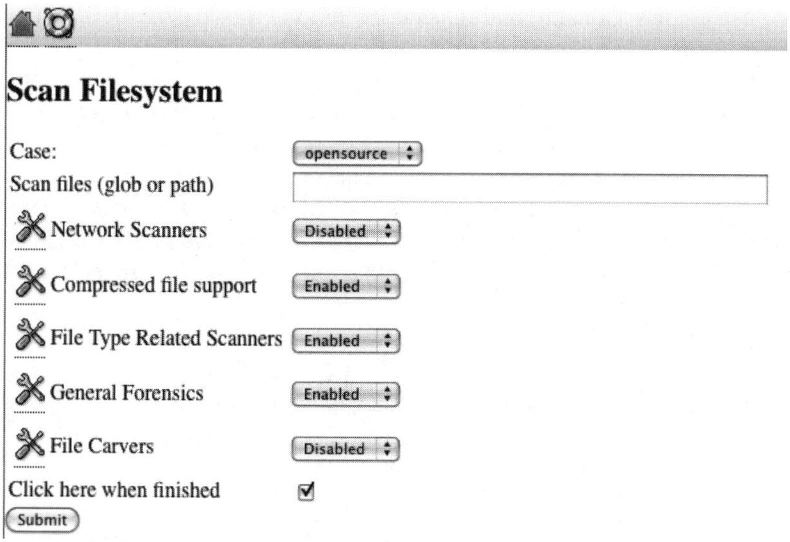

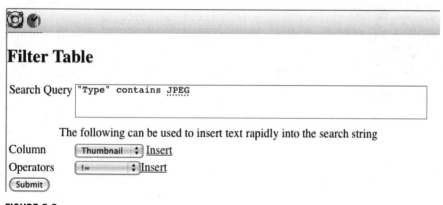

FIGURE 9.4

PyFLAG file system scanners.

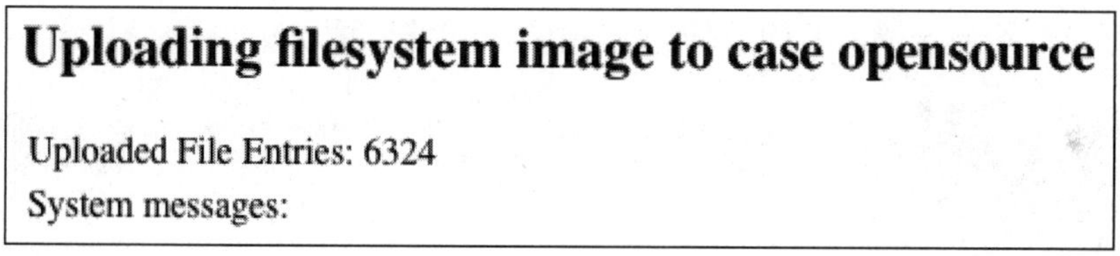

FIGURE 9.5

PyFLAG scanner progress.

FIGURE 9.6

PyFLAG filtering.

We can use the "Column" and "Operators" drop-downs to generate a Filter without knowing any SQL. Simply select the column or operator of interest, position the cursor in the Search Query field, and select "Insert." When the query is completed, click "Submit." See Figure 9.7 for a subset of the resulting JPEG-only output.

PyFLAG has another method for viewing files of a specific type under Disk Forensics -> Feeling Lucky. These are canned sets of queries useful for retrieving specific sets of data. In Figure 9.8, this was used to retrieve all graphics files from the file system.

As mentioned before, we can use the "SQL Used" button to force PyFLAG to "show its work," so to speak. The segment that follows is the SQL statement used in the graphics query in Figure 9.8.

```
select inode.inode_id as 'Thumbnail','inode'.'size' as
   'Size',file.link, concat(file.path,file.name) as 'Filename' from
   'inode' join 'file' on 'inode'.inode_id = 'file'.inode_id where
   ((1) and (( 'inode'.'inode_id' in (select inode_id from type
   where type like '%image%')) and 'inode'.'size' > '20000'))
   order by 'inode'.'size' desc
```

Note that this is but a small sampling of what you can do with PyFLAG. Many more extensive tutorials are available on the PyFLAG wiki.

FIGURE 9.7

PyFLAG—JPEG filtering results.

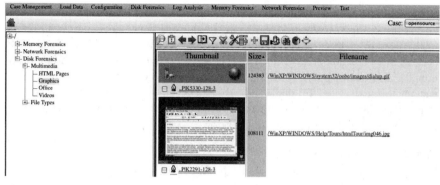

FIGURE 9.8

PyFLAG—all images search.

Digital Forensics Framework

ArxSys's Digital Forensics Framework (DFF) is a relative newcomer to the world of forensic GUIs, but it appears to be receiving a lot of active development at a fairly rapid pace [3]. At this time it does not have many of the features present in PyFLAG, but it does present a somewhat cleaner GUI and is quite simple to build and install on Linux, OS X, and Windows. In addition, it is quite extensible via scripts and plugins so a sufficiently skilled examiner can overcome any shortcomings that are discovered.

Virtual File System

Much like PyFLAG, DFF also creates a Virtual File System under which all subsequent items are loaded. DFF refers to unique items as *nodes*. The core of the DFF application is tasked with handling the creation of VFS nodes in memory. All display tasks are handled by a GUI layer, and populating nodes with data is handled by modules. The Virtual File System is viewed as a tree structure in the DFF GUI, with all nodes appearing as children under the root (/) or as children of other nodes.

Modules and Scripts

DFF modules are similar to PyFLAG's scanners. A module performs a discrete task and populates a node with the output of that task. The current version of DFF (0.8 at the time of this writing) comes with many modules that perform various tasks, including processing cell phone memory dumps, performing hash comparisons, viewing movies and images, and generating statistics about a node or set of nodes. Because all "analysis tasks" in DFF are performed via modules, the exposed application programming interface (API) has a great deal of functionality available. Additional modules can be written in C++ or Python. In addition, scripts can be generated on the fly using the built-in Python scripting engine.

GUI and Command-Line Capabilities

One of the strongest features of the Digital Forensics Framework is the clean, simple GUI. The familiar three-pane layout is a paradigm used by many GUI applications so even a novice should not have much trouble getting oriented in the application. Additionally, all functions performed via modules from the GUI can also be performed via the DFF shell. The DFF shell can be launched from within the GUI or can be used standalone. This allows the examiner to use the same tool whether she is connecting via a remote shell or sitting at a local desktop.

Installation and Prerequisites

DFF is available via a binary installer package for most Linux distributions and Windows and can be compiled from source on Windows, Linux, and OS X systems. In this example, we compile DFF 0.8.0 from source.

As always, first we need to install the program's dependencies. DFF's GUI is based on the QT4 library, so we will need to install a host of packages related to this. The following command will get us all the packages we need to build DFF successfully.

```
user@ubuntu:~$ sudo apt-get install swig1.3 cmake python-qt4-
   dev pyqt4-dev-tools qt4-qmake libqt4-dev libqscintilla2-5
   libqscintilla2-dev python-qscintilla2 python-magic python-
   qt4-phonon
```

DFF uses the cmake build system, so to start the process off we run "cmake" in the DFF's unpacked source directory.

```
user@ubuntu:~/source/dff-0.8-src$ cmake .
```

This will generate the makefiles we need to compile. Once complete, we can run make and then make install.

```
user@ubuntu:~/source/dff-0.8-src$ make
...
user@ubuntu:~/source/dff-0.8-src$ sudo make install
```

Usage

We will use the same image as before to explore the usage of DFF (WinXP2.E01). At this point, DFF does not support Expert Witness Format images; however, as demonstrated in Chapter 2, we can create a virtual mount point for the EWF container and expose the content as a "raw" image, which DFF can process using the following series of commands.

First we'll create a mount point for the container:

```
user@ubuntu:~$ mkdir ~/mnt
user@ubuntu:~$ mkdir ~/mnt/ewf
```

Next we will mount the EWF container:

```
user@ubuntu:~$ mount_ewf.py ~/images/WinXP2.E01 ~/mnt/ewf/
Using libewf-20100226. Tested with libewf-20080501.
```

Finally, we can confirm a proper mount by listing the directory we mounted the EWF to:

```
user@ubuntu:~$ ls -lath /home/user/mnt/ewf/
total 2.0G
drwxr-xr-x 3 user user 4.0K 2010-11-26 09:26 ..
dr-xr-xr-x 2 root root 0 1969-12-31 16:00 .
-r--r--r-- 1 root root 2.0G 1969-12-31 16:00 WinXP2
-r--r--r-- 1 root root 284 1969-12-31 16:00 WinXP2.txt
```

With this set up, we can start up DFF. We will pass the "-g" argument to tell DFF to start the GUI—without this flag, DFF defaults to shell operation.

```
user@ubuntu:~$ dff -g
```

Once the GUI comes up, the first thing we need to do is have it read in our image file. To do so, we will select "Add Dump" from the File menu (Figure 9.9). DFF uses "Dump" to refer to a bitstream image of a device, as opposed to a physical device.

After browsing to and opening our FUSE-mounted image file (/home/user/mnt/ewf/WinXP2 in our example), we get Figure 9.10. Note that adding the dump did just that, nothing more. We need to tell DFF to process the dump file further.

We can examine the attributes of the file on the right to determine that it is an NTFS volume. To process the NTFS structures in the dump, we can select Modules -> File System -> NTFS (Figure 9.11).

The NTFS parsing module has a few configurable options, as seen in Figure 9.12. Optional fields are off by default—the checkbox to the right enables editing them.

We provide a name for the node we are creating with this module (/WinXP2) and hit "OK." The Task Manager pane at the bottom of the window should provide

FIGURE 9.9

DFF adding image file.

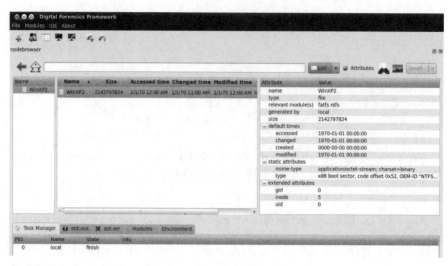

FIGURE 9.10

DFF raw image view.

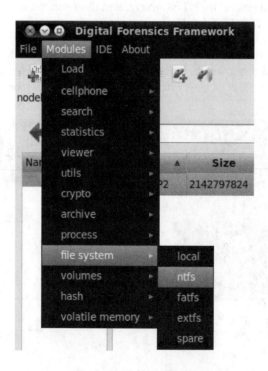

FIGURE 9.11

DFF NTFS parser.

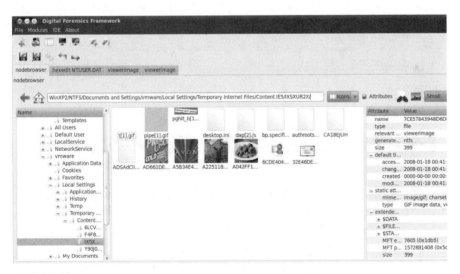

FIGURE 9.12

DFF NTFS parsing options.

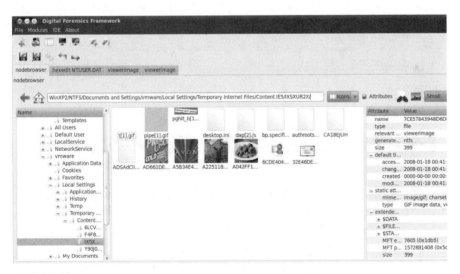

FIGURE 9.13

DFF file system browsing.

a status update as the NTFS processing tasks proceed. Once completed, we are presented with a standard tree file browsing structure, which we can use to examine the file system interactively. For an example of navigating DFF using the thumbnail view, see Figure 9.13.

One of the interesting modules included in DFF is the Fileschart module (Modules -> Statistics -> Fileschart). This performs cursory file analysis of all nodes and displays a graphical overview of the types of files present in the VFS (Figure 9.14).

DFF also includes a carving module. Currently the carving mechanism used is a simple header search, and the types of files supported are fairly limited. Figure 9.15 shows an active file carving process.

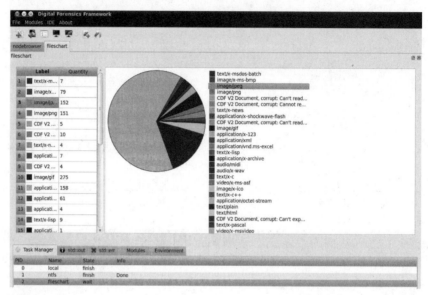

FIGURE 9.14

DFF file type statistics.

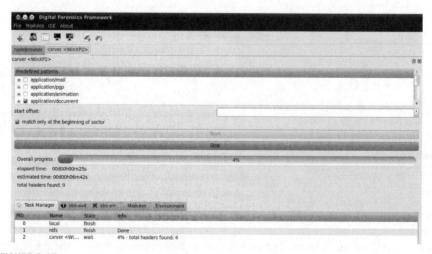

FIGURE 9.15

DFF carving.

Carved files will be added to the VFS under the node they were found in under a new directory named "carved" (Figure 9.16).

DFF contains a number of native viewer modules—an image viewer for graphics files, a movie player for video files, and a text viewer for text files. Unknown or binary files will be displayed using the hexedit module. Among hexedit modules features is the ability to search the file content for hexadecimal, ASCII, or Unicode strings. In Figure 9.17 we searched for "hbin" in the Adminstrator's NTUSER.DAT file and received 91 results. Clicking on the address of each results in the Offset pane in the lower right will jump to that hit.

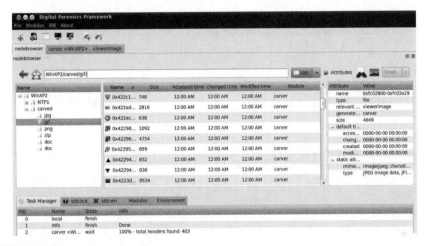

FIGURE 9.16

DFF-carved files.

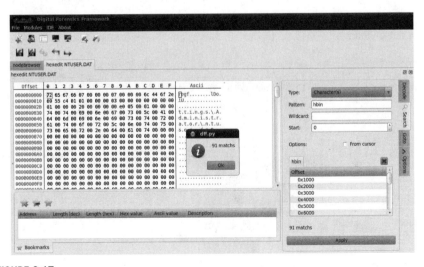

FIGURE 9.17

DFF Hex Editor search.

TIP

Hexedit View for Any File

While double clicking a binary or uncategorized file will use the hexedit module as the viewer for that file, you can use open any file with the hexedit module via the right-click context menu.

The hexedit module also allows the user to highlight and bookmark selected segments of data. In Figure 9.18 we have highlighted and bookmarked a registry key of interest.

The DFF unzip module (under archive) allows an examiner to examine the contents of a zip archive without extracting data first. In Figure 9.19 we launched the

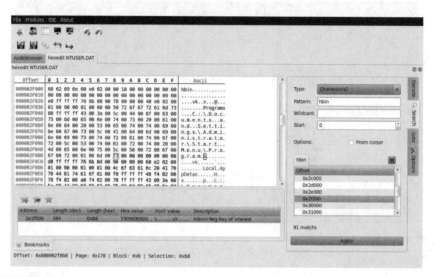

FIGURE 9.18

DFF bookmarking.

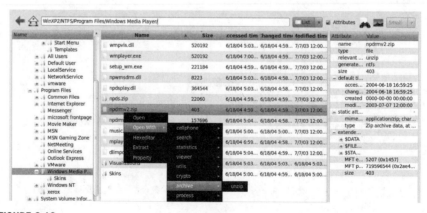

FIGURE 9.19

DFF unzip module.

FIGURE 9.20

DFF zip content view.

unzip module by right clicking on a Zip archive and selecting the "unzip" module from the context menu.

The archive content is added as a child node of the Zip archive under the VFS. We can now navigate down into the archive and examine the content, including the embedded time stamp (shown in Figure 9.20).

AUTOMATING ARTIFACT EXTRACTION

One of the constant challenges of forensic analysis is the amount of setup required before true analysis can be performed. If you are simply looking to identify and extract a specific file type, you still need to identify the partitions on image, identify the file systems, access their contents, locate files in question, and so on. The majority of this preliminary work is not interesting and not directly relevant to the purpose of the exam. The goal of automating artifact extraction is to reduce the amount of setup required before real work can begin.

Fiwalk

Fiwalk is a library and suite of related programs designed to automate much of the initial file system analysis performed during a forensic examination [4]. The name comes from "file & inode walk," which is effectively what the program does. Fiwalk's output is a mapping of a disk's file systems and contained files, including embedded file metadata if requested. The goal of the fiwalk project is to provide a standardized XML description language for the contents of a forensic image file and to enable more rapid processing of forensic data.

Because fiwalk inherits file system analysis capabilities from the Sleuth Kit, it is able to support any partition, volume, and file system structures the Sleuth Kit is capable of reading. In addition to its standard XML output, fiwalk can provide output in human-readable text, Sleuth Kit bodyfile format, the ARFF format used by the open-source Weka data mining system, and plain CSV for import into a spreadsheet program.

We can demonstrate the use of fiwalk by using it to generate a Forensic XML document describing the content of the ubnist1.casper-rw.gen3.aff file from Digital Corpora.

```
fiwalk -X ubnist1.gen3.xml ubnist1.casper-rw.gen3.aff
```

The resulting output is a 2.1-Megabyte XML document containing 2533 "fileobject" elements. An example fileobject element (for /etc/hosts) is shown here.

```
<fileobject>
  <filename>etc/hosts</filename>
  <partition>1</partition>
  <id>65</id>
  <name_type>r</name_type>
  <filesize>243</filesize>
  <alloc>1</alloc>
  <used>1</used>
  <inode>23065</inode>
  <meta_type>1</meta_type>
  <mode>420</mode>
  <nlink>1</nlink>
  <uid>0</uid>
  <gid<0</gid>
  <mtime>1231268387</mtime>
  <ctime>1231268387</ctime>
  <atime>1230469854</atime>
  <libmagic>ASCII English text</libmagic>
  <byte_runs>
  <run file_offset='0' fs_offset='528486400' img_
    offset='528486400' len='243'/>
  </byte_runs>
  <hashdigest type='MD5'>0a936719a10e067bab6fd92391776225</
    hashdigest>
  <hashdigest type='SHA1'>59bcce3e528094e1c7d09d32af788a5eb0f996
    0b</hashdigest>
</fileobject>
```

We can see that this element contains all the information we need to know about the file, including the three stored time stamps, ownership data, two hashes, a "libmagic" determination of the content of the file, and the location in the image where the file's content resides.

Fiwalk-based Tools

The main fiwalk program is written in C in the interest of speed. However, the fiwalk project also provides a Python module (fiwalk.py) so that forensic applications leveraging fiwalk's capabilities can be developed quickly and simply. To demonstrate this, several demonstration programs that use fiwalk.py are included. These can be used as is or as a basis for additional programs leveraging the fiwalk core.

One example is `iredact.py`, which is a disk redaction program designed to enable the intelligent removal of files meeting specific criteria from a disk image. The idea is to remove sensitive or otherwise nonshareable information from a disk image prior to making this image available to third parties. Altering a forensic image is always a fraught with peril, but because iredact.py is designed with forensic needs in mind, it avoids oversterilization or disturbing unallocated data.

Redaction is controlled by sets of condition:action pairs. Conditions can be a filename, a wildcard filename, a directory name, an MD5 or SHA1 hash, or file or sector content. Actions can be to fill the redacted content with a specific hex value, to encrypt the content, or to "fuzz" the content, which makes executables nonoperational but does not alter their strings.

TIP

Additional Python Sleuth Kit Bindings
Another project that provides Python access to the Sleuth Kit libraries is *pytsk*, developed by Michael Cohen of PyFLAG fame. At the time of this writing the project is in alpha and is available from http://code.google.com/p/pytsk/

TIMELINES

Timelines are a very useful analysis tool and have recently been discussed in various online forums and listservs. Perhaps more importantly, they are being used to a much greater extent than previously—say, 10 or even 5 years ago. In the past, most timelines have consisted almost exclusively of file system modified, accessed, and creation (MAC) times. More recently, however, the value of adding additional data sources has been realized, and analysts are taking advantage of this more and more.

As we're discussing timelines at this point, a couple of key concepts are in order. First, with respect to generating timelines, one of the key reasons for (and results of) adding multiple time stamped data sources (from within an acquired image, as well as from other external sources) to a timeline is so that the analyst can develop context around the events that are being observed. For example, with just the file MAC times in a timeline, the analyst may observe that a file was created, modified, or accessed, and that's it. However, adding multiple data sources allows the analyst to see other events that occurred around or "near" the same time, such as a user logging in or navigating the Windows Start menu to launch a program or open a recently accessed document. In addition to seeing a file accessed, the analyst may also see which user accessed the file, and perhaps even with which application.

In addition to context, a timeline provides the analyst with an increased relative confidence in data being observed. What this means is that some data sources are easily mutable (which is a fancy way for saying "easily modified"); on Windows systems, for example, file MAC times may be modified quite easily through easily accessible API functions. In fact, this happens quite often during malware infections, as well as intrusions. Other data sources, such as Registry key LastWrite times and Master File Table (MFT) $FILE_NAME attributes, may have time stamps associated with them that are not as easily mutable and would therefore be more reliable and provide the analyst with a greater level of confidence as to the overall data set. Also, consider other systems external to the compromised system, such as proxies, firewalls, and network devices that generate and maintain log data of some sort. The attacker may not even be aware of these devices, and their logs (as they pertain to the compromised system) can be included in the timeline, adding to the relative confidence of observed data. Further, data from multiple systems can be combined into an overall timeline, providing the analyst with a better view for correlating data across a number of systems. Analysts have used this technique to determine the initial attack that led to several systems being compromised, as well as lateral movement between systems once the attacker began to access the previously compromised systems.

Creating timelines from multiple data sources for analysis is a relatively new technique and not one that you'll see in commercial forensic analysis applications, as it requires extracting data that may be poorly documented, if it's documented at all.

While there aren't really any commercial applications that allow for the creation of multisource timelines, there are open source tools that are freely available. While some analysts employ custom tools and techniques to build their timelines, Kristinn Gudjonsson has developed the Log2Timeline framework (available on the Web at http://log2timeline.net), which can be installed on and run from a number of Linux variants, as well as MacOSX (the framework Web site includes an "Installation" section with various installation commands).

NOTE

Log2Timeline and SIFT

Kristinn's log2timeline framework is used to produce what are referred to as "super timelines," a phrase coined by Rob Lee of Mandiant and SANS fame. These timelines are referred to as "super" due to the amount of available data that can be included within the timeline.

Log2timeline and its associated tools are also included as part of the SANS Investigative Forensic Toolkit Workstation (SIFT) version 2.0 virtual machine [5].

Creating timelines is, at this point, a largely manual process, but can be accomplished with the assistance of open-source tools. Some analysts may choose to create the "super" timeline available through the use of log2timeline, while others may opt to take a more manual and minimalist approach, starting with file system metadata. These data can be extracted using *fls* from the Sleuthkit set of tools (referred to as TSK tools). From there, data from sources that make sense to add, based on the goals of the analysis, can be added. For example, the analyst may opt to add Windows Event Log data, unless the available event records do not cover the date in question (if the date is known). In the case of SQL injection where the Web server and database server were installed on the same system (which happens more often than you'd think), a timeline consisting of the file system metadata and relevant IIS Web server logs have proven to be all that is necessary to clearly demonstrate the attacker's actions.

Regardless of the method used for producing a timeline, resulting data can then be analyzed by opening it in a text viewer or spreadsheet application, depending on the analyst's preferences. Basic methods for performing timeline analysis is simply reviewing the items in the timeline sequentially, or performing simple searches for items of interest. To perform more meaningful analysis of timelines, the examiner must take into account the nature of time and various ways of extracting more meaning out of a temporal information. With that in mind, we will discuss some types of time information that may not be immediately apparent, some additional sources of time information, and some patterns of interest that may arise when examining a timeline.

Relative Times

Timeline review is generally performed by examining the generated timeline as a series of discrete time points, such as "December 4th 2010 at 11:05:23 PM UTC." Most reports of forensic analysis also follow this pattern as well. Unfortunately, this sort of review can lead to tunnel vision and a distorted view of the event that occurred. Since accurate event reconstruction is one of the goals of a forensic examination, this sort of thinking can be detrimental to an investigation. It is important to think of time as more than a set of points on a line. A program does not execute at a specific time—it *begins* execution at a specific time, *continues* execution, and eventually halts. While we may not always be able to recover all the artifacts covering the entirety of this time span, this is what actually occurred. The artifacts we uncover are just that: artifacts. Once again, *the map is not the territory*.

We can extend our understanding of timelines by thinking about four different types of relative times. We use relative times to discuss the relationship of one event or time point to another event or time point. There are three relative times to consider: *before*, *after*, and *during*. Any given time information can be referenced in relation to another using these time descriptions.

Before and After

Before and after are incredibly simple concepts, but can be applied to forensic examinations in interesting ways. Any discrete point in a timeline can be described as having occurred before or after any other point or event. Of course the converse is also true—an event (event B) dependent on another event (event B) occurring could not occur prior to that event. The canonical example of this is the creation of the file system being examined. This is the canonical "start point" for all file system time points. Any time information indicating a date before this is falsified, either intentionally or as a consequence of retaining original times during an archive extraction, as demonstrated in Chapter 8.

Another common example of this type of temporal investigation is examining all activity that occurred *after* a specific event of interest. In an intrusion investigation, this event will be the initial compromise time. This event can act as a stop point with regards to relevant time information—anything that occurred prior to the initial point of compromise is now irrelevant. This of course assumes you are able to make a definitive judgment about the initial point of compromise. In some investigations, this lower bound on time analysis may shift as new information is uncovered.

As expected, examination of items that occurred *before* a specific event is the opposite. In an intrusion investigation, the bounding event for this can be the last known traffic from an attacker's IP address. One of the goals of examining everything that occurred before an event is identification of the initial point of compromise. Given both time points, you can establish a finite window of time data that may be of relevance.

During

This describes a set of time data with a finite beginning and end—the *duration* of the event. The prime example of this sort of time information is the window of compromise during an intrusion. Given an attacker's entry, and the time of successful remediation, the time in between is the duration of compromise. This is often the largest time period of immediate relevance. Within this window, additional durations may be uncovered. For example, windows between logins and logouts of compromised accounts may provide additional windows of access to investigate further. This can help reduce the amount of time information of relevance the examiner needs to process.

This can also help reduce the amount of data considered to be compromised. For example, if sensitive data were not on a compromised system outside of the window of access, it may be reasonable to consider that there was no opportunity for data to be compromised. Conversely, identifying the window of access can be used to reduce the scope of investigation to data that existed on the system during this window. Limiting examination to a particular time window can also be useful when attempting to attribute particular activity to a certain user account. Any activity that has specific start and stop times can be used to partition a subset of time data.

Inferred Times

In many investigations, absolutely granular time points for data of interest may not be available or may be incorrect or misleading. If this is the case, *inferred time* may be the most accurate time available to you. Generally this will apply to deleted data. Data that have been deleted will either have no directly associated metadata structure or have a metadata structure that is tied only loosely to actual data content. Under these circumstances, it may still be able to infer additional temporal information

For example, in one investigation, metadata information for a deleted file ("file1.doc") on an NTFS file system indicated that the file was modified on

January 10, 2010. There were no signs of system clock manipulation, and the file name attribute time stamps were also consistent with January 10. However, the content of the file (a forecast of the Florida orange crop) appeared to be data that did not exist before March 10, 2010.

```
MFT Entry #: 4067
Path: D:\Temp\file1.doc
Deleted
Size: 5974865 (5.9M)
DATA MODIFIED: 01/10/10 02:21:58PM
ACCESSED: 01/10/10 02:21:58PM
CREATED: 01/10/10 02:20:27PM
MFT MODIFIED: 01/10/10 02:21:58PM
67 Data Runs
```

File1.doc is a $\approx$ 5.9-Megabyte file with 67 data runs. Given that the volume this file resides on was nearly empty at the time of examination, this is an inordinate amount of fragmentation. This leads to several suppositions. We can assume that the D: volume was nearly full when this file was created, which would account for the operating system placing the file content in any location it could find space. Once the original file1.doc was deleted, the MFT entry became "frozen" and its reuse never became necessary. Examining the data runs listed as allocated to the file1.doc entry yielded some of our Florida orange crop forecast. Examining clusters listed as purely unallocated that are adjacent to clusters listed as allocated to file1.doc show that this content continues for many contiguous clusters, which would not be the case if they were truly the data originally allocated to file1.doc.

Given this scenario, we have the following inferred timeline.

1. January 10 2010 2:20:27 pm—File1.doc is created on the system. MFT entry 4067 is populated with metadata relevant to File1.doc. File content for File1.doc is written to a nearly full volume, leading to a 5.9-Megabyte file with 67 fragments.
2. January 10 2010 2:21:58 pm—File1.doc is deleted, freezing the MFT entry. All clusters in the 67 data runs contain File1.doc data at this time.
3. {Sometime after March 10 2010}: The Florida orange crop report is created on this volume. An unknown MFT entry is created for this file, and clusters are allocated. Some or all of these clusters are in a run, which overwrites some of the data runs previously allocated to File1.doc.
4. {Sometime after entry 3}: The Florida orange crop report is deleted. The runs allocated to this file are left intact.
5. {Sometime after entry 4}: The MFT entry created for the Florida orange crop report is reused by a new file. Metadata and data run information contained in the MFT entry are overwritten and lost.

Note that while were are not able to assign fixed times to items 3 through 5 on our timeline we know that these had to have occurred sometime after March 10th due to the content of the document. Without this additional temporal knowledge, an examiner would simply have one set of incorrect time stamps to work with. In other cases, there may be two competing sets of time information. Without additional temporal knowledge gleaned from sources such as firewall logs, packet captures, or registry data, conflicting file system time stamps may simply end up being tossed out as inconclusive.

Embedded Times

We discussed the extraction of time information from file metadata in Chapter 8. Like information from devices external to the system, these time artifacts can be a very rich source of temporal data. The fact that they contain time information is frequently overlooked by or unknown to the actors that generate or transmit them. Embedded times can travel within the files as they move from system to system and cannot be manipulated directly with the same tools used to manipulate file system time data. They can retain their time information for recovery after deletion, even when the file system metadata structures have been removed.

File content may contain another source of time information as well: *embedded inferred time*. As an example, many PDF files will contain the name and version of the software used to generate them. The release date of this version of the software used to generate the document is the earliest date that the file could have existed. When examining office documents that may be of questionable veracity, the existence of printer make and model can be used to create a timeframe in which the document must have been printed.

> **WARNING**
> **The Unreality of Time**
> While it is certainly possible to manipulate or fake internal time information or other embedded metadata, this forgery generally appears in one of two forms. First, these data can be blatantly false: dates in the future, gibberish usernames, or application names that simply don't exist. This sort of "salting the earth" is found frequently in malware and other malicious files. It is obvious, but the point is to ruin investigative traces. The other form is used when the file in question is intended to be viewed as legitimate: forged legal documents, backdated financial information, and the like. Time manipulation of this sort is much more difficult to detect, and often in these types of cases detecting any inconsistency in data is exactly the point. It is highly unlikely that this level of tampering would occur on a document not intended to be passed off as a legitimate document.

Periodicity

Another concept useful in the analysis of temporal information is *periodicity*. Periodicity refers to the rate at which a given event or activity recurs. This is sometimes referred to as "frequency" but frequency can also refer to how often something occurs ("four times a day") as opposed to periodicity, which refers explicitly to the time that passes between repeated events. Periodicity is a useful signal when analyzing time data related to backdoor traffic. Most backdoor programs have a highly fixed period for beacon traffic back to their controllers. Unfortunately, many Benign auto-update programs also share this same characteristic. It should not be surprising then that periodicity can be used to classify automated traffic versus human traffic.

Even the most precise human will display some variance in their activity—their morning routine may be to fire up a Web browser, open their mail, and check a couple of Web sites, but the period between each of these activities will vary from day to day. Automated traffic will generally occur at fixed intervals. Analysis of fixed-length periods between recurring activities can help suss out automated activities intermixed with human activities. Analysis of the speed of recurrence can also yield positive results—activities that occur too fast for a human to perform in rapid succession are likely to be an automated process or a human running a script. Quasi-periodic activity can be of interest as well. For example, time information may indicate that a lab machine is accessed after hours, every Thursday night between 10 and 11 pm, with no discernible business purpose.

WARNING

More Human than Human

Be aware that some malicious backdoors will vary the timing of their beacon traffic to avoid detection via these mechanisms. In these cases, analysis of periodic activity will not be of much help, but other techniques [such as Least Frequency of Occurrence (LFO) analysis] may be of use.

Frequency Patterns and Outliers (Least Frequency of Occurrence)

"Least Frequency of Occurrence" is a term used by Pete Silberman of Mandiant at the 2008 SANS Forensic Summit to describe a characteristic of malware on systems; specifically, what he was referring to was that early on, malware would infect systems quickly, and many times, massively, continually scanning the network and infecting any vulnerable system. As such, many systems were infected and reinfected so many times that they quickly became completely unusable. As the development and goals of malware evolved and the direction moved to avoiding detection, authors began including the creation of a unique mutex to identify infected systems so that they would not be reinfected continually; after all, what was the point of completely denying the use of a system to anyone if you were after data, storage, or CPU cycles? As it happened, creation of the unique mutex led malware infection to being the least frequent event or action to occur on a system.

Consider this; during normal, day-to-day function of a Windows XP system in a corporate environment, a considerable amount of activity occurs on the system. In the morning, the user logs in, often after having only logged out and not powered the system down the previous morning. While the system is active on the corporate network, considerable activity occurs; files are created or modified as the user goes about his/her daily business. Even more activity occurs "under the hood"; on Windows XP systems, a System Restore Point is created every 24 hours, and a limited defragmentation of the hard drive occurs every 3 calendar days. In addition, the operating system and applications are updated automatically; in some corporations, systems are scanned for compliance regularly, and applications are updated accordingly. Given all this, it's easy to see how malware infections and even intrusions are often the least frequent activities to occur on systems.

The same is true for other systems, as well. Even on Windows 2003 or 2008 servers (database, file, web, etc.) and Windows 7 systems used in either the corporate or the home environment, malicious activity very often is the least frequent type of activity. So what does this mean for the analyst? Instead of looking for spikes in the number of files or increases in general activity on a system, an analyst is very often looking for a specific straw (based on color, length, texture, etc.) of hay in a haystack. Once found, the analyst will be able to provide context to that straw so that it will stand out from the other straws in the haystack.

Analysts need to consider LFO when performing analysis, particularly during data breach and intrusion investigations. Most systems have plenty of powerful tools installed for use by administrators, and these tools are equally useful for an intruder as well, particularly when it comes to determining what system they're on (*hostname*, *uname—a*), and what other systems may be "near" the compromised system (*ping, nbtstat.exe, net. exe*, etc.). As such, there really isn't an overwhelming need for a moderately knowledgeable attacker to download a massive set to tools and malware to the system. In fact, it seems that this is what most attackers want to avoid; more tools increase the likelihood that someone will notice their presence, either as the tools are downloaded, if one of them fails to run properly and generate errors, or if the installed antivirus application generates a warning based on detecting one of the attacker's tools.

Another aspect to consider is that in order to minimize changes made to compromised systems, attackers will generally opt to use already available user accounts (when it is necessary to do so) rather than create new ones, although creating a new user account or two is a great way to ensure that they can get back into the system(s) at a later date. In an infrastructure that may consist of hundreds or thousands of user accounts, what are one or two more? The answer to that is that they're the least frequency of occurrence, as it pertains to the user accounts.

The overall point is that instead of looking for the attacker who is doing the digital equivalent of driving a truck through your living room, analysts should consider LFO and look for those things that are slightly different, such as a few pieces of furniture that may have been moved. This is not to say that this is always the case; the authors are both very familiar with systems that have been compromised and turned into "warez" servers, making bootleg movies available to anyone with an Internet connection. In these cases, massive files have been uploaded, and the significant amounts of traffic generated by those downloading the files have slowed the victim infrastructure to a crawl. However, observing the nature of many attacks over the past several years, there seems to be a trend toward minimalization, in which the attacker or malware has the least effect possible on the compromised systems. Understanding this will assist analysts in investigating the incident.

SUMMARY

While it is certainly possible to run an entire investigation using nothing but command line utilities, integrated, the graphical forensic environments discussed in this chapter provide a host of benefits that make them compelling for an examiner. Being able to easily apply forensic processes inside of archives, indexed searching, and the ability to perform complex queries are powerful features that a clever examiner can use well. The fiwalk library and utilities reviewed demonstrate the power of using open source tools to automate and simplify data extraction and initial file-system inventory. Finally, we demonstrated a host of temporal analysis concepts and techniques that can be used to expand timeline analysis beyond simply searching through a listing of time stamp records.

References

[1] PyFlag. http://www.pyflag.net/, (accessed 18.12.10).
[2] M. Cohen, D. Collett, A. Walters, Digital Forensics Research Workshop 2008—Submission for Forensic Challenge. http://sandbox.dfrws.org/2008/Cohen_Collet_Walters/Digital_Forensics_Research_Workshop_2.pdf, 2008, (accessed 18.12.10).
[3] DFF: Open Source software for computer forensics & eDiscovery. http://www.digital-forensic.org/, (accessed 18.12.10).
[4] AFFLIB—fiwalk. http://afflib.org/software/fiwalk, (accessed 18.12.10).
[5] SANS—Computer Forensics and Incident Response with Rob Lee, Community:Downloads. http://computer-forensics.sans.org/community/downloads/, (accessed 18.12.10).

Free, Non-open Tools
of Note

- Disk and File System Analysis
- Windows Systems and Artifacts
- Internet Artifacts
- File Analysis
- Automating Analysis and Extending Capabilities
- Validation and Testing Resources

INTRODUCTION

As the title belies, the purpose of this book is twofold. First, we wanted to discuss digital forensics. Second, we wanted to demonstrate how to perform digital forensics tasks using open source tools. For some tasks, no open source tools are available. For others, open source tools are not the best tool for the job. With that in mind, we present a selection of free but non-open tools that can be used to supplement the tools discussed throughout this book. Unless otherwise specified, these tools are all Windows only.

This appendix is divided according to the chapter structure of the main book. Tools applicable to the techniques and artifacts discussed in a given chapter are discussed under that chapter's heading in this appendix. Note that some chapters present in the main text are not represented here due to either sufficient open source tools being available or the lack of any additional non-open tools worth discussing. Finally, we discuss some testing and validation resources that can be used to calibrate and verify the operation of your forensic tools. The tools described throughout this appendix should not be considered an exhaustive list, but instead a representative sampling of the available free, albeit non-open source tools that are available.

CHAPTER 3: DISK AND FILE SYSTEM ANALYSIS

Open source tools covered in Chapter 3 provide a wealth of capabilities. The following tools can be used in combination with these tools to augment and extend the analyst's capabilities.

FTK Imager

AccessData has provided FTK Imager as a free download for quite some time, and even updated the tool as time has passed. FTK Imager is an extremely valuable tool to any responder or analyst, allowing them to not only acquire images from systems (via the appropriate write-blockers or from live systems) but also to verify file systems of acquired images, be they raw/dd or "expert witness" (perhaps more popularly known as "EnCase") format, VMWare vmdk file format, etc. FTK Imager recognizes a number of file system formats, including not just FAT and NTFS, but ext2, ext3, and others, as well.

FTK Imager tends to come in two flavors. First is the full version that can be downloaded and installed on a workstation or laptop, and the second one is a "lite" version that includes the executable image file and necessary DLLs that can be copied to and run from a thumb drive or CD. This is often a very valuable resource, particularly during significant response activities. In such cases, responders are not limited by the number of imaging resources (laptops and write blockers) that they have available—rather, copying files to the root of external, USB-connected drives allows responders to perform live acquisition of a significant number of systems simultaneously.

At the time of this writing, the Lite version of FTK Imager is version 2.9, and the full version of the tool is at version 3. The most notable difference between the two versions, aside from the installation process, is that version 3 now provides the capability to mount an acquired image as a physical drive or as a logical volume (or volumes) on the analyst's workstation. You can mount images by choosing the "Image Mounting…" option from the File menu, as illustrated in Figure A.1.

As shown in Figure A.1, you can use FTK Imager 3 to do most of the things that you're used to doing, such as acquiring images, verifying file systems, and capturing memory, and you can now use it to mount images.

ProDiscover Free

Christopher Brown, the man behind Technology Pathways, LLC, makes a Basic Edition of his ProDiscover forensic analysis application available for free download. This free edition provides some basic functionality but does not include the more extensive capabilities of the full version. For example, the Basic Edition allows the analyst to create projects, as well as populate the Registry Viewer, the Event Log Viewer, as well as find Internet activity and conduct searches across the project, as illustrated in Figure A.2.

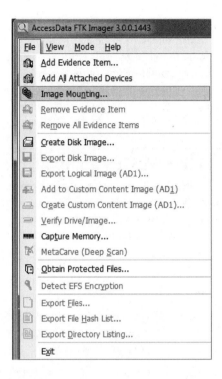

FIGURE A.1

FTK Imager 3 File menu options.

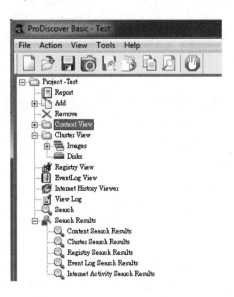

FIGURE A.2

ProDiscover Basic Edition project.

The Basic Edition (version 6.7.0.9 at the time of this writing) also provides the ability to perform secure wipes of drives and includes the imaging capability and image conversion tools found in the full edition. The Basic Edition does not, however, provide the ProScript functionality of the full edition, nor the remote access and imaging capability. A version of ProDiscover Basic Edition (version 5) is also available as a U3 install package so that it can be run from a thumb drive.

CHAPTER 4: WINDOWS SYSTEMS AND ARTIFACTS

Chapter 4 presented a variety of tools that can be used to process the numerous items of interest that can be found on a Windows system. The tools discussed here are purely supplemental. They do, however, have various characteristics that may make them appealing to an examiner. The first tool reviewed is "Windows File Analysis" from Michal Mutl.

Windows File Analysis

Windows File Analysis is a small, quite useful graphical Windows application used to parse and display five different items that frequently contain artifacts relevant during a Windows examination. These five items are:

- Thumbnail Database (Thumbs.db) files, which can contain thumbnail images of items that have been deleted.
- Prefetch files, which track the execution of programs on Windows XP, Vista, and 7 systems.
- Shortcut (LNK) files, which among other data can contain the locations for previously opened files and time stamps.
- Index.dat files, discussed in Chapter 7. These store Internet Explorer history information.
- INFO2 files, used by the Recycle Bin in XP.

Windows File Analysis can be downloaded from http://mitec.cz/wfa.html.

Event Log Explorer

Event Log Explorer is a robust application for interactively examining event logs from Windows systems. Event Log Explorer is free, but only for noncommercial, personal use. If you use this tool professionally you will need to purchase a license, but if you are a student or a hobbyist the free license should suffice.

By default the program opens Event Logs using the Windows application programming interface (API), but it has the capability of interpreting the file directly as well. To use Event Log Explorer to examine logs extracted from a forensic image, you will choose the "direct" option under "File → Open Log File" as show in Figure A.3.

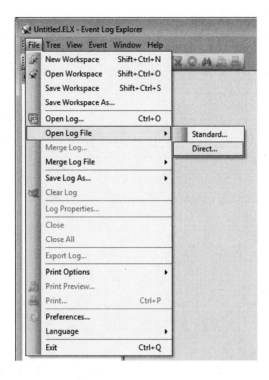

FIGURE A.3

Event Log Explorer—Open Direct.

Among the capabilities of Event Log Explorer is the ability to bookmark and filter by specific criteria, including time and date of the event, category of the event, and text in the description of the event. The Bookmark by criteria dialog is shown in Figure A.4.

When an interesting subset of log entries is located, the examiner can export them to HTML, tab-separated text, or an Excel spreadsheet.

Log Parser

Log Parser is a tool available from Microsoft [1] that allows you to run structured query language (SQL) searches across a variety of data sources, including ASCII text files, Event Logs (both .evt and .evtx formats), the Registry, and Active Directory. Log Parser is a command line interface (CLI) tool that is extremely useful. A very simple way to employ Log Parser is to use it to parse Event Log files into comma-separated value (CSV) format, using the following command:

```
C:\tools>logparser -i:evt -o:csv "SELECT * from System" >
   system.csv
```

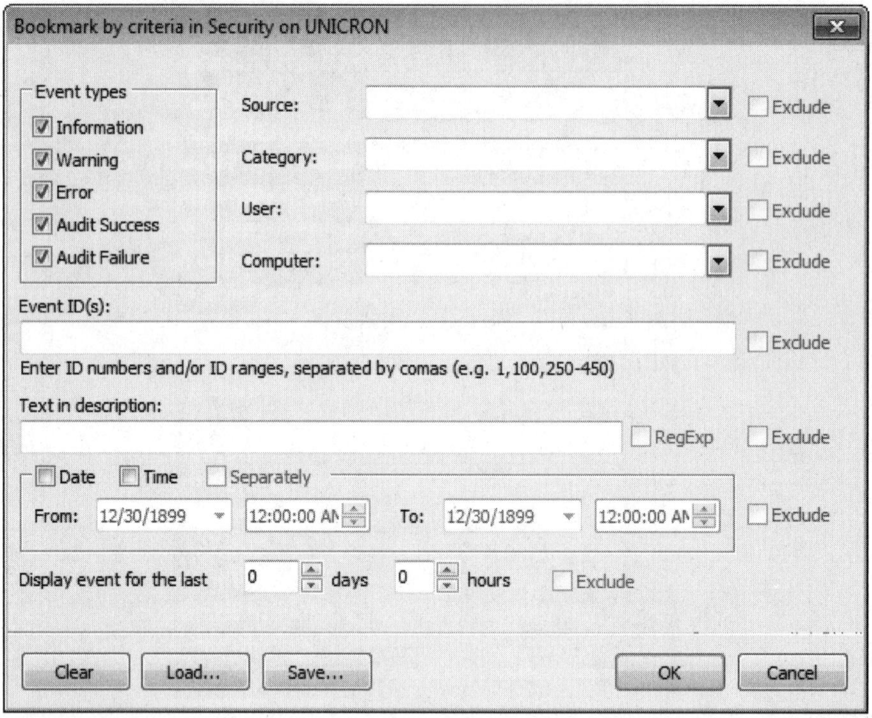

FIGURE A.4

Event Log Explorer—Bookmark search.

This command can be run on a live system and will parse the System Event Log and place all available information into a file format that can be opened in Excel. If you have extracted Event Log files from an acquired image and want to parse those, you would need to replace "System" with the full path to the extracted file; i.e., "D:\case\files\sysevent.evt."

It is very important to note that Log Parser relies on the API of the system that it is running on; therefore, you can only parse Event Log (.evt) files from Windows XP or 2003 on those systems; the same is true for Windows Event Log (.evtx) files from Vista and above systems.

Fortunately, you don't have to be an expert in SQL queries in order to take full advantage of Log Parser. Microsoft provides several examples of ways to utilize Log Parser [2], including producing graphs. A number of other sites on the Web provide examples of how Log Parser can be used; in addition, several graphical user interfaces (GUIs) are available for Log Parser, although these are not available from Microsoft. Perhaps one of the most popular is the Lizard GUI available from Lizard Labs (http://www.lizard-labs.net/log_parser_lizard.aspx). GUIs can make interacting with powerful tools such as Log Parser more intuitive and easier for new or novice analysts, allowing them to overcome the initial learning curve and avoid lots of typing.

CHAPTER 7: INTERNET ARTIFACTS

The growing use of SQLite as a data store by Web browsers is quite beneficial to forensic examiners using open source tools. In addition to the tools we reviewed, a wide variety of other SQLite applications can be used based on examiner preference. Additionally, the following tools provide some additional capabilities beyond what was discussed in Chapter 7.

NirSoft Tools

Nir Sofer provides numerous freeware tools at www.nirsoft.net, including a handful of utilities useful for forensic analysis of Internet artifacts from a variety of browsers.

The following tools are used to process the local caches of the referenced browsers:

- MozillaCacheView
- IECacheView
- ChromeCacheView

Each operates in a very similar manner and can be used as a GUI application or run from the console. This is quite useful if you are scripting the operation of the cache viewer program or need to process a large number of cached files. Via the GUI, tabular results can be exported as a text, HTML, or XML file. The elements recovered vary slightly depending on the type of browser cache being examined, but will generally include at least the URL the cached file was retrieved from, the MIME type the server supplied for the file, and the time the content was retrieved.

When executed via the command line, flags can be passed to copy the contents of the cache to another directory or to dump the results from parsing the cache out to the tab-delimited text, HTML, or XML. The utilities support arguments to restrict the files copied to those sourced from a specific URL or specific types of content. For more usage information or to download the applications, see http://nirsoft.net/computer_forensic_software.html.

Woanware Tools

Mark Woan has made a plethora of free forensic utilities available at www.woany.co.uk. We discuss two of them here: Firefox Session Extractor and ChromeForensics.

Firefox Session Extractor (or "firefoxsessionsextractor" as it is listed on the WoanWare site) is a simple console utility for parsing the sessionstore.js JSON file used by Firefox to maintain session state in the event of a browser crash or other improper close. This utility is nice in that because it is a console application, it can be used in a script and it will also process multiple sessionstore.js files in a recursive manner. It is available from http://www.woany.co.uk/firefoxsessionstoreextractor/.

ChromeForensics is, as the name suggests, an application for extracting artifacts left on a system by Google Chrome. As shown in Chapter 7, we can collect these artifacts directly using SQLite. ChromeForensics is an option if you are using Windows

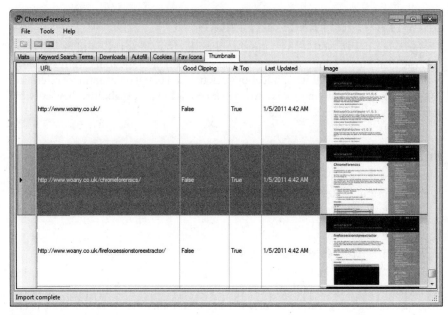

FIGURE A.5

WoanWare Chrome Forensics.

as your analysis platform and prefer a GUI application. It also has the advantage displaying Chrome's Web page thumbnails (shown in Figure A.5), with the ability to export them in an HTML report.

CHAPTER 8: FILE ANALYSIS

We covered the analysis of many different types of files in Chapter 8, including Microsoft Office binary files stored in the OLE/compound document format (Word Documents, Excel Spreadsheets, etc.). As we showed, these files are rich with valuable artifacts and can be of interest in many different types of examinations. This section presents three additional tools that can be used to perform additional useful analysis of these files.

Mitec.cz: Structured Storage Viewer

Michal Mutl has released a program for viewing the structure of Office binary files. In addition to interpreting the structure of streams and displaying metadata, individual streams can be viewed as text, raw data, image data, or others. For a demonstration of the Structured Storage Viewer being used to examine metadata from the infamous "blair.doc," see Figure A.6.

Mitec Structured Storage Viewer is available from http://mitec.cz/ssv.html.

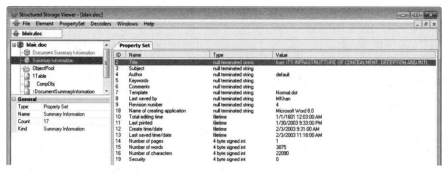

FIGURE A.6

Mitec.cz Structured Storage Viewer.

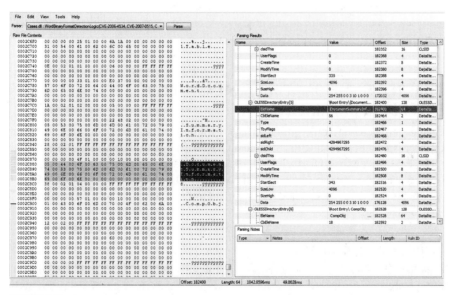

FIGURE A.7

Microsoft's OffVis.

OffVis

OffVis is a tool from the Microsoft Security Research Center that can be used to examine Office binary format documents. It is quite useful for browsing through the structure of an Office document interactively and has built-in knowledge of the Office binary internal structures. See Figure A.7 for an example of browsing the structure of a Word document.

OffVis is available from http://go.microsoft.com/fwlink/?LinkId=158791.

Note the text and hex view on in the left pane and the interpreted, structured view on the right. Each pane drives the other—double clicking an interesting area in the hex view will jump to the location of the structure in the right, and vice versa.

FileInsight

FileInsight is a hex editor from McAfee designed for analyzing malicious files. While FileInsight is used primarily for examining Windows executables, some of its features make it a good general file analysis editor. For example, examiners can apply data structures (C or C++ header files) to interpret files. This can be used to apply logic to the binary file format being examined. Prebuilt interpreters are included for Windows executables and Office binary documents, as well as a variety of date and time formats. The content of a file can be modified in-place using JavaScript, which can be useful to apply decoding functions or other content transformations. Finally, plugins can be developed using Python for more extensive tasks.

FileInsight is available from http://www.mcafee.com/us/downloads/free-tools/fileinsight.aspx.

CHAPTER 9: AUTOMATING ANALYSIS AND EXTENDING CAPABILITIES

Chapter 9 discussed some graphical examination environments and then went on to discuss concepts related to timeline analysis. This section looks at two different tools. First, we discuss a free, closed tool designed for examining text log data, which can be used to examine timelines quite successfully. Next, we review a tool that allows for secure and integrated management of the working notes produced during an examination.

Mandiant: Highlighter

Mandiant Highlighter is a free tool designed for the purpose of intelligent examination of log data. One of the problems with reviewing log data during incident response is the sheer volume of data involved. Highlighter attempts to tackle this issue in several ways. First, the pane on the right of actual log data is a graphical representation of the entire log. In Figure A.8 you can immediately see patterns in the length of logs, which can be of use in the investigation of many Web server attacks.

Highlighter provides line operations for any text file, but can provide field-based operations when analyzing a delimited file. For example, once a time and date field has been defined, the activity over time represented in the log file can be displayed as a histogram. Additionally, unique values found in a specific field can be highlighted in unique colors. This highlighting is displayed in the main log window, as well as in the overall view in the right pane. This allows the examiner to quickly identify patterns of access for highlighted IP addresses, usernames, or Web browser user agents, for example. For an example of some of these features in action, see Figure A.9.

FIGURE A.8

Mandiant Highlighter—log lines display.

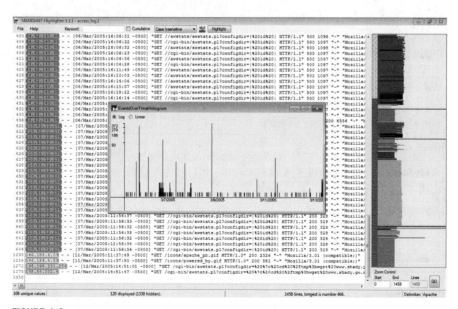

FIGURE A.9

Mandiant Highlighter—highlights and histogram.

Other prominent features of HIGHLIGHTER include the highlighting of named keywords, the removal of lines containing specific fields, and the management of these actions—the examiner can remove any change that has been applied at any time rather than relying on a serial "undo" buffer.

Highlighter can be retrieved from the Mandiant Web site, http://www.mandiant .com/products/free_software/highlighter/.

CaseNotes

Documentation is a key component in any case or examination, and there are a number of ways to keep notes of your work. One is to simply use a word processing application, such as MSWord, as this allows not only for formatting and pasting of images into the document, but is an accessible enough format that the document can be opened easily by other analysts. OpenOffice (from openoffice.org) provides a completely free suite of office applications, and the files produced can be saved in formats that can be opened by other word processing (MSWord) or document reader (Adobe Reader) applications. The key here is portability.

Another means for keeping case notes and documentation is with an application such as Forensic CaseNotes from QCCIS.com. This is a tabbed application that allows you to maintain contemporaneous notes about your examination; a sample test case open in Forensic CaseNotes (FCN) is illustrated in Figure A.10.

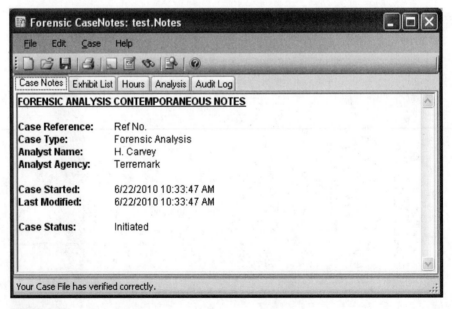

FIGURE A.10

Sample case open in Forensic CaseNotes.

As you can see from Figure A.10, FCN includes several tabs (up to four user configurable tabs) for maintaining various bits of case information. In the test case, an "Hours" tab has been added, as consultants generally need to track their time spent on cases on a daily basis, and having a separate tab (as with the "Exhibit List" tab) simply makes it easier to maintain this information. Each tab allows you to add and format text, add images, and so on, keeping complete notes.

Another useful benefit of FCN is that it maintains an audit log of activity, such as opening and closing the case, verifying the hash for the case notes file, and significant modifications to the case notes (adding tabs, etc.).

VALIDATION AND TESTING RESOURCES

Throughout the book we have mentioned validating and verifying tools. This can be challenging given the disparate data sets encountered during a forensic examination. To that end, we present the following resources that can be used to verify correct operation of any of the tools you use, not just open source tools.

Digital Corpora

We use items from Digital Corpora extensively in this book. Simply put, Digital Corpora is home to the most useful collection of varying, real-world files and file types freely available: the Govdocs1 collection. This is a collection of nearly one million files retrieved from government Web servers indexed via search engines. This is a tremendous resource for examiners looking to validate tool operation against a wide variety of files.

Additional available items include:

- Raw dumps from cell phones
- Disk images containing file systems that have undergone real or realistic use
- Complete investigation scenarios with supporting files

Digital Corpora files can be accessed at http//www.digitalcorpora.com.

Digital Forensics Tool Testing Images

The Digital Forensics Tool Testing (DFTT) Images collection is a set of carefully crafted image files designed to exercise particular capabilities of forensic tools. These images are terrific for testing the low-level function of file system processing tools and ensuring validity of operation when parsing things such as complex partition structures and unallocated data.

The DFTT Images collection is available at http://dftt.sourceforge.net.

Electronic Discovery Reference Model

The Electronic Discovery Reference Model (EDRM) provides a number of reference data sets specifically geared toward the calibration and verification of function of e-discovery tools and techniques. The most interesting data set provided by the EDRM is the Enron email data set. This consists of 107 Gigabytes of compressed email, available as PST archives as well as the open EDRM XML standard. This is a boon for any examiner looking to validate or expand the capabilities of email examination tools.

The EDRM can be accessed at http://edrm.net/projects/dataset.

Digital Forensics Research Workshop Challenges

Every year since 2005, the Digital Forensics Research Workshop (DFRWS) has presented a challenge to the forensics community. Each challenge is designed to spur development and documentation of new open source tools and techniques addressing a specific gap in forensic capabilities. These have ranged from memory images, to dumps from cell phones, to complete scenarios involving network traces, disk, and memory images from game consoles. These challenges provide a terrific baseline for examiners looking to test new or existing tools against interesting data sets.

Visit the DFRWS Web site at http://www.dfrws.org.

Additional Images

Acquired system images are also available for testing and validation, as well as for analysts to practice and maintain their skills from a number of locations. The National Institute of Standards and Technology site includes the Computer Forensic Reference Data Sets site, which offers an example image provided from a "hacking case" (found on the Web at http://www.cfreds.nist.gov/Hacking_Case.html).

The image can be downloaded as a single expert witness format (EWF, popularly referred to as "EnCase") format image or as several image segments.

Also, Lance Mueller provides several "practical" exercises through his Web site, forensickb.com. If you go to his site and search for the term "practical," you'll find references to several scenarios that include links to images of Windows XP systems that can be downloaded. You can then either try your hand at the practical exercise that Lance outlined or simply sharpen your examination skills.

Finally, the Honey Project provides a number of examples and includes materials through the Challenges page, found on the Web at http://www.honeynet.org/challenges. These challenges span a range of scenarios from image analysis (system images, diskettes, thumb drives, etc.), network packet captures (pcap files), log files, etc. All of these can be used to develop and sharpen skills or used for training or evaluation scenarios.

References

[1] Download details: Log Parser 2.2, Microsoft Download Center. http://www
.microsoft.com/downloads/en/details.aspx?FamilyID=890cd06b-abf8-4c25-91b2-
f8d975cf8c07&displaylang=en, (accessed 09.01.11).

[2] ScriptCenter Tools: Log Parser 2.2 Examples, Microsoft ScriptCenter. http://technet
.microsoft.com/en-us/library/ee692659.aspx, (accessed 09.01.11).

Index

Page numbers followed by *f* indicates a figure and *t* indicates a table.